Praise for *One Year Off*

"Sixty minutes into a thirty-minute commute one entertains the fantasy of selling the house, quitting the job, and taking off around the world. David Elliot Cohen and his young family did just that. Cohen chronicles their year of freedom with candor, boundless curiosity, and the sharp sense of humor that distinguishes the best traveling companion."
— Joan Ryan, columnist, *San Francisco Chronicle*

"Where would this country be if everybody took off mid-career for a voyage of discovery with their families? Much better off, I would imagine. David Elliot Cohen provides an engaging, inspirational road map to pulling up stakes and getting out."
— David Brancaccio, host of public radio's *Marketplace*

"Cohen makes a great case for the midlife sabbatical, and he does so with seductive heart and humor."
— Elizabeth Perle, author, *When Work Doesn't Work Anymore*

"Starting out as the kind of innocents abroad who cause the natives to snicker, they eventually make the tricky transition from tourists to travelers, and even if you would never want to do this yourself, they are charming travel companions."
— *People Magazine*

"The only regret I have about this marvelous book is that it ended too soon. If the family had decided to become the 'Traveling Cohens,' and continued their odyssey for years to come, I would have been happy to wait for the latest installment, because Cohen's printed voice is downright pleasant."
— *Denver Rocky Mountain News*

"Cohen proves to be a very capable writer, filling his narrative with interesting and amusing accounts."
— *The Christian Science Monitor*

Travelers' Tales Books

Country and Regional Guides
America, Australia, Brazil, Cuba, France, Greece, India,
Ireland, Italy, Japan, Mexico, Nepal, Spain, Thailand;
American Southwest, Grand Canyon, Hawai'i, Hong Kong,
Paris, San Francisco

Women's Travel
A Woman's Path, A Woman's Passion for Travel,
A Woman's World, Women in the Wild, A Mother's World,
Safety and Security for Women Who Travel,
Gutsy Women, Gutsy Mamas

Body & Soul
The Road Within, Love & Romance, Food,
The Fearless Diner, The Gift of Travel, The Adventure
of Food, The Ultimate Journey, Pilgrimage, 365 Travel

Special Interest
There's No Toilet Paper on the Road Less Traveled,
The Gift of Birds, A Dog's World, Danger!, Testosterone
Planet, The Penny Pincher's Passport to Luxury Travel,
The Gift of Travel, Family Travel, The Gift of Rivers,
The Fearless Shopper, Shitting Pretty,
Not So Funny When It Happened

Footsteps
Take Me With You, Kite Strings of the Southern Cross,
The Sword of Heaven, Storm, The Way of the Wanderer,
Last Trout in Venice, One Year Off

Classics
The Royal Road to Romance, Unbeaten Tracks in Japan,
The Rivers Ran East

ONE YEAR OFF

Leaving It All Behind for

a Round-the-World Journey

with Our Children

ONE YEAR OFF

Leaving It All Behind for
a Round-the-World Journey
with Our Children

David Elliot Cohen

with photographs by Devyani Kamdar

TRAVELERS' TALES
SAN FRANCISCO

Travelers' Tales and *Travelers' Tales Guides* are trademarks of Travelers' Tales, Inc., 330 Townsend Street, Suite 208, San Francisco, California 94107. www.travelerstales.com

Jacket Design: Jackie Seow
Jacket Illustration: John Segal
Interior Design: Ruth Lee
Interior Photos: Devyani Kamdar   •
Author Photograph: Doug Menuez
Page Layout: Cynthia Lamb, using the fonts Sabon and TradeGothic

Distributed by Publishers Group West, 1700 Fourth Street, Berkeley, California 94710.

Library of Congress Cataloging-in-Publication Data

Cohen, David Elliot, 1955-
    One year off: leaving it all behind for a round-the-world journey with
our children/David Elliot Cohen; with photographs by Devyani Kamdar
        p. cm.
    Originally published: New York: Simon & Schuster, c1999
    Includes bibliographical references
    ISBN 1-885211-65-1
    1. Travel—Anecdotes. 2. Children—Travel—Anecdotes. 3. Family
recreation—Anecdotes. 4. Cohen, David Elliot, 1955- I. Title: 1 year off.
II. Title.

G151.C638 2001
910.4'1—dc21   2001025015

First Edition
Printed in the United States of America
10 9 8 7 6 5 4 3 2 1

To my traveling partner—
with love and admiration

Contents

SOME PEOPLE HAVE RESOLUTE IDEAS ABOUT how their lives should unfold. As adolescents or young adults, they set goals and chart courses. When they encounter obstacles, they surmount them and move forward. If they stray from the preordained path, they always find their way back again. For better or worse, I've never been one of those people. Maybe I've never found my true métier. More likely, I just have a short attention span. But whatever it is, life has always seemed far more interesting when there is a healthy element of serendipity involved.

My young adulthood was shaped by this instinct for adventure. An otherwise lackluster career at Yale College was punctuated by two fairly unusual summer jobs—one as an assistant to a member of the British Parliament and another as an intern at the American embassy in Freetown, Sierra Leone. At the time, I didn't consider these positions great career opportunities. I just thought that listening to constituents' problems in a dreary Midlands housing project or touring an African bush town were great ways to sample the world.

In fact, when I graduated from college, I didn't have the slightest idea what sort of career I wanted. If someone had handed me an open air ticket along with my diploma, I would have gladly jetted off to Tibet or Timbuktu. But that didn't happen. Instead I ran into my father, and with the best intentions, he gently prodded me into law school. ("Even if you don't become an attorney, it's great mental training.") So with a vague sense of dread, I trundled off to law school with the rest of the living dead. I still remember sitting in a huge classroom on the first day of school with 150 or so eager novitiates. The dean—a noted contracts scholar—strutted across the stage like a puffed-up peacock and boomed, "We're going to change everything about the way you think!"

My first reaction to that was, "Not if I can help it, buddy." And of course that set the stage for a truly gruesome year, where I proved two theories fairly conclusively: 1) the first year of law school isn't the preferred venue for contrarian thinking, and 2) you can't learn torts and civil procedure through osmosis. No one was sorry to see me go.

After that, I served an undistinguished stint as a salesclerk in a Pittsburgh bookstore. I thought it was a great job, since I got to spend most of my time browsing the inventory and chatting with customers. But eventually, my parents prevailed upon me to try something more ambitious, so I bought a copy of *The New York Times* and scanned the want ads. The very first notice that caught my eye called for publicity director at a small photography book publishing house called Aperture.

Aperture published some of the world's finest art photographers—giants like Robert Frank, Edward Weston, Dorothea Lange, Edward Stieglitz, and Minor White. I always admired Aperture's lavish publications when they turned up at the bookstore, and more important, I thought it would be exciting to live in New York for a while. I applied for the position and got it.

Six months later, the talented martinet who ran the place

fired me for unconscionable indolence and general insubordination. In retrospect, I'd have to say he was justified on both counts. I believe the breaking point came when he spent half an hour expounding his philosophy of life and art to me, and I replied, "But Michael, that's just Plato's *Myth of the Cave* repackaged." No one likes a smart-ass, and I quickly found myself living in Manhattan with no job, no income, no prospects, and roughly four weeks' savings.

You might think this condition would have humiliated and frightened me. (It certainly would now.) But at the time, I wasn't all that worried. I'll be the first to admit that I didn't take full advantage of the educational opportunities offered at Yale, but I did learn the most important thing they taught there—baseless self-confidence.

It's a lesson that can't be underestimated. Most of my classmates and I departed our graduation ceremony on the Old Campus fully convinced that we were incapable of anything short of rousing success. In fact, the joke among the underachieving set was that if you did manage to graduate from Yale (which is almost a given), you could never become a bum—merely an eccentric. Over time, life's vicissitudes have convinced nearly all of us that we can fail as well as the next guy. But at twenty-three, I was still well inoculated with Ivy League bravado and roundly sure that if I got fired, it was only because the boss was a cretinous jerk, and something better would turn up the following week.

In this case, it actually did. When I had about $200 left in my bank account and a $292 rent payment due, I got a call from Guy Cooper—a totally hip British picture editor who lived in Harlem and played the guitar like Mark Knopfler. Guy's wife, Lela, was from my hometown of Erie, Pennsylvania, and I used to date her sister. Anyway, Guy said he was leaving his position at a small, prestigious photo news agency called Contact Press Images in order to become associate picture editor of *Newsweek*. Guy's boss—a roguish, charismatic photo guru named Robert Pledge—told Guy to find a replacement before he left. So Guy ransacked his Rolodex looking for someone, anyone, who might be vaguely qualified for the job. Fortunately, Cohen is near the beginning of the alphabet.

I hoped that Pledge (everyone called him just "Pledge") wouldn't hold my recent dismissal against me, but he couldn't have cared less about the blots on my copybook. Pledge worked from the gut, and he figured that we would get along well and I'd work like a *campesino* if I liked what I was doing. In turn, I saw the blustering, bearded forty-year-old Frenchman as a kindred spirit, and I admired his panache. Pledge worked when he wanted to—which was often all night. He dressed like a slob. He turned down lucrative jobs because he didn't like the people offering them. And without benefit of any discernible management skills, he commanded a ragtag band of ten highly talented, fiercely loyal photojournalists, who roamed the earth covering stories in the name of truth and justice.

For a twenty-three-year-old kid in search of excitement, Contact Press Images was the best possible place to land. I earned a subsistence wage, but I scarcely noticed because every day was a new adventure and every breaking news story seemed to concern me personally. I loved the little yellow boxes full of slides that were rushed back to New York from Irian Jaya and El Salvador. I loved the adrenaline rush when we landed a scoop or made a magazine deadline by minutes (which, because of Pledge's management style, was fairly routine). And I secretly relished the late-night phone calls when Pledge would growl in his throaty, accented English, "The Shah of Iran's been overthrown. Find David Burnett in Manila and get him to Teheran."

Most of all I liked hanging out with the photographers between assignments. They always knew where to find the best Ethiopian restaurant in New York, and they always had the best possible war stories. It was like having a big dysfunctional family of dashing, larger-than-life older brothers (and one older sister—Annie Leibovitz). Our office was like a clubhouse where the favored traits were quiet bravado, savoir faire, and cynicism.

Once in a while, the photographers even dragged me along when they went on assignment or covered a big celebrity. One of my favorite photographers, Douglas Kirkland, always brought me signed Polaroids of the countless beautiful women he photographed. He convinced various stars and supermodels to write bogus inscriptions to me like, "David, you're the best lover I ever had, Morgan Fairchild" or "I'd leave Billy for you in a minute, Christie." I posted these ersatz testimonials on a big bulletin board in my kitchen where they rarely failed to impress my dates.

After I'd been at the agency for about two years, Contact's youngest photojournalist, a gifted and prodigiously charming con artist named Rick Smolan, asked me if I wanted to come to Melbourne, Australia, to work on a photo book project. Smolan's grandiose scheme was to bring one hundred of the world's best photojournalists to Australia, spread them across the country, and have them all snap pictures on a single day. This extravaganza, modeled after a *Life* magazine special issue, was supposed to produce a lavish coffee-table book called *A Day in the Life of Australia.*

Incredibly, Smolan had convinced several major corporations to back his scheme, but he said he needed "some management help" to actually pull it off. This turned out to be an understatement. After a grueling twenty-hour flight, I discovered that the *A Day in the Life of Australia* project headquarters consisted of a bedroom and dining room in a run-down little house in a marginal Melbourne neighborhood. Smolan and his Australian partner had no budget, no workable accounting system, no filing system, and they were practically broke. They did have a Tandy personal computer—which was pretty high-tech for 1981—but it lost the entire contents of its memory whenever someone switched on the vacuum cleaner—which from the looks of things, wasn't often.

Still, the project had a rare can-do spirit, and with Smolan in command, we bluffed, maneuvered, and equivocated our way to success. When Smolan and I arrived in the Western Australian city of Perth with no money for a hotel room, we traded the manager of the local Sheraton one hundred copies of our nonexistent book for three weeks' worth of free lodgings. When thirty-six publishers in Australia and America rejected our can't-miss book idea, Smolan convinced a bank to lend us $250,000 at 21 percent interest. We used the money to print the books ourselves. Then we sold them through newspaper ads.

Fortunately, *A Day in the Life of Australia* was a great success. One hundred top photojournalists from twenty countries all showed up in Sydney. Their photographs were inspired. The book won several awards and eventually became a number one bestseller in Australia. This enabled us to retire our debts—as opposed to going to jail for fraud. But when the dust settled, everyone involved swore up and down that they'd never, ever do anything remotely similar again. (Our office manager actually ended up in the psych ward of a Sydney hospital for two weeks.)

But a year later, in 1982, the state of Hawaii called and offered Smolan and me a free trip to the islands if we would consider doing *A Day in the Life of Hawaii*. We ended up spending eight idyllic months there, and Smolan invited me to become his partner in Day in the Life, Inc. From that point forward, our small Day in the Life crew adopted a nomadic lifestyle, traveling from country to country, producing a new book every year. By 1986, we had four moderately successful projects under our belt and were casting about for a fifth. I wanted to go for the brass ring—*A Day in the Life of America*. Smolan agreed, somewhat reluctantly, and a few months later we announced the project. The day our press release went out, the phone lines in our Denver office lit up like a Christmas tree. At one point, our publicist, Patti Richards, breathlessly announced that she had all three major television networks on hold simultaneously.

It only got crazier from there. None of us believed that *A Day in the Life of America* was the best book we ever did, but with Reagan in the White House, the stock market booming, and America feeling its oats, a book celebrating the U.S. of A. was the right product at the right time. All the cosmic tumblers fell into place and *A Day in the Life of America* became the first coffee-table book ever to hit number one on *The New York Times* bestseller list. It settled on the list for fifty-six weeks, selling more than 1.4 million copies—one of the best-selling nonfiction books of the decade. Shortly thereafter Collins Publishers bought Day in the Life, Inc., and Smolan and I became young millionaires (barely) with profiles in *The New York Times,* a piece on *20/20,* and a feature story in *People* magazine. (*People* wanted to photograph us with dollar bills falling out of the sky, but we managed to convince them that was bad taste—even for the eighties.)

My long-suffering parents were shocked and vastly relieved that their chronically underachieving son had staged what had to be characterized as a remarkable, Prince Hal sort of turnaround. But my mother, upon seeing *A Day in the Life of America* at the top of the bestseller list, said something strangely prescient. "I wonder what happens," she said, "when the pinnacle of your career occurs when you're only thirty-one years old."

As things turned out, her concerns were justified. I wouldn't say that a huge early success ruined my career. But trends come and go, cut-rate competitors move onto your turf, and new corporate parents have a way of institutionalizing and dumbing-down even the most entrepreneurial of projects. Smolan reacted by withdrawing to his computer screen and the conference circuit, where he was a stunningly good speaker, and I was left to tend the nuts and bolts of the *nouveau régime.* Over time, Smolan became increasingly alienated, and I felt as if I were doing all the heavy lifting. After a while our very successful, symbiotic partnership faltered. Smolan left first, and a year later, I followed him out the door.

As my career unraveled, my home life improved. Back when I was in Tokyo doing *A Day in the Life of Japan,* I met a beautiful American translator named Devyani Kamdar. Devi (pronounced "Davey") was a recent Stanford graduate who was using her fluent Japanese to earn enough money to backpack around Asia. Her father was Indian, her mother American, and the first time I saw her, I experienced a hormonal frisson. We met at one of our famous Day in the Life group dinners. (At the time, we tended to graze in herds.) The bad news was that I got blazing drunk on Japanese potato vodka and ended up in the back of a Shinjuku taxicab singing "We Are the World" at the top of my lungs. The good news was that one of our young interns, Torin Boyd, noticed the chemistry and showed enough initiative to get Devi's phone number for me. (I believe he also offered up some plausible excuses for my boorish behavior.)

After a first date at a very elegant Japanese restaurant where they served elaborate little seafood dishes on huge antique *imari* plates, we became a couple and spent most of our free time together. In fact, we were so compatible that I could often sense, telepathically, when she was near. I used to amaze Smolan by saying, "Devi's here," and a few minutes later she'd walk through the door. Unfortunately, Devi was in Tokyo only long enough to assemble her travel fund. And even if she could have stayed longer, I had to rush back to New York for postproduction work on *A Day in the Life of Japan.* We left Tokyo about the same time, and I figured I'd never see her again.

But over the course of the next several months, I started to think about Devi more and more, and eventually I decided to track her down. I called her mother in Eugene, Oregon. She didn't know where Devi was, but she thought maybe she'd show up in Bali sometime in the near future. I wrote a letter to Devi saying that I was desperately searching for her and addressed it to:

Devyani Kamdar
Poste Restante
Denpaser, Bali

Theoretically, the Balinese post office would hold this letter and give it to her if she ever showed up asking for mail. I had my doubts about this scheme, but a few weeks later I got a crackly phone call from halfway across the globe. I told Devi to stay put, and I'd meet her in Bali within a week.

Before it was fully developed by the tourist trade, Bali was a magically romantic place to court. Devi and I holed up in a thatched cottage at the old Tanjung Sari Hotel overlooking Sanur Beach. We spent hot days exploring the island and turning brown on the sand. In the cool evenings we lay in bed listening to the exotic gamelan music that wafted through our hut on scented breezes. Eventually, I had to go home, but Devi promised to join me in New York when she finished her Asian tour.

We lived together in Manhattan for several months. Then, one day, Devi decided to take off on a tour of Europe with three of her girlfriends. She was gone only about three weeks, but given her proclivity to wander, I began to worry. The day she returned I got down on one knee and proposed. We eloped to Hawaii and were married on a thirty-foot sloop off the beach at Waikiki.

Ten months later, our daughter, Kara, was born. Devi hated the freezing New York winters, and neither of us wanted to raise children in Manhattan, so I persuaded HarperCollins to let us move its new Day in the Life division to San Francisco. Soon after we arrived, our second child, Willie, was born. When Lucas arrived five years later, we were comfortably settled in a big brown-shingled house in leafy, suburban Mill Valley.

By then, I'd more or less left HarperCollins, but I was still producing coffee-table books from a small cottage next to our house. The books weren't big bestsellers like *A Day in the Life of America*, but as long as I kept churning out titles, I could make a pretty good living. Devi paid the company bills and balanced the checkbook each month. She drove the children to their myriad activities, played tennis, and gardened. We had three wonderful children, two Labrador retrievers, a sport-utility vehicle and a thirty-five-inch TV. And that should have been that—a reasonably smooth and successful transition from a wild and adventurous youth to a mature, content adulthood with all the suburban trappings.

Or so I thought. Shortly after my fortieth birthday, I began to experience the first twinges of spiritual uneasiness. I suppose you could call it a midlife crisis or nostalgia for the swashbuckling days of my youth. Whatever it was, slowly and inexorably, the old spirit of adventure reasserted itself. I quietly began to dislike the big house and the sport-utility vehicle and the mediocre coffee-table books I was making. I started to realize that it was pretty stupid to work all the time making money to buy things we didn't particularly need. I couldn't have put it into words at the time, but in retrospect, I think I began to mourn the loss of the free spirit that once roamed the world, worked for passion, and ran off to Bali on a moment's notice.

Of course, I knew I couldn't turn back the clock, so initially I tried to suppress these seditious sentiments. I said to myself, "Grow up. Be sensible. This is a natural process. You get older. You have kids. You settle down. You work for a living. Passions dim. People change. Life goes on." But over the course of several months this very sane, very rational line of argument lost its fizzle, and I realized that I liked the old spirit better. In fact, the more I thought about it, the more I realized that the only truly sensible thing to do was to embrace the old spirit and strike back out into the world in search of new adventures and fresh experience.

Then came the reality check. I mean how was I going to do this big adventure travel thing when I had a wife, an eight-year-old daughter, seven- and two-year-old sons, a mortgage, and a business to run? I couldn't just close everything down and yank the kids out of school, could I? But if I didn't sell the house and close the business, would I really be cutting the ties? Wouldn't that just be a long vacation? That wasn't what I was trying to achieve. What I wanted was a clean break, a blank slate, ground zero. A new start with no preconceived plans, no itinerary, no time limit. Somehow, in this agitated state, I decided that the only way to truly purify my life and reclaim my old spirit was to sell our house, close down the business, liquefy our possessions, and take off around the world for an indeterminate length of time.

Now there was just the small matter of telling my wife of nine years that I wanted to stop working, sell everything we owned, and drag the whole family off on a rambling trip to God knows where. I thought it might be too great a shock to spring this on Devi all at once. So over the course of several weeks, I began to propose increasingly ambitious plans. First, I talked about a trip to Australia. Then gradually, over time, I started adding countries. This strategy turned out to be completely unnecessary, because when I finally worked my way up to the big casino—the part where we got rid of everything and became global vagabonds—Devi listened patiently to what most wives would consider a masterpiece of insanity and essentially said, "Yeah. That sounds like a pretty good idea."

Initially, I was amazed at her reaction, but then I remembered who it was I married. *Of course* this sounded like a good idea to her. I mean why would Devi, the original free spirit, be any more enamored of suburban quotidia than I was? She missed her old life, too. She wanted to roam the world the way she did before we met. And as she reminded me, her own formidable mother had taken her—and her three siblings—on a low-budget round-the-world trip when Devi was only six years old.

So I discovered that my wife actually liked this deranged concept. I also discovered that we could pay for the trip with proceeds from the sale of our house and cars, and that we could legally take the kids out of public school and home-school them on the road. (And, of course, the journey would be a great education in its own right.) Interrupting my career wouldn't be a problem, because I didn't care about my career anymore. So other than a sudden illness in the family, there was only one possible stumbling block: losing our nerve. I mean it's one thing to dream up a scheme like this and quite another to maintain your resolve. And if there was ever a plan that lent itself to chickening out, this was it. I figured the best way around this pitfall was to boldly announce our agenda to all our friends and family. That way we'd be too humiliated to call it off. So in December 1995, Devi and I dispatched a holi-day e-mail that went like this:

Subject: Ready, Fire, Aim
Date: Friday, December 15, 1995
From: daylifers@aol.com (David Cohen)

Mill Valley, California

Dear Friends:

Devi and I are writing to you for three reasons. First of all, we want to wish you a Merry Christmas, Happy New Year, Happy Hanukkah, and joyous *dewali*. (That last one's for Devi's Indian relatives.) Secondly, we want to tell you a little bit about the kids and how they're doing this year. And finally, we want to tell you about a big decision we've made.

First the kids. We can't believe it, but Lucas is nearly two already. He's now a roly-poly little guy with a husky voice and an infectious laugh. He recently sprouted a riot of curls that make him look like a cross between Lyle Lovett and a Raphaelite angel. He's also learned to say a few dozen words, and some—like "Hay-lo, Man" (Hello, person of either sex) and "Ni-Ni Wawa" (Good night, Kara)—appear to be English even to the casual observer. Others, like "Ma-dai" (food), "Ya-yee" (liquid), and "Dow" (motor vehicle), don't seem to derive from any of the major Indo-European language groups. Still, we all manage to communicate with Lucas on his own terms. When we eat in a restaurant, we say things like, "Give Lucas some *ma-dai* and put some *ya-yee* in his cup," and people at neighboring tables think we're Romanian.

Our big boy, Willie, is now nearly seven. He has large eyes the color of semisweet chocolate, and he's the spit and image of his mother. Willie has a sweet, cuddly nature punctuated by flashes of temper that always land him in trouble. He's slightly small for his age but very intrepid. He skis black diamond slopes with abandon, and stands on his toes to evade the height requirements at amusement park roller coasters.

Kara recently turned eight. She's fair and slight—somewhat pixieish—with a bright, happy face and a quick wit. She's painfully shy around strangers, but she now has a trio of best friends and an active social life. Kara recently conned her grandmother into buying her a speaker phone with speed dial. So now she trades second-grade gossip and fashion tips at the touch of a button. ("What are you going to wear?" "I don't know." "What are you going to wear?") Fortunately, she hasn't shown any interest in boys yet, so I've put off buying a firearm for at least another year.

Devi and I are also doing reasonably well—both at home and at work, but we recently decided to make some—how should we say it?—radical changes in our lifestyle. I know this is going to sound insane, but we've decided to sell our house, close down Cohen Publishers, Inc., take the kids out of school, and travel internationally for a while. At this point, we're not sure exactly how long we'll be gone—maybe a year, maybe more—or even where we're going. Devi wants to take a train across India and a riverboat up the Amazon River. I'd like to visit the annual elephant rodeo in Thailand, and Kara and Willie both want to go on an African wildlife safari. I suppose we'll try to do all of these things and just knit them together as we go along.

Now I do realize that many people—perhaps even most people—resolve to quit their jobs and take off for foreign climes at some point in their lives. I also realize that good sense usually prevails sometime before they leave, and they have second thoughts about the whole affair. Believe me, Devi and I have had second thoughts, too—about the cost of the trip, about its effect on our marriage, and about spending twenty-four hours a day with three young children. We realize that the trip could go horribly wrong. And then we'd have to come back to no house, no job, no school. (Not to mention the fact that we'll be completely mortified.)

That being said, we do have a few things going for us. First of all, Devi and I are both committed to this idea in fairly equal measure. In other words neither of us dragged the other one into this. Secondly, we've both traveled very extensively, so we have a reasonably good idea of what we're getting into. Finally, we have a comforting precedent. Thirty years ago, Devi's mom took Devi and her three siblings around the world all by herself. She used standby tickets, stayed in inexpensive hostels, and made meals on a hot plate. Somehow, she managed to find her way through India, Iran, Turkey, Austria, France, and Denmark. And aside from losing one kid for a while in Istanbul's Grand Bazaar, there were no major mishaps.

If Devi's mother could do all this by herself thirty years ago when international travel wasn't so commonplace, Devi and I figure we have a fighting chance now. And if we can make this work, we believe the rewards will be worth the risk. We'll have the opportunity to spend a long period of undistracted time together. We'll see the world through our children's eyes. And with luck, we'll expand their horizons for the rest of their lives.

Of course, much of this edification will be lost on little Lucas. For him, a safari in Zimbabwe isn't that different from a trip to the Safeway. But the timing's right for Kara and Willie. As they get older, they'll be less willing to abandon their friends and activities for a long trip with Mom and Dad. At this point, at least, Willie's all gung ho and Kara, though skeptical, seems willing to be convinced.

Anyway, that's our big news for the year. I know this all must sound fairly bizarre. It does even to us. But we know that if we consider this particular leap of faith too long or too carefully, we'll never do it—and someday we'll regret that. Of course, we want to keep in touch with you while we're gone, but since we won't have any fixed address, we'll have to rely on e-mail. If you want irregular updates from the far corners, let us know, and we'll stay in touch.

Best wishes, the Cohens

The response to this letter was distinctly mixed. Some of our friends thought it was a wonderful idea. A few even seemed jealous. Others—generally the ones who told us how brave we were—actually thought this was the single stupidest thing they ever heard in their lives. One PTA mom said to me, straight out, with a horrified look on her face, "That would be my idea of hell." But for the most part, the response was positive. I was heartened by the fact that older people—folks in their sixties and seventies whose kids had left home—were the most encouraging. I think they wished that they'd done something like this when they were younger. But no matter what people thought about our expedition, everyone was curious how it would turn out, and they all signed up for our periodic progress reports.

In the end, I wrote twenty-three of these e-mail updates. They described our travels by airplane, ship, bus, car, van, train, camel cart, oxcart, and elephant howdah through sixteen countries on six continents. They recounted the times we got hopelessly lost in Rome and Cape Town, how we rushed our daughter to the emergency room in Bangkok, how we escaped a charging hippo in Botswana, how Kara nearly died in Australia, and how I stumbled upon a bit of enlightenment in a cave in rural Laos. They described what it was like to live out of a suitcase for more than a year and how we managed to coexist as a family in tight quarters twenty-four hours a day.

As you read these adventures, anecdotes, and minor epiphanies, I hope you get the sense that these letters were sent to you, or better yet, that you traveled with us during our one amazing year off. If you have any questions or comments as you read these letters—even before you finish them all—send them to me at daylifers@aol.com. I would love to hear from you.

ONE
YEAR
OFF

June 15, 1996
to
July 7, 1997

C h a p t e r   1

Subject: What Have We Done?
Date: June 15
From: daylifers@aol.com (David Cohen)

Tiburon, California

Dear Friends:

In December, Devi and I announced that we were trading in our quiet suburban life for a long rambling trip around the world. Well, I'm sorry to report that this transition has taken far longer than we expected. I actually thought we'd be sipping *vin rouge* on the *rive gauche* by now—but we haven't even managed to leave town yet. Put it this way: Disengaging from your normal routine and establishing an entirely new way of life is a full-time job for months on end.

That being said, I think we're nearing the end of the process. We closed the business, sold our house and cars, and the rest of our things have either been given away, put in storage, or thrown in the trash. Our telephones, TVs, and stereo are all gone—ditto, the mortgage, the water bill, and the property tax notices. In fact, our lives have now been simplified to the point where each of us is left with only one suitcase, a backpack, an economy-class round-the-world ticket and a passport.

I thought we might have second thoughts about shedding all our possessions, but it's turned out to be a very liberating act. I'm not saying that we're all going to become Buddhist monks or move to Walden Pond when we get back. But I now realize how much time, money, and mental energy we spend acquiring and maintaining material goods. When we finally emptied all our closets, drawers, and storage spaces, I was frankly shocked to see how much pure crap we've accumulated over the years. In fact, my favorite part of this whole disengagement process was filling a dumpster the size of a swimming pool with all the flotsam and jetsam of our lives and dispatching it into the sunset.

Planning this trip has also been far more complex than I anticipated. When I first came up with this mad scheme, I thought we could just buy some open, round-the-world tickets and make the trip up as we went along. But then Devi—the voice of reason—convinced me that showing up in a foreign country in the middle of the night with three small children and no place to sleep might be a bit *too* footloose. Devi said we should have a basic plan—as a fallback position—even if we eventually changed everything along the way.

That made sense, so we decided to consult a travel agency. Again, I thought we could stroll up, tell the agent our plans, and two weeks later she'd send us a fat envelope full of tickets, itineraries, and colorful brochures. Not even close. Our usual travel agency was okay for cheap business travel, but a year-long trip around the world put them completely out of their depth. A month after we first called, they still hadn't organized our air tickets. We finally had to fire them and call the airline ourselves. It took three or four hours on the phone, but we eventually got some cheap round-the-world tickets*—and enough potential frequent flyer miles for a free trip on the space shuttle.

---

*Approximately $3,000 each on United.

After striking out with the low-end travel agency, we went to the other extreme, and engaged a very tony adventure travel boutique. We met with some of their expert travel planners over a pot of Earl Grey in a well-appointed conference room. They all seemed competent and knowledgeable, so we asked them to organize one of the most logistically difficult portions of our trip—a month-long passage through Southern Africa. At that first meeting—and at least three times afterward—I asked for an estimate, even a ballpark estimate, of what something like this might cost us. But the woman in charge kept saying that she couldn't possibly quote any prices until all the arrangements were tied down.

Three weeks later, she got back to us with a very exciting, beautifully crafted itinerary. We'd be met at every airport and escorted to each hotel. We'd never have to drive a car, confirm a flight, or carry our own luggage. And, of course, we'd visit only the best possible game-viewing sites. That was the good news. The bad news was that this extravaganza was going to set us back somewhere in the neighborhood of $40,000. Once I regained consciousness, I sheepishly asked her to scale back the expedition—radically. She got back to me the following week cheerfully announcing that she'd sharpened her pencil and worked up a modest $31,000 program. These folks were obviously used to working with the carriage trade—and it was with some degree of embarrassment that I was compelled to inform them that their ends were far beyond our means.

So at that point we'd pretty well struck out with a cheap, incompetent travel agency on the one hand, and a very competent, wildly expensive one on the other. But just when things looked bad Devi stepped into the breach and started making the bookings herself. She found out rather quickly that she could put together a very good African itinerary for a small fraction of what the travel boutique would charge us. From that point forward, we steered clear of the professionals, and Devi became our in-house travel agent. For a few esoteric bookings—like a canal boat in Burgundy or a villa apartment in Tuscany—she used a service that specializes in international vacation rentals.* Other than that, Devi usually found it quicker, cheaper, and easier to make reservations herself.

Devi's indispensable tools in this effort were a three-foot shelf of good, up-to-date guidebooks and a fax machine. With these, she was able to book rooms at a Botswana game lodge, a cheap pensione in Rome, and even a tent at the Pushkar camel festival in Rajasthan. Every night, after the kids went to bed, Devi pored over her *Fodor's* and *Lonely Planet* guides and cast faxes into the ether. Each morning at the crack of dawn, she leapt out of bed to see what she caught. On good days, she rushed back into the bedroom clutching a sheath of faxes from around the globe. On bad days, when no one wrote back, she fretted a lot. But slowly over the course of several months, Devi cobbled together an itinerary with a workable balance of cost, convenience, and adventure.

So here's our plan—at least the one we're heading out the door with: We're going to visit thirteen countries on five continents. These include—in chronological order—Costa Rica, France, Italy, Greece, Turkey, Switzerland, Botswana, Zimbabwe, South Africa, India, Thailand, Australia, and Hong Kong (whew!). We've booked accommodations in advance for about half the trip. Almost all of these bookings can be changed on twenty-four-hours' notice. When we don't have bookings, it's usually because we have insufficient information or we're doing something unusual—like taking local ferries from Venice across the Aegean Sea to the coast of Turkey. This will inevitably cause the journey to unfold in unexpected ways. And that's fine with us, because the whole purpose of this journey is to open ourselves to new experiences and genuine adventures.

That being so bravely said, do we still have concerns about this expedition? In a word, yes. As we get closer to the departure date, each member of the family has an updated list of

*Hideaways International.

fears and phobias. Devi is very well traveled, but she's always roamed around by herself, so she has genuine concerns about too much family togetherness. She's spoken to, or heard of, six other families that have attempted this sort of journey. Four of them had a marvelous time, and the trip brought them closer together. The other two couples were later divorced—though it's not clear that this was due to their travels.

Devi is also concerned that she and I won't find any private time away from the kids. Apparently, there are very few reasonably priced "family suites"–type hotels outside North America and Australia, and few European hotels of any kind allow five people to stay in a room. The kids are too young to sleep by themselves. So that means that Devi and I would have to sleep in different rooms for most of the trip. That's okay for a few weeks—but not for a year or more—so in a bow to realism, we've asked our regular baby-sitter, Betty, to join us for at least the first part of the trip. Betty, who's single and in her mid-thirties, loves to travel, and she's thrilled with the prospect of a round-the-world journey. Fortunately, she's willing to work for room, board, air tickets, and some pocket money, so that makes it practical for us to bring her along. It does feel a bit like cheating, but we've decided not to be doctrinaire about this—especially if it means giving up intimate relations for a year.

Devi's other major fear is that two-year-old Lucas will fall off something—like an Italian balcony or a French canal boat. To mitigate this hazard, she bought a toddler leash and forty feet of nylon netting. Devi honestly believes that she can child-proof our shifting environment as we travel around the world. I have my doubts, and I'm only glad that Lucas isn't old enough to be humiliated by the leash.

Eight-year-old Kara's two main concerns are losing contact with her friends and being devoured by a wild animal. The other day she greeted me at the breakfast table with a stern expression and a copy of the *San Francisco Chronicle*. The headline read, "Marin Girl Mauled by Hyena," and it described a local eleven-year-old who was attacked while camping in Kenya. Kara pointed at the story, and said accusingly, "And you *still* want to go to Africa?" I assured her that we'd do everything in our power to protect her, but Kara remained stubbornly skeptical until Devi found a place in Western Australia where she could swim with wild dolphins. In Kara's mind, that made up for a multitude of sins.

Willie, as usual, is gung ho for any adventure that might come his way. Being seven and male, his social life is far less complex than Kara's, and he's genuinely delighted to miss a year of school. If anything, Willie helps reassure Kara that this madness will all turn out well in the end. I think at this point, if we told Willie we were all going to the backwoods of Borneo for the rest of our lives, he'd say, "Okay, let's do it."

Lucas, who's now speaking in full sentences, also seems comfortable with the trip—at least to the extent he understands it. He'll have his mommy, his daddy, and his blankie with him twenty-four hours a day. So for him, this is the best of all worlds.

As for me, I do have this strange fear that the kids will contract some vile disease in India. It may be coincidence, but almost everyone I know who's gone there has come down with some sort of illness, from dysentery to malaria. To avert this, Devi faxed the Centers for Disease Control in Atlanta. They sent back some advisories saying if we went to India—or Botswana for that matter—we should be inoculated against polio, tetanus, hepatitis A, hepatitis B, and typhoid. Plus we should take the antimalarial drug Lariam. According to the CDC, Lariam's side effects can include psychotic behavior. That sounded worrisome, so when we went to get our shots, I mentioned it to the doctor. He said not to worry, that full-blown psychosis occurs only in a small minority of cases.

As you might expect, Willie took the vaccinations like a trouper. No tears—just a stoic grin and an immediate demand for compensation from Dr. Joe's treasure chest of ten-cent toys. Lucas, on the other hand, was stunned and offended that we could just stand by and allow him to be violated like that. Then he burst into tears. As for our eldest, I'm chagrined to say that she threw herself into a full-scale panic. She started crying even before the doctor came into the examination room. Then she bolted from the office and ran screaming down the hall. I actually had to drag her back into the examination room and hold her down while she got her shots.

Aside from my disease phobia, I also have to admit that being homeless and out of work—even by choice—is somewhat disorienting. It's odd to realize that from now on, wherever we happen to be on a given day is our home, and that there's no single safe haven to which we can return. It's also strange to suddenly relinquish all your structures and schedules—all the chores, routines, and rituals that define and organize your life. When you follow these routines, it's possible to live most of your life on autopilot. It's like driving to work without even thinking about the route. But when your routines are disrupted—especially this radically—you become very conscious of your actions, your surroundings, and your relationships. Everything seems new and unsettled. But again, that's one of the goals of our trip—to disrupt our usual patterns so thoroughly that we'll be receptive to new options and possibilities.

To do that fully, we have to let this transformation from conventional to nomadic life take place on its own terms. We have to observe the changes and be conscious of them, but we can't limit the outcome or cling to old routines and old ways of thinking. Sometimes that's difficult, because all our friends and acquaintances constantly question us about the future. They ask, "How long will you be gone? Where will you live when you get back? Will you go back to the same job?" I try to tell them that the whole purpose of this journey is to see new possibilities, and that if we predetermine the outcome at the start, that purpose will be defeated. But most people are uncomfortable with that answer. They seem to crave certainty in their own lives, and they consider it imprudent to place one's family in such an ambiguous position. To that I can only reply that any sense of certainty we have in life is ephemeral at best. That was revealed to us this month with savage clarity.

Devi and I have two friends, Curt and Alma. They don't know each other. Curt was my roommate at Yale, and Alma was Devi's friend at Stanford. Curt has been HIV-positive for nearly twelve years, and two of his former lovers have died from AIDS. His doctors, his friends, his parents, and everyone else have always known it was only a matter of time, and probably a short time at that. Alma, on the other hand, was a happy, healthy, vibrant woman who participated in two very successful Silicon Valley start-ups. She recently married the man she loved. They were building their dream house, and she was eight months' pregnant with twins.

Curt and Alma were both on fast tracks, moving in opposite directions. Then, all of a sudden, Curt starts responding to a new cocktail of AIDS drugs and his virus-load drops off the chart. For all intents and purposes, after waiting to die for twelve years, Curt is "cured." Alma, on the other hand, is riding home from work with her husband, seat belt stretched over her big belly, when a guy in a pickup truck falls asleep at the wheel, crashes across the median strip, and hits their Mercedes head-on. Alma is killed instantly. The emergency room doctors try to deliver the twins, but they die, too. Alma's husband was sitting behind an air bag, and he walks away without a scratch.

Here's another twist. Alma's funeral, which should have been the saddest event on the face of the earth, was attended by more than a thousand people, and it was one of the warmest, sweetest, most life-affirming events Devi and I ever attended. Her husband, her father, and her brother all delivered eulogies that made us realize that this woman, cut down in the fullness of life, had actually been blessed. Her life was important to so many people. Curt, on the other hand, has gone into therapy. He didn't think he would live very long, so for the last twelve years he's led his life as if he were already dead. Now that he's "cured," he's not sure what to do.

So if you ask me about certainty, I'd have to say it's a cruel illusion. And if you ask us how this trip is going to turn out, and what we're going to do when we get back, I'd say the purpose of this journey is to open ourselves individually, and as a family, to a world of possibilities, because tomorrow…well, who knows about tomorrow?

Love from all,
David

P.S. About the only thing we did more quickly than we anticipated was sell our house. We still have about a month before we leave the country, so we're driving down to L.A. to visit friends, then over to Arizona to see Devi's mom. We'll come back via the Grand Canyon, Death Valley, and Yosemite. It'll be sort of a trial run for the big trip. Besides, I hear that the weather in Arizona is lovely in July.

C h a p t e r   2

Subject: We Never Get to Go Anywhere
Date: August 1
From: daylifers@aol.com (David Cohen)

Stinson Beach, California

Dear Friends:

Only one day to go until we leave the good ole U.S. of A. I don't feel particularly jittery yet, just relieved that this endless transition period is nearly over and that we're finally getting on the wretched plane and going already. The other day, a friend of mine said, "You know, it's really tough to miss you if you won't leave." He's right. It's time to get out of Dodge.

We've been back in the Bay Area for about ten days now. This, after a month-long drive down to Arizona and back. It was an illuminating preview of the year to come. I thought I knew my children pretty well. After all, I worked at home, and I saw them regularly during the course of a day. But, believe me, spending twenty-four hours a day with your kids for a month takes matters to an entirely new level. First of all, Kara and Willie fought constantly. By constantly, I don't mean three times a day. I mean three times an hour. And it was always over the most incredible issue like "Her hand's on my side of the line," or "She breathed on me," or my personal favorite, "He called my stuffed dog idiotic." Devi and I both fought with our siblings when we were kids, so this month-long car ride was karmic vengeance with a passion. Had they witnessed it, I'm sure my parents would have been deeply satisfied that what goes around comes around.

When the usual threats, time-outs, and quiet times stopped working, we had to get creative. Devi read about a guy who bought a huge bag of candy whenever he went on a road trip with his children. First, he displayed the bag lovingly to the children, and told them it could all be theirs at the end of the trip. Then, every time the kids started fighting, he silently grabbed a handful of candy and tossed it out the window. The kids would stop fighting immediately. I thought it was a great idea—very direct, very graphic—but Devi said it might be too difficult to explain this particular child-rearing technique to the highway patrol when they pulled us over for littering.

Instead, Devi devised a simple but fiendishly clever system of bribery. She got hold of some old checkbook registers and credited one dollar to each kid's account for every hour they behaved passably well in the car. She deducted a dollar for every argument, piercing scream, or act of naked aggression. In practice, Kara earned about $4 a day; Willie, about $2.50. These were the only funds the kids had to buy postcards, costume jewelry, giant Grand Canyon pencils, and fake Navajo rugs. Which brings us to the second salutary effect of this system. Instead of saying, "No, you may not buy that $19.95 inflatable Sea World killer whale," fourteen times a day, we just said, "Sure, go ahead...*but, remember, it comes out of your account.*" As soon as the kids figured out it was their hard-earned money that they were squandering, they quickly evolved from rampaging shopaholics to fiscal conservatives.

At this point, I'm sure some of you are thinking, "You mean you're *paying* your children not to fight with each other instead of exploring the root causes of their aggression and developing effective conflict resolution skills?" Okay, you're right. I don't recall any chapters entitled "Bribing Your Children" in Brazelton or Spock. But I also doubt those guys ever spent twenty-four hours a day with their children for a month.

Once we contained the internecine warfare, Devi and I turned our attention to the food issue. Namely, that Willie's list of acceptable sustenance has gradually dwindled to a precious few. Willie has now declared himself a vegetarian (though he doesn't actually like very many vegetables either, so he's more like a potatotarian). He won't eat fish, pork, or poultry in any form, and he won't eat beef...unless it happens to be shaped into a sausage or enclosed in a taco. There is no rationale for this—at least, none deducible by adults—but believe me, it's impossible to persuade Willie that hamburgers and tacos are crafted from the same substance.

Devi and I suspect that Willie is hyper-fussy about food in order to carve out his own special niche in the family. After all, two-year-old Lucas has first call on everyone's attention. When he needs feeding or changing, he gets it, and everyone else waits. Kara's the oldest and most verbal, so when Lucas isn't fussing, she dominates the scene. Poor Willie is stuck in the middle. Some kids develop psychosomatic allergies or wet their bed to attract attention, but I think Willie's using his diet. If that's the case, he's been wildly successful, because when it's time to eat, all eyes are upon him.

Devi, Betty, and I all say solicitous things like, "Will you eat a hot dog, Willie? It's almost like a sausage. How about pasta with marinara sauce? There's no meat in it. Vegetarian ravioli? Pasta with butter and Parmesan cheese? French fries? Rice with soy sauce?" Then, when the food arrives, we all wait with bated breath to see if the young prince approves.

All this extra attention naturally threatens Kara's sense of primogeniture, so she's been subtly undermining Willie's position as the family vegetarian since the beginning of the trip. During our premeal interrogation, she usually tosses out something like, "Why are you a vegetarian, Willie? Are you opposed to killing animals, or do you just hate meat? If you're opposed to killing animals, you shouldn't wear leather."

Or, after we've spent ten minutes painstakingly persuading Willie to eat an egg roll or soup or some other concoction where the meat is obscure, Kara will pipe in with something like, "You know, Willie, the broth in that soup is actually made from meat, so if you're really a vegetarian, you shouldn't eat it."

Devi and I know that if we put our foot down and serve Willie only what everyone else is eating, he'll eventually get hungry enough to expand his repertoire. But for now, we're inclined to concede him this peccadillo. The only problem (aside from the fact that we have to eat at Taco Bell all the time) is that later in the trip it may be difficult to find tacos and french fries in India.

Something else we learned about our children during this practice run. Namely, what impresses them is entirely different from what impresses us. This was best illustrated by our first encounter with the Grand Canyon. We arrived just before dusk, and as the sun set, every color in the desert palette played across the canyon walls. I stood on the rim of the abyss transfixed by its grandeur. I'd seen only photographs and films before, and these don't begin to convey the Grand Canyon's vast scale and majesty.

"Well, kids," I said. "There it is. The Grand Canyon. One of the Seven Wonders of the World. Isn't it magnificent?"

To which Kara replied, "Wow, look at this chipmunk, Willie. Isn't he cute." When I turned around, I saw all three of our children with their backs to the canyon totally engrossed by a small brown chipmunk rendered tame by a summer-long parade of blasé children.

On the way to Arizona and back we also witnessed the majestic coast of Big Sur, the stark beauty of Death Valley, and the splendor of Yosemite. Kara and Willie found all of these wonders mildly interesting—better than school, perhaps, but not as good as a *Rugrats* cartoon. In fact, there was only one place we went that truly impressed the children—a place so fabulous that the b-word* was never mentioned. I am, of course, speaking of the magnificence that is Las Vegas. The moment Kara walked into the MGM Grand Hotel, her jaw dropped and stars danced in her eyes. And as the slot machine bells rang and the coins clanked and the hundred-foot video display morphed endlessly over the check-in desk, all she could say, over and over, was "A hotel with five thousand rooms, and its own theme park. Its... own...theme...park."

Devi and I were horrified. I mean here we had just quit our jobs and sold our house in order to drag our children around the world to see a vast array of natural, cultural, and historical sights which, in the final analysis, might not interest them quite as much as, say, the souvenir shop at the MGM Grand. This was a sobering notion full of unpleasant implications for the year ahead. Still, we took a deep breath and decided not to panic—at least not yet. After all, we're the ones who brought the kids to Las Vegas in the first place. And who can really blame them for falling in love with mock pirate battles, fake erupting volcanoes, and animatronic dragons that shoot propane fireballs from their mouths? Devi and I decided it would probably be unnatural for young children to like Big Sur and Yosemite as much as the MGM Grand and Universal Studios.

Kids come into the world hardwired to love theme parks and chipmunks. Apparently it takes time and training to appreciate the Grand Canyon, Yosemite, or the Louvre. Still you have to start the learning process some time, so we're going to drag these children through the Uffizi and the Acropolis whether they like it or not. And by the end of this trip, we hope there will be room in their hearts for Botticelli and the Parthenon as well as the Vegas Strip.

*Boring.

Speaking of unrealistic expectations, Devi and I also found ourselves from time to time asking Kara and Willie, "Do you realize how lucky you are? What a great opportunity this is? How few children get to do this?" When tears of gratitude didn't stream down their cheeks, we realized that no, they didn't understand how unusual this journey was—and they probably wouldn't for a long time to come. In fact, within a matter of three weeks or so, living in a different hotel room every night and traveling from one place to another every day seemed to be completely natural to them—like they did it all the time. One evening, near the end of our trial run, Devi and I decided to leave the kids in the room with Betty and go out for dinner by ourselves. As we were walking out the door, Kara asked, "How come you aren't taking us?"

I explained that Mommy and Daddy needed some time alone and that we'd be back in a few hours. Now, the fact that Kara had been to five cities, four national parks, and two dozen restaurants in the past three weeks didn't for one second deter her from saying, "Ahh...We never get to go anywhere."

It's not that Kara and Willie have forgotten their old life. They clearly remember living in a house in the suburbs and going to school and down to the swamp to play with the neighbor kids. But, unlike Devi and me, they don't seem to cling to their old ways as a fixed frame of reference. To the kids, that was then, and this is now. We used to live in one place. Now we move every few days. We used to watch television and play with toys. Now we go to national parks and sit in the car. At this point, I think if we decided to stay in Paris for a few years, they'd become French, God forbid. And if we toured the country with Barnum and Bailey, they'd become circus people.

Our friend Susan Wels tells the best anecdote about kids this age and how well they adapt to new environments. Several years ago, she, her husband, Dave Hagerman, and their two young girls moved into an old Victorian in San Francisco's very gay Castro district. One day, Sue was walking home from the store with her six-year-old, Casey, in tow.

Casey suddenly yelled, "Look, Mommy, look…" Sue glanced up to see two men holding hands and walking a dog. One of the men was wearing a tight leather skirt, fishnet stockings, and a mustache. Sue was bracing herself to explain the facts of alternative life when Casey piped up and finished her thought. "Mommy, their dog is wearing a sweater!" After only a few months in the Castro, Casey was completely unimpressed by guys in dresses. For her, the dog in the sweater was the novelty.

Apparently two-year-olds take a little longer to adjust—at least Lucas has. I thought Lucas would be perfectly content so long as he had his mommy, his daddy, and his blankie. But as soon as we started moving from place to place every day, he began to worry that one of these times he was going to be left behind. Whenever we packed our suitcases in the morning, Lucas would hold on to Devi's leg like a baby monkey or sit on top of a suitcase so he wouldn't be forgotten.

Of course, we reassured him that this would never, ever happen—that he was our precious boy, and we would take him with us wherever we went. But our credibility suffered a serious blow when we all piled into the car in Palm Springs one day, did a head count, and realized that Willie had been left behind. The poor little guy went into the bathroom just before we all walked out the door. As soon as we discovered we were short one seven-year-old, I jumped from the car and ran back to our room. Willie was standing just inside the door with one small tear in the corner of his eye. It would have broken your heart to see him.

The other mistake we made with Lucas was taking him on the Universal Studios tour. It's a terrific ride, but to really enjoy it you should be old enough to grasp the concept that the five or six natural disasters you encounter along the way are lifelike illusions. This was Lucas's first bus ride of any kind and during the space of thirty minutes, he was assailed by King Kong, a flash flood, an avalanche, an earthquake, and a collapsing bridge. For the most part, he was not amused. The next time we tried to get him onto a bus—at the San Diego Zoo—he made it perfectly clear that he would never board this sort of conveyance again.

After nine and a half years of marriage, and for the first time since we courted, Devi and I are learning how to be with each other every hour of the day. Of course, even with Betty along, we're not really with each other in any real sense more than three or four hours out of every twenty-four. The rest of the time at least one of the kids needs feeding, watering, cleaning, comforting, conciliating, bathroom stops, diaper changes, or some other sort of custodial attention. I've noticed, however, that I now rely upon Devi for nearly all of my adult feedback. Before we left home, I was always on the phone, interacting with a small group of adults. Within that circle, we told jokes, gave advice, exchanged confidences, and listened to gossip. Now I do all of these things exclusively with Devi. At home, we lived parallel lives that met and digressed according to a rhythm developed during nearly a decade of marriage. Now, those rhythms have been disrupted, and we share everything— one path, one experience, one life, one bathroom. To be all things to each other places a heavy burden on the relationship, and I find that Devi's comments, her praise and criticisms, carry far more weight than they used to—probably more than they should.

I think Devi knew instinctively that changing our life this way would force us to reexamine and realign our relationship. She tried to tell me this in a subtle, empathetic fashion, but of course, I had to discover it for myself. I'm sure we'll find a new equilibrium over time, but until we do, we both have to devote time and attention to a modus vivendi we've taken for granted for years.

> Best wishes,
> David, Devi, Kara, Willie,
> and Lucas

Chapter 3

Subject: The Sex Life of Butterflies
Date: August 4
From: daylifers@aol.com (David Cohen)

Arenal Lodge, Costa Rica

Dear Friends:

Greetings from Costa Rica. You have to love this country just on principle. Even though they're wedged between Nicaragua and Panama—pretty turbulent nations in recent decades—the Costa Ricans have no armed forces of any kind. Instead of blowing their colones on Apache helicopters and Sidewinder missiles, they've bet the country's future on education, health care, and ecotourism.

And that's why we're here—to tour Costa Rica's pristine beaches, towering volcanoes, and dense tropical rain forests. Since saving the rain forest is pretty much the cause célèbre amongst the elementary school set these days, Devi and I thought a trip to the jungle would be a good, kid-friendly way to launch our journey. Furthermore, this is the only leg of our trip that was organized by travel professionals—so we thought that might get us off to a smooth start.

Anyway, that was the plan. In reality, things didn't work out so well. We took off from San Francisco at 11:00 A.M., and with a five-hour layover in Mexico City, we didn't arrive at our small, but not-so-charming Costa Rican inn until 2:00 in the morning. By that time, Devi and I were shattered, and the kids were utter zombies. No one was even mildly amused when the night clerk said he had only one double bed and one single for the six of us. The clerk—who spoke only Spanish—insisted nothing else was available, and we should just make the best of it.

I couldn't believe it. This was the very first night of a *year-long trip around the world,* and our reservations were already screwed up. Fortunately, Devi speaks Spanish very expressively, and she made it perfectly *claro* that we all required a bed. After an hour of spirited conversation—largely incomprehensible to me—we ended up commandeering the staff dormitory. Of course, by that time, it was nearly 3:00 in the morning.

As a consequence, we weren't nearly as cheerful as we could have been when we joined the rest of our tour group over a 7:00 A.M. breakfast. Fortunately, they were a copacetic lot. There was a middle-aged Jewish couple from Long Island, a folksy South Dakota professor and his twenty-two-year-old son, a lovely older couple from California's Central Valley, their teenage granddaughter, plus Lloyd and Philippa—young marrieds from a tony London suburb. Lloyd and Philippa turned out to be quite pleasant—particularly at the cocktail hour. Still, Devi and I couldn't help noticing that they seemed to regard our children as small petlike beings—interesting in an anthropological sense, but wholly unsuitable as dinner companions—which unfortunately, they were. Every time Lucas did something particularly simian, like mashing a banana into his hair, I saw Philippa take a silent vow that no child of hers would dine in public before the age of twelve.

Our crew also included an earnest young tour guide named Miguel and our bus driver, Oscar Gómez. Apparently, many ecotourists come to Costa Rica specifically to see the rare tropical birds here, and Oscar, the bus driver, had a preternatural ability to spot *rara avises* obscured in trees fifty meters off. This would have been impressive in its own right, but Oscar could pull this deft trick while navigating a bouncing bus down a winding, pothole-strewn road.

Every twenty minutes or so, Oscar would suddenly hit the brakes, point out the window, and mumble something to Miguel. Miguel would then activate the loudspeaker and say, "Oscar has just spotted a rare and beautiful crested karakara in that cinchona tree over there on the left." Bob from Long Island would break out his new foot-long 300 mm lens and deftly snap the bird. Then Kara and Willie would pull out their own cheapo point-and-shoot cameras and fire off several shots of the magnificent bird, which would subsequently appear as a minuscule black dot on numerous 3 x 5 prints. Finally, Miguel—who was clearly an overachiever amongst Costa Rican tour guides—would check the bird off in a small notebook and announce, "That makes fourteen bird species and eight different mammals we've seen since the beginning of the trip."

In this manner, we bumped and jolted out of Costa Rica's Central Valley up through the highlands toward Poás Volcano. Since the whole family was wildly sleep-deprived, the little bouncing tour bus had a powerfully soporific effect. Devi, the kids, and I all stretched out in our seats, napping in short snatches until Oscar spotted a roseate spoonbill or a band of howler monkeys. Then we all sat up, rubbed our eyes, and gazed blearily out the window before falling back to sleep.

In Costa Rica, different crops grow at different altitudes, so each time we woke up, we saw an entirely different landscape. In the lower elevations, there were plantations full of wide-leafed banana trees and stately coconut palms. Higher up, there were extensive *fincas* with countless rows of lush, dark green coffee bushes. Then there were small roadside strawberry farms and ferny woods. Finally the road—and I use the term loosely—was bounded by virgin cloud forest and alpine meadows.

After three or four bone-shaking hours, we reached the summit of Poás Volcano. When we stumbled out of the bus, we were treated to a stunning sight—a gaping caldera more than a kilometer across complete with steaming vents and a small, scalding-hot blue-white lake at the bottom of the crater far below. We stood on the rim, gazing down at the boiling lake. Then I snapped every conceivable family combination in front of the crater. Of course, I didn't have Devi's complete attention. Bringing little Lucas to the rim of an active volcano was her worst nightmare come true. Most of the time we were there she clutched Lucas in her arms, and when she did put him down, she wrapped the baby leash around her wrist so tightly I thought it would cut off all circulation to her hand.

Kara and Willie, on the other hand, were as bored by this wonder of nature as they were with the Grand Canyon. They glanced perfunctorily over the rim a few times, then immediately looked around for something better to do. When I asked Kara to share her impressions of the volcano with me, she said, "It's nice"—like she saw giant steaming craters every day on the way home from school. I know it's hard to believe, but for some reason Kara and Willie seemed to like the fake volcano on the Las Vegas Strip better than the real thing. When we reboarded the bus, Devi buckled Lucas back into his seat and breathed a huge sigh of relief, and the kids just yawned and went back to sleep.

The next morning, we were supposed to take a three-hour hike through the Monteverde Cloud Forest Preserve. Clearly, this was going to be a long hard slog, so we left Lucas back at the lodge with Betty. But since we came to Costa Rica specifically to show Kara and Willie the rain forest, we decided to bring them along. When we got to the trail head, ringed by towering trees, it was already drizzling, and the forest path was melting into wide ocher puddles. Not only would Kara and Willie have to march seven kilometers through the jungle. They'd have to do it in the rain and mud.

Furthermore, there was a certain element of danger attached. At the outset of the hike, Miguel emphatically warned everyone—particularly the kids—not to eat any berries or touch any plants or insects without consulting him first. Apparently, the cloud forest was teeming with toxic flora and fauna. According to Miguel, this was especially true of flowers, berries, and insects that were either bright red or bright yellow. Miguel said this flamboyant coloration alerted birds and animals to a particular flower or berry's poisonous nature. Of course, it has the opposite effect on children, so before we set off, Devi and I drilled Kara and Willie about this peril.

"Okay," I said. "What do you do if you see a red or yellow insect?"

"Don't touch it," replied Kara and Willie in unison.

"And what if you see a red berry?"

"Don't touch it."

"And . . ."

"Don't eat it."

"And what'll happen to you if you do touch it?"

"We'll get a rash."

"And what'll happen if you eat it?"

"We'll die a horrible gut-wrenching death."

Excellent. We were ready to go.

So wouldn't you think a huge steaming volcano would be an excellent bet for kids, and a four-mile hike down a muddy jungle path would be a disaster? I did and, of course, I was completely wrong. Kara and Willie turned out to be avid explorers, and for them, the dripping cloud forest and every mud puddle in it were filled with wonder. They were delighted by the towering trees, babbling waterfalls, and small forest pools ringed by bamboo, ferns, and philodendrons. They found wild coffee bushes decked with ripe red beans and banana flowers the size of hanging lanterns. Miguel showed the kids how epiphytic plants latch on to tree trunks and pull nutrients from the air around them and how strangler figs wrap their vines around healthy trees and slowly envelop them.

Along the path, we also saw poisonous yellow and black millipedes half a foot long, red bugs clustered together by the hundreds to resemble poison berries, and a rank of ants carrying angular leaf segments ten times their size. Kara knew all about these leaf cutter ants from school. She told our whole group how the ants brought leaves back to their tunnel and made compost heaps where they grew edible fungus. Both kids, but Kara in particular, seemed to have a natural affinity for the rain forest, and Devi and I were astonished when they hiked the entire length of the puddle-strewn trail with nary a complaint.

The best cloud forest marvels came at the end of the hike. The first occurred at the continental divide—the razor's edge of the Central American cordillera. There, we suddenly emerged from the trees and found ourselves perched on a precipitous cliff high above a verdant jungle valley. Just a few feet in front of our eyes a never-ending stream of wispy, windborne clouds shot past us, one after another, at more than twenty miles per hour. It was a superhighway for clouds, and the children were delighted by the phenomenon.

They were even more delighted when we returned to the information booth at the head of the trail and found this bizarre Dr. Seuss creature waiting for us. It was a big South American raccoon-type beast with a furry tail and a long pointed nose. Officially, it was called a coatimundi, but Lucas, who met us at the end of the hike, dubbed it a "long-face," and that appellation stuck. The long-face was a semi-tame little mendicant, that requested (and received) most of our children's lunch. As far as the kids were concerned this creature, by itself, was worth the trip to Central America.

The following morning, we took one more cloud forest hike. The highlight for Kara and Willie was a rustic little coffeehouse along the trail. It was really just a shack, but behind the shack lived an entire colony of cheeky, garbage-swilling coatimundis—about three dozen in all. Now, if one of these little beggars could enchant our children, imagine what a whole pack could do.

When coatimundis get together, they communicate in improbable high-pitched squeals, and if someone is misguided enough to throw food into the crowd, these squeals escalate into a screeching, ululating frenzy. The coatimundis were shy at first, discreetly peeking out from behind the shack. Then a few adolescents crept into the open. Then all three dozen gradually emerged, standing on their hind legs, brazenly begging for food and methodically encircling us. At that point, one of our fellow tourists—the young fellow from South Dakota named Aaron—recklessly tossed some of his beef jerky into the crowd. When he did that all hell broke loose. Coatimundis screamed, wrestled, and mugged each other for the beef jerky. They circled around Aaron's back, climbed his leg and stuck their paws into his pockets. Aaron gave them everything he had, but when his beef jerky supply gave out, he had to retreat up the trail with a pack of keening coatimundis in pursuit. Kara and Willie practically fell down laughing.

Another real winner in the kid department was the nearby Monteverde Butterfly Garden. It was really more of a makeshift insect zoo. Aside from the butterflies, they had live poisonous caterpillars, bugs that looked like sticks, giant horned beetles, and cabinets full of cocoons and chrysalises that slowly yielded gorgeous winged creatures.

One of the best attractions at the butterfly garden was a simple 10 x 10 foot section of wall, painted white and illuminated by some sort of big high-tech light bulb. There was a big sliding screen door a few inches in front of the wall. At dusk, the entomologists pushed back the screen and switched on the purplish light, and a stunning variety of moths flew in from the surrounding forest. At dawn, they pulled the screen closed, and *voilà*—a live moth exhibit. There were hundreds of moths in all shapes, sizes, and colors. Some were as large as your hand, others the size of your fingernail. Kara's favorite was a moth that played dead the moment you touched it. Even if you brushed it lightly, it fell right off the wall like a dead leaf. Then it waited around for a few minutes until the coast was clear.

I figured this was a once-in-a-lifetime opportunity to ask a professional moth guy a question that's nagged me for years. Namely, why are moths mindlessly attracted to light bulbs? I'm sorry to report that, despite his evident erudition, the tropical entomologist didn't provide a satisfactory answer. He proffered a fairly tentative story about how moths navigate by the light of the moon and become confused when they see another bright object. Devi bought it, but I didn't.

One thing this guy did know about was the sex life of butterflies. Our tour of the butterfly garden concluded with a discussion of lepidopteran procreation that was PG-13, bordering on R. Our three little angels were all standing in the front row with bright upturned faces when the entomologist tapped his chart with a pointer and asked the group, "Now what are the three requirements for any species to have sex?"

Now, on one level, it might have been appropriate for the kids to learn about the birds and the bees from a bug expert. But I really didn't want Kara and Willie clued into life's sweet mystery by some hippie lepidopterist in the backwoods of Costa Rica. Okay, if the truth be known, I didn't want them clued in at all. Willie's seven and a half and Kara's nearly nine. So we'll probably have to give them the old sex talk sometime before the trip's over. I also know, intellectually, that both of them are old enough to handle the information now. The problem is I can't handle their understanding the information, because it's bound to go something like this:

1. Children learn how babies are made.

2. Children are inevitably grossed out (as in, "He puts what in where?").

3. Children remember they, too, were once babies.

4. Disturbing mental images of parents pop into children's head.

At this point, at least, Kara and Willie are still in the dark, so when the bug guy said, "What are the three requirements for any species to have sex?" a chill shot down my neck, and I immediately interrupted him.

"Excuse me," I said. "But some of us aren't entirely conversant with the whole S-E-X concept, if you know what I mean."

"Oh, I see," said the lepidopterist, looking at the children thoughtfully. "Well, in that case, let me put it this way. The interesting thing about this particular species of butterfly is that after the male inserts his, well, whatever, he plugs the female's, uh, you know, in order to prevent other male butterflies from...can we say mating? Yes, thank you, we can...to prevent other butterflies from mating with her."

To his credit, he was able to explain quite a bit about the sex cycle of butterflies without using any key words or giving away any big secrets, and thanks to him, Devi and I remain virgins in the eyes of our children.

Hasta luego,
David, Devi, Betty,
and the kids

C h a p t e r   4

Subject: Pura Vida
Date: August 10
From: daylifers@aol.com (David Cohen)

San José, Costa Rica

Dear Friends:

When we last left our intrepid travelers, they had narrowly escaped the hippie lepidopterists of the Monteverde Butterfly Garden, fiends who would have inadvertently—but fiendishly nonetheless—revealed to their innocent children the mysterious facts of life. Having deftly dodged that bullet, it was time for lunch.

Apparently the proprietors of the restaurant we went to had the same prudish attitude toward sex as I did, because there was a large hand-printed sign inside the front door that read, *"En este restaurante no se permiten escenas amorosas."** That message was somewhat undercut by the fact that it hung right next to a 2 x 3 foot beer calendar adorned with a life-sized picture of a woman's rear end in a thong bikini. Still, the meal was delicious, or as Kara loudly announced to the

---

* "No amorous scenes are permitted in this restaurant."

assembled tourists and Costa Ricans alike, "That sure was good Mexican food."

Our next stop was Arenal Lodge, which was located near the very active Arenal Volcano. The lodge was only about twenty-five miles from Monteverde as the crested karakara flies, but we denizens of the tour bus had to rattle four hours and a hundred miles across a mountain pass to get there. Aside from not wasting money on armed forces, the Costa Ricans have apparently been skimping on road repair, and my kidneys barely survived the ride.

Our room at Arenal Lodge featured a magnificent view of the famous volcano that blew its top in 1968, killing somewhere between sixty and eighty people and around twenty thousand head of cattle. The day we arrived, the mile-high cone loomed ominously above the jungle canopy, wearing a mantle of white clouds and an iron-gray crown of volcanic smoke. It rumbled ominously every half hour or so, and after dark, we could see dull streaks of glowing orange lava flowing viscously down its side. It was like an old *King Kong* movie, and I expected to see Fay Wray fleeing the jungle at any moment.

Since traipsing our children through the venomous cloud forest had gone so well, we decided to push our luck and bring everyone—including two-year-old Lucas—on the volcano hike the following morning. This trek took us across old lava flows and partway up the cone. As we picked our way through the steaming basalt boulders, it occurred to me that a large-scale eruption at this point would be inconvenient to the point of cremation. Strangely, nobody else seemed the least bit concerned.

Sitting comfortably at home, you probably think that a three-mile hike on a narrow path through vast fields of jagged lava rock would be a rather bad place to bring a two-year-old...And, boy, would you be right. I mean, really, what were we thinking? The only thing that could have made matters worse—aside from an actual eruption—was a driving rainstorm. And sure enough, an hour into the hike, the heavens opened, drenching our clothes and making the rocks as slippery as...well, wet rocks. I'd still be picking my way back down through the lava fields with Lucas on my shoulders if it weren't for Oscar, the bus driver. Add "agility of a mountain goat" to "eye of an eagle" on Oscar's list of James Fenimore Cooperesque attributes, because he carried Lucas at least halfway down the mountain for me.

Later that afternoon, we found a mellower way to enjoy the volcanic ambience. At the base of the mountain, there was a funky old hot springs resort called Tabacón. It had five steaming pools heated by Arenal's magma core. The largest and warmest pool had a long water slide for the kids and a Hawaiian-style swim-up bar for parents. Devi and I stood in the hot green water with our backs to the mossy old bar languidly sipping margaritas and watching the volcano above us spew steam and ash. Every thirty minutes or so, it tossed up some pretty good-sized boulders, and as dusk approached, red lava flowed torpidly down its side. This was simultaneously pleasant and disturbing. Actually, I think the word would be decadent. Even for Californians used to life on the fault line, it seemed awfully hubristic to be standing around in a swimming pool sipping margaritas immediately beneath an erupting volcano.

I'd always wondered how the citizens of Pompeii had been caught so off guard. Now I know. Someone probably said, "Gee, Mount Vesuvius seems awfully active today." And everyone else said, "Don't worry, Marcus. Have another margarita."

Our last stop in Costa Rica was Tortuguero National Park, located on a long, nearly uninhabited stretch of Caribbean coastline. Its name derives from the fact that Tortuguero is one of only two spots in the western Caribbean where giant green sea turtles waddle ashore to lay their eggs.

Up until this point, the Costa Rican roads had been pretty wretched, but that was no longer an issue because there was no road whatsoever between Arenal and Tortuguero—or between anywhere and Tortuguero for that matter. There were only two ways to get there: drive to the Caribbean port of Limón and hire a boat, or take a light plane over the mountains to a small airstrip near the lodge.

There were several good reasons not to take the airplane. First of all, before we left home, my sainted mother called specifically to say, "Son, I realize you are traveling around the world for God knows how long, that you're going to India and Africa and God knows where. And I understand that you feel compelled to take our grandchildren away from us for a year or more. But promise me this one insignificant thing: that you won't fly around Third World countries in small airplanes." Then she told me a story about another young couple, just like us, who went to Africa, and when the guy's mother came to visit she was killed in a small plane crash and her body was nearly eaten by lions. ("They'll have to live with that guilt.")

Anyway, we didn't have much choice. The tour operators, in their wisdom, decided to fly us to Tortuguero from a small rural airstrip, and it would have taken an extravagant display of cowardice to weasel out of it. That being said, I was still taken aback when Miguel asked us to pare our baggage down to ten kilos. I mean, honestly, do you really want to fly in a plane where a few kilos either way makes a difference? I also couldn't help noticing that the airstrip in Río Frío Sarapiquí wasn't exactly what you'd call a real airport. There was a sixteen-seat propeller-driven plane and a strip of blacktop that might pass for a runway. But otherwise, there were none of the usual accoutrements one associates with modern air travel. I didn't miss the X-ray machines and the line at the check-in counter, but there is something reassuring about a tower and radar and whatever else they have that keeps one airplane from colliding with another.

We took off over a patchwork of lush jungle and

cultivated fields. Despite my misgivings, the flight was remarkably smooth, and within twenty minutes we sighted the azure Caribbean hemmed by tall palms and a gleaming strip of white beach. We descended alongside the Río Tortuguero and landed on an airstrip hacked from the coastal jungle. Brakes squealed. The plane shuddered, and we rolled to a halt. We all got out and humped our luggage across the runway, through a palm grove to an old-fashioned flat-bottomed boat powered by a sputtering outboard motor. Then we crossed the wide crocodile-infested river.

On the other side, we found simple accommodations reminiscent of summer camp. The lodge looked as if it might blow over in a stiff wind, and its builders were apparently unfamiliar with the concept of right angles, but in my present ascetic state of mind, I was delighted to find someplace without air conditioning, telephones, televisions, radios, or minibars. The most anomalous and pleasant aspect of the lodge was the fact that there was no parking lot or any sort of road leading in or out. Automobiles, trucks, and the wheel in general were completely useless here, and this gave Tortuga Lodge an old-fashioned Graham Greene sort of appeal. We'd clearly left civilization behind, and that was good for a cleansing sigh of relief.

Our first scheduled trek was a boat trip into the coastal rain forest. After a hearty lunch, our entire party piled back into the little blue scow that brought us over from the airstrip. As we headed upstream, the river gradually narrowed. The mud-brown water turned black, and the trees closed in around us obscuring the heavy gray sky. Webs tended by monstrous black spiders hung from bank to bank only a few feet above our heads, and from time to time the screech of an eagle or the subwoofer grunt of a howler monkey pierced the hot, heavy air.

As we chugged up the river, movie scenes kept popping into my mind—first *The African Queen,* then *Apocalypse Now.* At first, I thought that was sort of romantic, connecting our little adventure with these grand cinematic images. But then it struck me that popular culture—even good popular culture—has so thoroughly pervaded our lives that it's now practically impossible to experience new places and adventures without immediately comparing them to something we've seen in a movie or on television. Fortunately, Kara and Willie don't have this problem—at least not yet. When they were four and five years old, Devi enrolled them in a Waldorf preschool.* The school asked parents to insulate their children from television and movies and not to buy them clothes festooned with cutesy media characters. Initially, I thought these rules were elitist nonsense—a sort of cultural superiority—but in the end I realized that they kept the delicate garden of a child's imagination from being weed-whacked by violent action figures or the latest Disney confection.

Because of this early training, I believe that Kara and Willie can still encounter new places and experiences with imaginations that are largely unsullied by seductive processed Hollywood imagery. That's one of the many nice things about bringing our children on this trip. They give Devi and me a rare opportunity to step outside the hive-mind and see new places through their fresh eyes.

On our last day in Tortuguero we had the rare opportunity to observe giant green sea turtles as they shuffled ashore to lay their eggs. At ten o'clock on a moonless night, the whole family hiked and stumbled along a pitch-black Caribbean beach strewn with rocks and logs. We were led by a whispering guide carrying a half-watt penlight. His number one rule was "Do not annoy the sea turtles." Bright lights and talking of any sort—even whispering—were strictly forbidden.

---

*Based on the teachings of Rudolf Steiner (1861–1925), Waldorf schools encourage children to develop their natural spirituality without imposing structures on their learning.

Even though they weigh four hundred pounds and are the size of large ottomans, green sea turtles are actually fairly difficult to spot in the middle of the night. First of all their dark color blends pretty well, and secondly, they use their big flippers to bury themselves halfway into the sand. This process takes several hours, after which the turtles go into an hour-long trance and lay dozens of gleaming white eggs that look like small Ping-Pong balls.

Half an hour into the hike, we finally stumbled across a sea turtle. We all circled behind her. (Rule number two: Never stand between a sea turtle and the sea.) Our guide gently lifted her rear end, and we all took turns glancing at her big pile of white eggs. Devi and I were rewarded with big silent "Wows" from the kids.

Afterward, as we hiked back up the beach, the guide held up his hand. We held perfectly still while another giant sea turtle shambled across the sand and slid silently into the tepid Caribbean. She would never see her children. After a few months in the warm sand, the hatchlings would make their way into the shallow water, where 95 percent would be eaten by predators. The few survivors would roam as far as Florida and Venezuela, then they would return to Tortuguero to repeat the cycle. When we got back to the lodge, in the middle of the night, the children shook the sand from their shoes and fell asleep, enchanted by the evening's revelations.

So was the first leg of our journey a success? On one level, yes. Less so, on another. Certain moments, like observing the laying sea turtles and watching Kara come alive with joy and knowledge in the Costa Rican cloud forest, were worth all the coffee in Central America. But there were also philosophical problems with this segment of our trip. First of all, we traveled in a hermetic group that somehow managed to avoid any substantive contact with real live Costa Ricans. Granted, this was billed as a nature expedition, not a cultural experience. But there's something wrong about rambling around a country for eleven days and never meeting anyone outside the tourist trade.

And while one of the primary goals of our journey was to search for adventure, we found the whole concept of an "adventure tour" somewhat oxymoronic by nature. An adventure is supposed to involve challenges, surprises, and an element of risk. When you begin an adventure, you're not supposed to know how it ends. But tour operators—even adventure tour operators—have to do everything possible to eliminate risks and surprises. Their job is to deliver an experience that matches the advertised itinerary as closely as possible.

The organizers of our tour did a fine job, and with Oscar and Miguel at the helm, we undoubtedly saw more sights and learned more facts than we ever would have done on our own. Furthermore, adventure tours, such as they are, tend to attract easygoing traveling companions—not the sort who whine if the soup isn't hot or there's a cockroach in the sink. But any way you cut it, this was still a preplanned, prepackaged, predestined experience—and on that level, it was ultimately unsatisfying. Devi and I are both glad that this was the only part of our trip that was professionally planned and organized. Within the bounds of safety and reason, the journey we want to take will be full of screw-ups, wrong turns, blind alleys, and missed opportunities—things that tour operators do their best to avoid.

If you ask a Costa Rican, *"Qué pasa?"* and things are going reasonably well, he'll invariably answer, *"pura vida"*— pure life. It's the first phrase they teach you when you stumble off the plane in San José. *Pura vida* is what we're searching for on this trip, and unfortunately, it can't be sold as a package.

Mucha suerte,
David, Devi, Betty, Kara,
Willie, and Lucas

Chapter 5

Subject: Those Lovable French
Date: September 1
From: daylifers@aol.com (David Cohen)

Paris, France

Dear Friends:

After eleven days in Costa Rica, we boarded a plane and flew to Washington, D.C. We had to go to Washington in order to catch our flight to Paris, and as long as we were there, we spent a few weeks visiting East Coast friends and relatives and showing our kids the star-spangled sights in Boston and Washington. As you might imagine, Devi and I weren't looking forward to a seven-hour transatlantic flight with three small children. But to tell you the truth, it wasn't that bad. We got lucky and flew across the pond in a brand new 777. We were in coach, of course. But the plane had plenty of legroom, comfortable seats, kid's meals, and little television screens in the back of every seat. Those mini-TVs were a godsend. As soon as we took off, all three children slipped slack-jawed and drooling into video-induced comas. At home, we usually get out the crash cart and revive them after a few hours—but not on our flight to France. This was the first flight since we left home where our children weren't fighting, kicking the seats, crawling down the aisles, dumping their drinks, or trying to stand on the fold-down trays.

When we landed at Charles de Gaulle Airport, we collected our luggage, and went outside to organize a ride into town. There were six of us, plus a dozen bags, and we had no idea how to get where we were going by bus. So we either had to take a limo or two cabs. I spotted a limo first. The driver had a neatly trimmed mustache and wore a smart gray suit. As I approached him, he regarded my jeans and running shoes with high Gallic disdain. I asked what it would cost to take the six of us to Trocadero. He said 550 francs—the equivalent of $110, plus tip.

Since I'd only been in Paris for ten minutes, I still thought that was a lot of money. I sucked in some air French style and said in my high school Français, *"C'est très cher, Monsieur."** I thought maybe he'd lower the price a little, but he just stuck out his lip and shrugged his shoulders expressively. I asked him to wait a second and ran the length of the sidewalk to find out how much two cabs would cost. Uh-oh. It was $120— plus two tips. The limo was actually cheaper. I hightailed it back to the limo, but by that time the driver had consummated a deal with two slick Euro-tycoons who probably never even asked about the fare. The driver saw me coming, raised his chin and said, in the most haughty way possible, "You 'ad your shawnce."

I just had to laugh, because it was so gorgeously French. I replied in my high school patois, "Monsieur, there is always another chance." As if he cared. He sped off with the two chic executives, and we stuffed ourselves into a $120 taxi convoy.

Forty minutes later we pulled up outside the Citadines Aparthotel—one of Devi's great guidebook finds. There, for half the price of a typical Paris hotel room, we got two bedrooms, a small living room with a fold-out couch, and a kitchenette. Our

* "It's quite expensive, sir."

little apartment was clean, pleasant, and brilliantly situated in the heart of the stylish sixteenth arrondissement. We dumped the bags, showered, and took a three-hour nap. When we woke up groggily in the early afternoon, we set out to stroll the tree-lined boulevards of Paris.

Only three cities in the world—New York, Paris, and Hong Kong—give you such a buzz just walking down the street. They're completely different, of course. In New York and Hong Kong, you're mesmerized by the kaleidoscope of humanity. In Paris, you're seduced by what D. H. Lawrence called the "man-made nobility" of the place. But in all three cities, you can wander the streets for hours on end buoyed by the ever-changing spectacle.

We left our hotel and walked north to Avenue Foch, the broad tree-lined boulevard girded by luxurious apartment buildings. We strolled several blocks to the Arc de Triomphe, and turned right into the very elegant Avenue Victor Hugo. All along the avenue, there were perfect little shops—some famous, some not—but all with gorgeous window displays that were works of art in their own right. One little store sold nothing but doorknobs and drawer pulls. I know that doesn't sound too scintillating, but this hardware was so exquisitely displayed that it looked like the crown jewels of England. (Probably cost the same, too.)

We stepped into a very fancy chocolate shop. It must have been the most beautiful chocolate shop in the world. It had cases full of exquisite truffles and floor-to-ceiling mahogany shelves that held artful papier-mâché candy boxes in soft shades of rose and turquoise. The entire place was suffused with the aroma of cocoa. The kids were transfixed. We allowed each child to pick out a single truffle—about a twenty-minute procedure—then, an elegantly dressed shop lady carefully wrapped each piece to go. The price was absurdly high, but in this case, worth it.

Speaking of prices, Devi and I were soon confronted with an incontrovertible fact. Our food budget for Paris was hopelessly insufficient. Back home, in a flash of naïveté, we allocated $60 a day for food in most places, and $100 a day in expensive cities like Rome and Paris. That seemed like a lot of money at the time, but we now realized, with six of us, that came to only $16 per person per day. To put that in perspective, one family lunch at La Tour d'Argent would have wiped out our whole four-day Paris food budget and then some. Of course, we weren't eating lunch at La Tour d'Argent. They probably wouldn't let us in. But even the corner bistros exceeded our modest means.

What's more, we got the distinct impression that Paris restaurants don't welcome small children with open arms—especially at supper time. And who can blame them? They've got this very elegant thing going with starched white tablecloths, dessert carts, and waiters in black jackets. Then along come the Cohen kids, screaming at 120 decibels and sticking bread sticks in their ears. Our children aren't demure by American standards, but in a Paris restaurant, they were like rampaging Visigoths. Devi and I spent most of our first dinner in Paris shushing the kids and saying, *"Pardonnez-nous, Madame, Pardonnez-nous Monsieur,"* to all the people around us. Everyone was fairly understanding, but by the end of the meal, we felt obliged to tip heavily.

We obviously needed a new plan. Our little apartment had a kitchenette, so we went on a grocery shopping expedition. It was a very pleasant adventure. The neighborhood shops were small and highly specialized. They had the best of everything, lovingly displayed, and the proprietors spoke precisely no English. Devi speaks four languages fluently,* but French isn't one of them. My French is rudimentary, but aside from making a few perplexing requests, like asking a butcher for a slice of *jambe* (leg), instead of *jambon* (ham), things went reasonably well.

---

*English, Japanese, Spanish, and Italian.

After that, we ate about half our meals in the room, and Devi and I even slipped out for a few suppers *sans enfants.* This way, we found a bit of Paris romance, avoided a great deal of Gallic opprobrium, and only exceeded our food budget by 50 percent. Good thing, too, because with fabulously overpriced Venice and Zurich ahead of us, we'll probably be scrounging for berries and witchetty grubs by the time we get to Australia.

On our second morning in Paris, we took another superb walk. This time, we strolled down to the Seine River along the Right Bank to the Tuileries Gardens and the Louvre. Initially, the kids were skeptical about the itinerary. When I told them where we were going, Willie asked suspiciously, "What's the Loove?"

I was sort of hoping the kids wouldn't inquire too closely, but now there was no way around it. "Well," I said, 'fessing up. "The Louvre is a gigantic art museum."

"What!"

"An art museum. You know, paintings, sculptures, drawings, that sort of thing."

"No, Daddy," Willie groaned. "Please don't take us to an art museum. Anything but that! I mean it. I'll even go to a church." His anguish was truly poignant.

"Look," I said, "this isn't your normal, run-of-the-mill art museum. It's the greatest art museum in the world. They have the *Mona Lisa* there, the *Venus de Milo,* the *Nike of Samothrace.*"

Willie perked up slightly at the mention of Nikes, but both he and Kara were clearly poised to sulk.

Fortunately, Devi had anticipated this reaction. She told Kara and Willie that they could each pick out five postcards at the Louvre gift shop. Then we'd have a competition, and whoever found the most pieces of art depicted on their postcards would win a treat. Having a winner and a prize made all the difference. Kara and Willie could now engage in their favorite hobby: sibling rivalry. They also figured any place with a gift shop couldn't be all bad.

Now everyone was anxious to get to the Louvre, but to get there, we had to walk through the Jardin des Tuileries. This urban oasis of formal flower beds, ancient trees, and cement ponds was a perfect place for the kids to cut loose. Kara and Willie raced up and down the crushed granite paths, watched elaborate model sailboats tacking across the ponds, and even found a big Henry Moore sculpture that was good for climbing.

Lucas scampered around the Tuileries as well, but he was held in check by the baby harness Devi bought back in San Francisco. I'm sure you've seen this contraption. It's sort of like a dog leash for kids, and it was actually quite serviceable for keeping Lucas out of the Paris traffic. But the reaction of the French citizenry in the Tuileries suggested this device is not in general use here. As we strolled down the broad central path with Lucas straining at his leash, everyone started pointing and laughing at us. It took a few minutes to figure out what the problem was, and by that time, even Lucas was becoming self-conscious. We figured we'd better restore his dignity, so we unclipped the leash and let him scamper off with Kara and Willie. Still, I'm sure that several dozen Parisians went home that night and regaled their families with stories of the wacky Americans who walk their children like dogs. (*"Oui, c'est vrai!"*)

And speaking of dogs, what's the story with dog poop in this town? Paris is one of the most immaculately groomed cities in the world. Every hedge is trimmed and every facade scrubbed. But the entire town is blanketed with dog feces, and apparently no one expects the dog owners to scoop it up. Dogs also ride in taxis, sit in restaurants, and are generally treated with more kindness and affection than people. In my next life, if I happen to slip down the karmic ladder a few rungs, I hope to return to earth as a Parisian dog, nibbling gourmet table scraps and gaily crapping my way down the Champs-Elysées.

In the face of all this canine excrement, the kids developed a new sport. Each time they spotted dog droppings, they pointed and yelled, "Poo-poo, poo-poo," like a cuckoo clock to warn the other members of our party. But even with this early-warning system in place, it was nearly impossible to navigate three small children through the fecal minefields without a few minor mishaps. So after we traversed the Tuileries, we had to clean up the kids' shoes before ushering them into the Palais Louvre. Fortunately, there was a drinking fountain nearby, so we did a pretty good job of it.

When we finally got inside, we ate lunch, made a bathroom stop, and thoroughly inspected every square centimeter of every gift shop under the I. M. Pei pyramid. By the time the kids picked out their postcards for Devi's "Find the Masterpiece" game, we barely had time to skim the Louvre's gargantuan collection. Still, we were able to find most of the show-stoppers, and we even managed to elbow our way through the coterie of Japanese tourists gathered reverently around the *Mona Lisa.*

The competition was a great success. As we wandered the wide marble hallways of the Louvre, dwarfed by heroic Delacroix and lush Fragonards, the game compelled the children to cast at least a perfunctory glance at every work of art we passed. They even discovered a few pieces that captured their imagination. And whenever they found a painting or sculpture that matched one of their postcards, they were in seventh heaven. Miraculously, the kids didn't want to leave—even when a guard tapped us on the shoulder and told us it was closing time. Kara had the bad luck to choose three postcards from a touring exhibit that had recently departed for another venue. So, much to her chagrin, Willie won the competition. Cheated by fate, Kara desperately wanted to return the next day for a rematch.

On the way back to the hotel, we learned another fact of Parisian life. Namely, unless you enjoy sitting gridlocked in a crooked medieval street helplessly watching your net worth diminish, don't take a taxi at rush hour. Luckily, our driver knew a slew of tunnels, shortcuts, and back alleys. But when we finally got to the hotel and shelled out a few zillion francs for the fare, we resolved, from that point forward, we'd either walk or take the métro like everyone else.

Back in the room, I spoke to an old friend of mine who runs Paris's renowned Magnum photo agency. He invited us to his apartment for dinner on Sunday and suggested a few places we might dine in the meantime. One that sounded particularly intriguing was called the Brasserie Balzar. It was located on the *rive gauche* near the Sorbonne. Devi and I decided to give it a try.

As it turned out, the Brasserie Balzar had a celebrated past. It was a hive of anti-government activity during the 1968 student uprising, and it had a rich literary and philosophical tradition as well. William Shirer, who wrote *The Rise and Fall of the Third Reich,* ate there regularly, and Jean-Paul Sartre used to drop in to argue passionately—and apparently quite loudly—with Albert Camus about Existentialism, Marxism, and the Absurd.

When we entered Brasserie Balzar, the maître d'hôtel immediately recognized us for what we were and escorted us to an obscure corner of the restaurant reserved for uninteresting people. There, we sat next to two fiftyish schoolteachers from Minnesota who were in Paris on a two-week holiday. These ladies undoubtedly wanted to dine next to a couple of Sorbonne classics professors, or at the very least, some *rive gauche* roués. So when Devi and I arrived, their faces fell, and they weren't particularly interested in speaking to us. What's more, the food was heavy and old-fashioned, and the service was perfunctory, at best.

Anywhere else in the world, this would have added up to a disagreeable dining experience. But Devi and I discovered that when you're sipping a smooth red wine in the Quartier Latin on a cool autumn evening, none of these things matter too much. The lights in the fin de siècle restaurant glowed soft and yellow, burnishing the brass rails and dark oak. The silken patter of French conversation swirled and eddied around us, and waiters in crisp black-and-white darted to and fro importantly among their favored clients. Devi and I relished this sumptuous scene for hours and left with a warm sense of contentment. Afterward, we bought a baguette and strolled together, hand in hand, down cobblestone streets in the City of Light.

> *À bientôt,*
> *la famille* Cohen

C h a p t e r   6

Subject: Awkward Moments
Date: September 3
From: daylifers@aol.com (David Cohen)

Dôle, France

Dear Friends:

The kids had been lobbying to go there from the moment we arrived, but we didn't make it to the Eiffel Tower until our third day in Paris. The tower was originally built as a temporary engineering display for the 1889 Universal Exposition, and not everyone liked it. In fact, no less a personage than Émile Zola called it "an insult to the city of Paris." But Zola would have gotten quite an argument from Kara and Willie. They haven't been so impressed by anything since we left Vegas. Willie, in particular, was anxious to hop aboard La Tour Eiffel's glass elevator and zip all the way to the top.

There are actually three classes of elevator tickets available at the Eiffel Tower. You can visit the first level—about thirty stories up—for 20 francs. If you're more adventurous, you can go to the middle level for 38 francs or the crow's nest near the top of the thousand-foot spire for 55 francs. We promptly split into three factions. Fearless Willie and the intrepid Betty got tickets for the top. Devi and Lucas took the middle ground, and Kara and I were the chickens.

Incidentally, if you don't like heights, the glass elevator at the Eiffel Tower won't inspire confidence. The elevator car itself seems fairly modern, but the mechanism at the base of the tower is exposed, and it all looks like original nineteenth-century equipment. As we stepped into the elevator, Kara started crying, and Lucas announced, "I'm scary, Mommy." But then the doors closed, and the car whisked silently up through the latticework.

When the infernal contraption reached the first level, Kara and I yelled *au revoir,* and leapt out before it could take us any higher. Then we wrapped our arms around each other and tried to stay as far as possible from the edge. At first, Kara was pretty panicky, but then she discovered there were souvenir stores up there, and the prospect of shopping for tchotchkes instantly assuaged her fears.

We were all supposed to regroup on the first level at noon. Devi and Lucas showed up a little early. As Kara made some tough last-minute buying decisions, Lucas cuddled in Devi's arms and gazed out over the red-tile rooftops of Paris.

"Where's the White House?" asked Lucas, who evidently thought he was still in Washington. Devi gently explained that when you sit in an airplane for eight hours, you generally end up in a different country.

Another thirty minutes passed and Betty and Willie still didn't show up, so we decided to wait for them on terra firma. We zipped back down the leg of the tower and sat near the exit where we could see everyone who came out. Every ten minutes or so, another group of happy tourists emerged from the elevator, but Betty and Willie were never among them. After an hour, Devi decided that she'd better go up and take a look while I waited by the exit with Kara and Lucas.

The moment Devi disappeared from view, Kara announced, "I'm hungry, Daddy."

I looked at my watch. It was 1:30—well past her lunchtime.

"Look," I said. "I understand you're hungry, but we have to wait here until Mommy comes back with Betty and Willie. Then we can all go to a restaurant together."

I knew this argument wouldn't succeed, because when Kara gets hungry, she musters a passion not usually found outside the opera hall. "I'm *really* hungry, Daddy," she moaned plaintively.

Then Lucas took up the cry. "I'm really hungry, too, Daddy."

"I believe you—both of you," I said. "But unless we wait here, we're going to miss Mommy, Betty, and Willie when they finally get off the elevator."

"I'm so hungry," moaned Kara, "that I have a stomach-ache—a really bad one."

As Kara well knew, I could only stand this pitiful display for so long. "Okay," I said. "What do you want to eat?"

Negotiations had now commenced, so Kara set forth her opening position.

"How 'bout an ice cream cone, Daddy?"

"No way. Not before lunch."

"What about candy?"

"Come on, Kara!"

"Okay, then. How 'bout french fries."

"Fine. You can have french fries," I said. "You see that food truck over there? It sells french fries. Here's twenty-five francs. Go straight to the truck. Ask for *une grande portion de frites*. That's 'oon gran portion de freet.' Then come straight back here. And don't wander off. I mean it, Kara. I'm watching you."

That was actually difficult to do, because I now had to alternate my glance between the elevator in front of me, Kara behind me, and Lucas all over the place. I felt like a spectator at Wimbledon. Needless to say, I lost sight of Kara almost immediately, and she didn't reappear for nearly twenty minutes. During that time, I felt fairly irresponsible not knowing the exact whereabouts of two out of my three young children in the middle of Paris. When Kara did finally show up, she was carrying a little cardboard tray of french fries slathered in approximately a liter of ketchup.

"I couldn't work the ketchup thing right," she said.

"I can see that," I replied. "Did you get any napkins?"

"I don't think they had any napkins. Do you want me to go back and look?"

"No, that's okay. I don't want to lose you again. But listen," I said. "You both have to be very careful not to get ketchup all over your clothes. We're going to a restaurant for lunch, and I don't want you guys to look like slobs."

"Okay, Daddy."

I actually thought that last admonition might be futile, but Lucas took it straight to heart. As soon as his hands were completely covered with ketchup, so much so that ketchup was actually dripping into the dirt beneath the Eiffel Tower, Lucas decided to clean himself up. I glanced up, and to my utter horror, I saw him wiping his red sticky hands on the beige linen trousers of a meticulously dressed thirty-five-year-old Asian woman. Both legs.

"No, Lucas," I cried. But it was too late. The prim lady stared at her trousers in disbelief. Then Lucas looked up and gave me a tentative smile.

I walked over, picked up Lucas, and said to the lady, "I'm sorry. I am really so sorry. Oh, God, Lucas. That was very bad..." But it didn't really matter what I said, because the besmirched lady didn't speak any English. She just gave me a sad reproachful look and walked away.

About that time, Devi, Betty, and Willie finally emerged from the elevator. Betty and Willie had been delayed by the crowds on the upper level. Willie surveyed the scene and moaned, "Ohhh, french fries. How come I didn't get any?"

So there we were at the Tour Eiffel. Under my capable tutelage, one kid got lost, the other two were covered with crusty red ketchup, and one of those had a dirty diaper. It was now past two, and the kids hadn't eaten lunch. Plus, Lucas had just ruined some Chinese lady's vacation. Being a parent keeps you humble. For days at a time you can fool yourself into thinking that you've got everything nicely under control. Then, without warning, it all veers off into sheer raging chaos. I suppose the trick is to realize that these awkward moments are actually the good times.

We did many other things in Paris, though not nearly enough. We walked through the hushed medieval nave of Notre Dame and admired the cityscape from Sacre Coeur. We rode a painted carousel in the Jardins du Trocadero and visited a crowded little square in Montmartre where Kara and Willie had their portraits sketched in chalk and charcoal.

Our only other mishap occurred when we tried to leave town. We took a cab to the Gare de Lyon where we were supposed to catch the 11:20 TGV* to eastern Burgundy. When we arrived at the station, two good-natured porters examined our tickets and offered to take our luggage to the appropriate platform. With great effort, they hauled our mountain of green canvas through the length of the station and up a long flight of stairs to Track G.

Unfortunately, there was no train on Track G, which confused the porters no end. After some rapid-fire conversation, the small, wiry one ran downstairs to see what the problem was. He returned ten minutes later and told the tall, stocky porter that it wasn't Track G we wanted; it was Track J. The big fellow slapped himself on the forehead and reshouldered our bags.

We trudged back through the station up another long set of stairs to yet another platform, where we found not one, but two sleek TGVs. The porters looked confused again, but then an old

---

*The TGV, or Train à Grande Vitesse, is a 160 mph bullet train.

bandy-legged stationmaster came over, mumbled something, and pointed to the train on Track I. The porters loaded the bags onto the train, wiped their brows and patiently waited for their tip.

But as I fumbled with the French currency, a young, dark-haired train conductor approached, and asked to see our tickets. He examined them gravely, shook his head and said (in French), "I'm terribly sorry, monsieur, but this isn't the train to Dôle; it's the express to Lausanne, Switzerland. The train to Dôle is across the platform on Track J."

When the porters heard this bit of news, they broke into a loud chorus of *"Non, non. Ce n'est pas possible!"* But the conductor assured them it was, so for the third time in twenty minutes, they gathered up our bags and schlepped them back across the platform.

The minute that was accomplished, the old stationmaster scurried back and yelled, "What are you doing?"

The young conductor replied matter-of-factly. "The Americans' luggage was on the wrong train. The TGV that stops in Dôle is on Track J."

"You don't know what you're talking about," said the stationmaster, pulling out a well-thumbed schedule. "The train to Dôle is on Track I."

"Don't you think I know where my own train is going?" asked the young conductor.

"You should," sniffed the old guy. "But obviously...you don't."

"Are you saying I don't know where my own train is going, you, you...*imbécile?*"

At that the old guy's face went beet red. *"Imbécile? Moi?* Listen you young fool. I've been working at this station for twenty years and you, *mon ami,* are the *imbécile.*"

At that point, all hell broke loose. The porters leapt into the fray and everyone started yelling, gesticulating, and poking fingers into each other's chest. Devi thought the old stationmaster was going to have a coronary, so she decided to intercede. But the moment she opened her mouth, the stationmaster turned his fury on her and screamed in heavily accented English, "You...shuddup! Just shuddup ah tell you!"

Naturally, I felt honor-bound to defend my spouse, so I put my hand on the stationmaster's shoulder and cleverly replied, "Hey, *you* shut up, you jerk!" That wasn't helpful either. The stationmaster used several French colloquialisms I've never heard before. (I believe one translated as "anal rapee.") Then he stalked down the platform spitting invectives. Kara, Willie, and Lucas looked dumbstruck.

In the end, we took the young conductor's advice and boarded the bullet train on Track J. But as the sleek TGV slipped noiselessly from the station, we weren't exactly sure whether we'd end up in Burgundy or Switzerland. We figured either one would probably be fine. After all, as John Steinbeck wrote, "People don't take trips. Trips take people."

C'est la vie,
David

Chapter 7

Subject: Speak French or Die
Date: September 8
From: daylifers@aol.com (David Cohen)

Saint-Jean-de-Losne, France

Dear Friends:

As it turned out, the young conductor at the Gare de Lyon was right, and we ended up in Burgundy—just as we intended. Our specific destination was the ancient town of Dôle, situated in a fecund agricultural region called the Franche-Comté or Free County of Burgundy. Since Dôle is a rather small place, the TGV stopped there for precisely two minutes. That was barely enough time to gather the children and literally throw the bags off the train. As the TGV whooshed eastward toward Besançon, the whole family was left standing breathlessly on a thin strip of tarmac by the side of the track with our luggage scattered all around us. When we looked up, we noticed that there were two full sets of rails between us and the station, and the crossing was thirty yards down the track.

We had two choices. Someone could run over to the station and try to find a porter, or we could just pull the suitcases behind us on their little two-inch plastic wheels. Since we couldn't see any porters from where we stood, we decided to line up the suitcases and form a convoy. Kara, Willie, Devi, and I each pulled a large suitcase on wheels with a smaller bag piled on top, and Betty pushed Lucas in the stroller. We made it down the narrow strip of tarmac to the crossing with no trouble at all. Then we looked both ways, and began to cross the tracks.

Unfortunately, nobody really considered what might happen when the little plastic wheels on the suitcases hit the big steel rails sunk into nine-inch-wide furrows. Some made it further than others, but eventually all the big bags got stuck in the furrows, and they all tipped over. Then the little bags fell off the big bags, and the whole convoy broke down irretrievably, leaving green canvas luggage scattered all over the tracks.

Few things in life focus your mind so well as getting stuck on the railroad tracks—particularly when the tracks in question are plied by 160-mile-an-hour bullet trains. When their suitcases got terminally bogged down, I yelled at the kids to get off the tracks and leave the luggage behind. They grasped the situation immediately and ran for cover. Then Devi and I dashed back and forth like idiots plucking the bags off the rails one by one.

This was all good entertainment for the three local geezers hanging out by the train station. One laughed so hard, I thought he might expel a lung. But between this episode and the morning fracas at the Gare de Lyon, Devi and I were pretty frazzled. So we were relieved to find two taxi drivers outside the station who understood my fractured French and agreed to take us across town to the Doubs River boat docks.

We were going to the docks to pick up a houseboat we rented six months earlier. When we made that reservation, it seemed like a smashing idea to loll away seven bucolic days on the scenic waterways of Burgundy. I was still excited by the big picture, but now that the moment was at hand, I felt a bit nervous about the details—specifically, the fact that we had hired a drive-it-yourself houseboat. In theory that sounded like fun, but in truth neither Devi nor I had ever set foot on a houseboat, let alone driven one. We weren't exactly sure what skills were required, but it did seem like you should have some sort of training before you navigated a floating house down a canal.

It wasn't just a matter of crashing into another boat or running aground. Every few kilometers or so, the canals were interrupted by locks that raised or lowered the boat as needed. I've seen ships go through locks on television, and the narrator always says something like "the experienced captain deftly maneuvers the vessel into position." I knew we weren't piloting an oil tanker through the Suez Canal, but this still didn't seem like a job for dilettantes.

When we arrived at the boatyard, we found a manicured green lawn, beautiful gardens, and a fleet of eighteen matched cabin cruisers. Apparently, these were the houseboats. We checked in at the little marina office, where we found the manager, a bright-eyed middle-aged fellow chatting away on the phone and chain-smoking pungent Gitanes. He acknowledged our presence with a nod, but it took him another fifteen minutes and two more cigarettes to wind up his call. The marina manager realized my French was basic, so he spoke to me very slowly and deliberately, like I was mentally deficient. And if I didn't understand a particular word or phrase—usually a boating term or something to do with the paperwork—he repeated it even more slowly and deliberately, like I could get it if I only tried harder. By the end of our parley, Devi and I apparently put down a hefty deposit on the boat, bought a book of canal charts, and made arrangements for a driving lesson. After that, we inspected our new home on the water.

The *Chalon,* as she was called, was a well-designed ten-meter craft with a tiny sundeck in the back and a roomy main salon that included a gray L-shaped banquette, a large

Formica table, a small refrigerator, a sink, and a tiny range. There were three "bedrooms"—a small trapezoidal master bedroom squeezed into the bow and two other sleeping spaces slightly larger than coffins. The Iron Maiden–sized bathrooms were equipped with pump-it-yourself maritime toilets and a hose-and-nozzle contraption you could pull out of the sink to give yourself a shower, although that looked like it might be difficult unless you happened to be double-jointed or a circus acrobat.

Once we toured the houseboat and brought our bags aboard, a bearded young deckhand named Jean-Michel showed up to give us our boating lesson. Apparently, Jean-Michel couldn't speak one word of English because he looked baffled when Willie said "Hello." Don't get me wrong. I don't expect the neighborhood grocer in Paris to speak English any more than I would expect the checkout clerks at the Mill Valley Safeway to speak French. But you might think a guy who teaches Americans and Brits how to drive houseboats for a living might know a few key words like "bow" or "stern"— if only to protect the company assets.

I'll tell you one thing. If I'd known twenty-five years ago that the lives of my wife and children would someday depend on my ability to understand French, I would have paid a lot more attention in high school. As it was, I must have slept through the class where they covered nautical terms and control panels, because to me the whole lesson sounded like this:

"If you have a problem with your *bluh-bluh-bluh,* make absolutely sure that you never touch the *bluh-bluh.* That is extremely important. Also, if you find smoke coming from the *bluh,* it usually means that your *bluh-bluh* is *bluh-bluh,* and you should turn the *bluh-bluh* and disconnect the *bluh.* Is that clear?"

Sure. Why not?

By the time Jean-Michel finished the lesson, it was nearly 4:00 P.M., and we were thoroughly intimidated. The locks shut down at 6:30, so we decided to spend our first night in the marina and leave the next morning. We were relieved when Jean-Michel said he'd come back at 8:00 A.M. to help us negotiate the first lock.

Since the pressure was off till morning, we walked into town to provision the boat. As we strolled the narrow cobblestone streets of Dôle, the birthplace of Louis Pasteur, we found it to be a remarkably charming place. There were lovely little shops and restaurants, meticulous autumn gardens, and handsome eighteenth-century houses with sprays of red geranium at the windows.

Buying supplies for the boat was an exceedingly pleasant chore. We strolled from shop to shop collecting crusty baguettes, ripe pungent cheeses, spicy sausages, country patés, and a wide array of fresh garden produce. As you might imagine, there was a plentiful selection of inexpensive Burgundy wine. That evening, we prepared a simple dinner from superb ingredients. When Betty and the children went to sleep, Devi and I drank ruby red wine in the cold air under the stars.

When we woke up the next morning, we knew that we couldn't put it off any longer. Like it or not, we had to muster our courage, untie the boat, and push away from the dock. I did a contortionist act washing up in the bathroom and had a quick breakfast of *pain au chocolat* and hot *café au lait*. At eight o'clock sharp, Jean-Michel rode up on his bicycle, his breath steaming in the cold morning air. He loaded the bike onto the small stern deck, then he cast off the lines and brought the rumbling engine to life.

As he maneuvered the cabin cruiser onto the glassy river, Jean-Michel reeled off a few more incomprehensible instructions. I just nodded, mumbled *"Oui"* a lot, and hoped he wasn't saying anything crucially important. A few minutes after we shoved off, we came to a fork in the waterway. Jean-Michel told us that an unnavigable section of the Doubs River continued off to the left, and the Canal du Rhône au Rhin was on the right. We wanted the canal, of course, but Devi and I noted with some trepidation that there weren't very many road signs out here on the river.

It wasn't long before we spotted our first lock off in the distance. We could see black iron gates, stone and concrete embankments, and the old lockkeeper's house. Well in front of the gates and slightly off to the left was a tall metal post sticking out of the water. The post had an arm extending from the top, so it looked like a gallows. But instead of a noose, there was a long red and white striped rod dangling from the arm. Apparently, this was the mechanism that activated the lock.

Jean-Michel deftly maneuvered the boat alongside the contraption. Then he nimbly scampered onto the deck and twisted the rod clockwise. (Or was it counterclockwise?) Further up the canal, a red light turned green, indicating that we could proceed. We cruised forward slowly, passed through the heavy gates, and came to a standstill between the old stone walls of the lock.

The lock wasn't much wider than the boat itself and about twice as long. Jean-Michel put the engine in neutral and hopped ashore. Devi threw him the bowline. He wrapped it once around a heavy iron bollard, and handed it back to her. Then he took the stern line from Willie and swiftly lifted his bicycle from the deck. Oh no! He was going to abandon us!

At that point, the doors clanged shut, and the water began to fall rapidly. In less than two minutes, it dropped fifteen feet, exposing the mossy walls of the lock. Well above us now, Jean-Michel stubbed out his cigarette, hopped on his bicycle, and nonchalantly waved good-bye. Devi and Willie pulled in the lines, and the gates in front of us opened slowly. We were on our own.

Our first test came soon enough, because there was another lock only a few kilometers up the canal. As we approached the gates, everyone was in a state of high anxiety. Now that I was driving instead of Jean-Michel, the entrance to the lock looked incredibly narrow. A little too narrow, in fact, because when I tried to put the houseboat into the lock, I bounced the starboard bow solidly off the right-hand gate. Fortunately, there were big rubber fenders all around the hull, so I didn't do any real damage, but this maneuver didn't reassure the crew. In fact, it was at this point that Betty decided the whole operation was entirely too risky. She grabbed Lucas and ducked into her tiny bedroom.

This was a so-called manual lock, which meant a lock-keeper had to come out of her old stone house and work the gates by hand. It's hard to believe, but every time some yahoo tourist comes floating down the stream, this poor woman has to drop whatever she's doing, put on thick leather gloves, and crank the huge iron gates open and shut. It was sort of charming and old-fashioned, but even Kara mentioned this couldn't be cost-effective for the French government.

Oh, and guess what the locals do for entertainment in these parts. That's right. Instead of demolition derbies, they come out and watch the tourists crash their way through their first few locks. It's sort of like *Burgundy's Funniest Home Videos*. I'll tell you what, though, the fearless crew of the *Chalon* didn't give the Bourguignons that much to laugh about. I'm not saying we were perfect, but after that first little ricochet off the gate, things got progressively smoother. I managed to stop the boat in roughly the right place. Then Devi and Willie tied it up like professional deckhands (more or less). As the water dropped, they pulled the lines in smartly. Then we cruised proudly out of the lock, and a big cheer went up on the *Chalon*. Okay, it was more like a big sigh of relief. The point is, we made it.

After that, we mustered the crew every few kilometers or so, and ran the drill all over again. Once we got the hang of it, it was actually a lot of fun. The whole family worked together as a team, and the kids enjoyed the hustle and bustle. Willie was particularly proud of his part in the operation. He knew that everyone was genuinely nervous about getting the boat through the locks in one piece, and I think it meant a lot to him that we trusted him to handle the stern line and keep it taut as the water level dropped. He took his job seriously and executed it with a sweet earnestness. I'm no child psychologist, but this seems like the sort of thing that builds a child's self-esteem. He knows we have confidence in him, and that helps him believe in himself.

After the terror of the first few locks subsided, we sat back and enjoyed the scenery. For the rest of the morning, we cruised past thick green forests and grassy fields dotted with white sheep and cream-colored Charolais cattle. Since autumn was upon us and we weren't far from Dijon, there were fields of yellow mustard flowers everywhere. Every so often we passed a small hamlet—a few stone houses clustered around an old Romanesque church. But generally, the only people we saw were the lockkeepers—friendly, weathered men and women engaged in an obsolete profession.

That isn't to say that they weren't entrepreneurs. Nearly every lock had a little stand offering local produce, wine, and honey, along with the usual array of soft drinks and ice cream. We bought a few items from a lockkeeper who was particularly helpful, and I was pleased to note that a bottle of decent red wine cost less than a can of Coke.

As noon approached, we reached the end of the Canal du Rhône au Rhin and entered the broad Saône River. For no particular reason, we turned upstream instead of down, and as we pulled away from the last lock, a pair of swans flew in close beside our boat. They glided alongside for a while,

then touched down softly on the water escorting us onto
the river.

>   Yo ho ho from the crew of
>   the houseboat *Chalon,*
>   David

Chapter 8

Subject: Finding Our Stride
Date: September 11
From: daylifers@aol.com (David Cohen)

Nice, France

Dear Friends:

Life aboard our houseboat in Burgundy was peaceful and languorous, and it wasn't long before we settled into an agreeable daily routine. Every morning, we woke up moored in another picturesque river town. There were always handsome old stone houses with red-tile roofs, spreading green willows, and a rubber-booted fisherman or two tending stout fifteen-foot poles.

Devi usually got up first and brewed a pot of fragrant *café filtre*. Then she strolled to the local *boulangerie* for fresh, warm baguettes and flawless croissants. After breakfast, we hunched over the waterways chart and set our course for the day. Then we filled our water tanks, strapped the kids into their life jackets, and cast off the lines.

During the morning and early afternoon we cruised the Saône River at a leisurely pace. The houseboat's top speed was only eight miles per hour, so there was never any temptation to rush. We just floated along, savoring the scenery and stopping randomly at gorgeous little riverine villages. It was like meandering inside a Constable painting.

At mid-afternoon, Lucas went down for his nap, and Devi shepherded Kara and Willie through their lessons. Up until this point, I'm afraid we've been pretty lax in the home schooling area, but once the cool days of autumn were upon us, the old rhythms kicked in, telling us it was time for class. Devi tutored Kara and Willie, while I drove the houseboat, sipped red wine, and admired her infinite reserve of patience.

As dusk fell, I kept an eye out for a place to moor. The moment we landed, Kara and Willie jettisoned their schoolbooks, leapt off the boat, and chased up and down the docks like little maniacs. They even had playmates for a few days—a brother and sister from Bath, England, who were cruising the Saône on another family houseboat.

While the children played under Betty's watchful eye, Devi and I wandered into town to shop in the local markets. We carefully selected autumn produce, crusty baguettes, salamis, and ripe cheeses. I usually prepared dinner, and Devi read the kids a bedtime story by the dim yellow light of the boat. By nine o'clock, everyone was drowsy, so we snuggled under our comforters, and were gently rocked to sleep by the soft, lapping waves of the river.

We floated along for seven days cruising up the river to the friendly village of Auxonne, where Napoleon served as a young artillery officer, then rambling on to Gray, a handsome town decimated by warfare and plague throughout the Middle Ages. When we got that far, we came about and drifted downstream to the ancient village of Seurre, where Caesar pitched his camp during the Gallic Wars. By that time, the tourist season was long gone, and only a few straggling houseboats were still on the river.

All in all, our week on the Saône was placid and uneventful—a sweet interlude when we could savor the aesthetic pleasures of Burgundy and catch our breath after three months on the road. It was also a time when we made important strides as a family. Remarkably, all six of us—even Kara and Willie—managed to live together harmoniously in a space no larger than our kitchen back home. It's not that the children suddenly began to treat each other with unbounded respect and affection. That's still a long way off. But for the first time since we left home, they seem to be moving in the right direction.

There was another transformation during this period that was more subtle, but just as significant. I think I can explain it best by saying that our journey, up until this point, felt as if it were a diversion from our real life. Like what we used to do—living in a house, going to work, taking the kids to school—was "normal," and this trip was a respite. But sometime this week, while we were floating down the Saône, our life in motion began to feel more normal and comfortable. Maybe it's because we were doing everyday activities like shopping, cooking, and teaching the kids to read. Or maybe I just stopped comparing everything we do now to the way it used to be. But more than anything else, I think it just took time—three months to be exact—to fully relinquish our old routines and embrace a new way of life. I should say that it took Devi and me three months to make this transition, because the children seemed to manage it much more quickly.

At the end of the week, we sailed back to Dôle. According to our rental agreement, we had to return the boat by 9:00 A.M. sharp or risk losing our deposit. Just to be sure, we arrived the night before, and moored at the little marina beneath Dôle's venerable basilica. When we first picked up our houseboat, Devi and I were charmed by this photogenic arrangement—our little boat framed by the majestic cathedral. But there was a drawback, and it revealed itself Monday morning at the crack of dawn.

Each September morning on the river had been getting progressively colder, but Monday was the coldest by far. According to the ship's French-language manual, there was a heater on board, but either it was broken or we didn't know how to use it. Either way, the boat felt like a walk-in freezer. Consequently, Devi and I were buried deep under the duvet when the basilica's prodigious bells began to toll...and toll...and toll. *Bong, bong, bong.* It was unimaginably loud, like we'd somehow awakened inside the belfry. After a few minutes of this skull-rattling tintinnabulation, Devi peeked out from under the covers and said, "What's going on?"

"I don't know," I replied. "Maybe the town's being sacked by Huns. We should probably flee."

"No, I'm too tired to flee," said Devi, closing her eyes again. "It has to stop soon."

But it didn't. It just went on and on for twenty minutes or more. I groaned and covered my head with a pillow. When that didn't work, I surrendered and jumped out of bed. It was so cold, I could see my breath, so I started hopping around the tiny cabin trying to generate some heat. The ceiling was only about five feet high, so I had to hunch over. Between the hunching and the hopping and the pounding bells, I began to feel like the hunchback of Notre Dame. So, I started doing my Charles Laughton–Quasimodo imitation. I hunched over Devi, contorted my face and said, "I call the big bell Marie."

Even though she looks the part, Devi was disinclined to play Esmeralda. She moaned and said, "Oh, no. Get out of here. I can't stand this anymore."

Then, one by one, Kara, Willie, and Lucas wandered into the room rubbing their eyes. They were bewildered by the bells, but they liked the Quasimodo routine, so soon there were three more little hunchbacks bounding around the bed. Devi retreated to the bathroom, and I got all three kids to yell, "Esmeralda, Esmeralda. Fear not our hideous aspect." Alas, we were all spurned in favor of the fair Phoebus, or at least a hot shower, and incredibly, the basilica bells kept right on tolling. I have no idea whether they ring like that every

Monday morning at the crack of dawn, but if they do, only the drunk and the dead sleep late in Dôle.

When the racket finally subsided, we were wide awake and ready to head south toward Beaune, the wine capital of Burgundy. We picked up a grey Citroën minivan at the only car rental agency in town, loaded the bags, and bid a fond farewell to our trusty houseboat. I haven't driven a standard transmission car for more than a decade, so Devi took the wheel. We found the autoroute out of town, and Devi quickly cranked the van up to 140 kilometers per hour.* We reached the Beaune turnoff in no time. Devi parked the van, and we set off to explore the old walled city on foot.

Beaune's present-day circumstances were largely deter-mined five centuries ago when Burgundy was the largest coun-try in Europe, encompassing most of present-day Belgium, Luxembourg, Alsace-Lorraine, and the Netherlands. At its zenith of power, Burgundy's ducal chancellor, Nicolas Rolin, decided to build a great hospital in Beaune. To insure its future, he endowed the Hospices de Beaune with expansive vineyards and a salt works. The salt works didn't turn out to be any great shakes, but five hundred years later the vineyards still produce some of the finest wines on the face of the earth.

Devi knew all this from her guidebook, and she deftly steered us toward the Marché de Vins, the expansive eleventh-century wine cellars operated by the Hospices de Beaune. A woman at the front desk gave each of us our own *taste-vins* (those dimpled shell-shaped cups that sommeliers wear) and an impressive *carte de vins* listing twenty-two rarefied offerings. Then we ducked our heads and crouched down a cramped spiral staircase made from stone slabs. When our eyes adjusted to the underground darkness, we found ourselves standing at one end of a very long

*Equivalent to about 85 mph.

passageway lit only by candles set in shallow wall niches. The passage was lined with polished oak barrels, three feet in diameter, and every thirty feet or so it widened into a small room.

We walked slowly down the shadowy corridor to the first room, where we found a six-foot wine rack and three upturned barrels. Atop each barrel was a lit candle, a bottle of wine opened to breathe, and another in reserve. There was also a carafe for spitting out the wine after you tasted it. Of course, there was little chance of that. I mean here we were essentially unescorted in one of the world's greatest wine cellars, encompassed by countless cases of Montrachets, Meursaults, and Mazis-Chambertins. It was a scenario I could only dream about at home, so I wasn't going to take just one tiny little sip and spit it out. I filled the *taste-vins* time and again, lingering for seconds and thirds. There were a dozen sublime wines to taste in the cellar and another ten upstairs in a cavernous old chapel. The chapel was an appropriate venue, because by the time I got there, I was having a religious experience. (Bacchanalian, but religious nonetheless.) I felt as if I were embraced in a red velvet fog, and I said to Devi over and over, "This must be the best place on earth. No seriously, Devi, there has never been a better place than this."

Since Devi was driving to Nice after lunch (and she's a pretty light drinker anyway) I didn't press too much grog on her. Still, this was the sort of epiphanous experience I wanted to share with someone, and after a while, I noticed I was sharing it with Willie. I heard myself saying things like, "This is a very nice one, Willie."

Then Willie would sip a magnificent Chambolle-Musigny '87 from the *taste-vins*, nod thoughtfully and respond, "Mmm. Yeah. That one's pretty good."

It was only after another American couple started staring at us pointedly that I remembered Willie was only seven and a half. He'd had only seven or eight sips from the *taste-vins*, so he wasn't drunk or anything, but I figured I better cut him off.

After all, if Willie's first experience with wine included the finest vintages Burgundy had to offer, it would probably spoil him for life.

When we emerged from the Marché de Vins, blinking in the sunlight, Betty and the kids desperately wanted to shop for more souvenirs. At this point in the trip, Devi and I can't even look at another souvenir shop, so we gave the troops lunch money and ducked around the corner for a proper French lunch. We chose an old-fashioned place with burgundy-velvet walls, brass fixtures, and tufted banquettes. We ordered the old standbys from the *prix fixe* menu: escargot, then rack of lamb followed by cheese, fruit, and dessert. Everything was superb.

As we were finishing our *tartes tatin,* three French men entered the restaurant accompanied by two young American women in miniskirts. The oldest man, obviously the alpha-male, was in his late fifties. He was bald with a thin gray mustache, and he wore a camel-colored cashmere sport jacket with an expensive green and gold tie. The moment this fellow sat down, he began to hold forth expansively about life and love in heavily accented English while the young women made a good-faith effort to appear enthralled.

"I am so very bored when I travel," he said loudly enough for everyone in the room to hear. "When I travel, I am always weteeng for somesing. I wet foh zee 'otel room. I wet foh zee aeroplane. I wet foh zee taxi." Then he paused for effect, and said, even more loudly, "What can you do when you travel, but wet and wet and mek love seven times a night?"

When I heard that seven-times-a-night thing, I twisted around involuntarily and found myself staring at the guy. I guess I was looking for traces of irony, but *monsieur* was dead serious. To their credit, both young women managed to maintain straight faces. The other men just puffed on their cigarettes as though they'd heard this all before.

When we walked out of the restaurant, I apologized to Devi. "I'm sorry," I said. "We've been traveling for three months now. We've wetted foh zee 'otel rooms...foh zee aero-plane...foh zee taxis. And never once, in all that time, have I ever made love to you seven times a night."

"That's all right," said Devi. "I'm not that bored with traveling yet."

"Good thing," I replied, and we ran off to find Betty and the kids.

In vino veritas,
David

Chapter 9

Subject: Gluttony without Tears
Date: September 17
From: daylifers@aol.com (David Cohen)

San Teodoro, Sardinia

Dear Friends:

After our sybaritic stopover in the wine cellars of Beaune, we leapt back on the autoroute and blazed south toward the warm Mediterranean seashore. Our plan was to spend three days sightseeing on the Côte d'Azur before heading off to the rugged island of Sardinia, where Devi's father lives.

It was a long drive from Burgundy to Nice, and we didn't arrive until well after 9:00 P.M. Since our modest hotel wasn't exactly a local landmark, we drove up and down the dark city streets for more than an hour until we finally found it, then we fell into bed exhausted. When we woke the next morning, it was a warm, sparkling day on the French Riviera. After the gray skies of Burgundy, we were all glad to feel the sun on our neck—especially Devi, whose spirits always warm with the weather.

We had a nice enough time on the Côte d'Azur. The tourist season was long gone, so we didn't have to battle the teeming crowds of August. Still, the whole time we were there, I felt as if we'd wandered into someone else's private club, where we didn't really know the rules. After all, this is a pretty glamorous corner of the world, and after three months without benefit of dry cleaning, Devi and I didn't feel particularly glamorous. So our short stay on the Riviera didn't include any black-tie evenings at Monte Carlo or candlelight dinners at the Carlton. Once in a while, we poked our heads into a fancy joint like the Hotel Négresco in Nice. But mostly, we just played in the park, swam on the few free public beaches (most of them charge an arm and a leg), and strolled along the promenades in Nice and Cannes.

When it came time to leave, we boarded a huge yellow ferry to the island of Corsica. Devi's father was supposed to meet us there and drive us down the coast and across the Bocche di Bonifacio to the neighboring island of Sardinia. Pete—or Prabhakar, as he's known in his native India—works as an aeronautical engineer for the Sardinian airline, Meridiana. He is, without a doubt, one of the most gracious, generous men I've ever had the pleasure of knowing, but dependability isn't his defining characteristic. Devi tried to call Pete several times from Nice in order to confirm our meeting in Corsica, but she never managed to reach him. So as the ferry steamed away from the French coast, we weren't entirely sure whether Pete would be waiting for us when we arrived or how we would get from northern Corsica to Sardinia if he didn't show up.

Our lack of faith was entirely unfounded. The moment we landed, we saw Devi's father waving from the pier exactly as he promised. He wasn't alone, either. By his side, kissing all the grandchildren on both cheeks, was a bombastic dark-haired woman in her early forties named Franca. Franca had a deep voice and dancing eyes, and she spoke Italian at the speed of light.

While we were loading our suitcases into the van, I mouthed the words to Devi, "Who's that?"

Devi shrugged and said sotto voce, "Maybe she's from Meridiana Airlines."

Whoever she was, Franca was a gregarious whirlwind of a presence. Try as I might, I could not convince this woman that I didn't speak Italian. Franca and I had long, one-sided conversations, sometimes for ten minutes at a time. Her Italian had a lovely, mellifluous sound, but I didn't have a clue what she was saying. And God help the man, woman, or child who innocently said to Franca, "Oh, you're Italian."

This happened three or four times while we were in Sardinia, and each time it did, Franca's impressive bosom rose defiantly and her eyes flashed with indignation. "I am not Italian," she said. "*I* am a Sard." This reflected the proud Sardinian sentiment that the mainland Italians were only the latest in a three-thousand-year series of foreign aggressors who had temporarily conquered their island.

My favorite moment with Franca came when we were all driving in the van one evening. Franca was speaking to her ten-year-old son, Paolo, on a cellular phone, and apparently, he wasn't eating enough dinner. (This, we later learned, is a relative concept in Sardinia.) Anyway, Franca was vigorously urging Paolo to finish his meal. It was a long discussion, and after a while Franca was no longer holding the phone to her ear. She just held it in front of her face with her left hand and gesticulated at it with her right. We all stared in amazement as Franca screamed at her cell phone.

"Eh, Paolo, Mangia! Mangia!"

We heard a tinny little reply from the phone. Then Franca showed the cell phone the back of her hand and yelled, *"Mangia, Paolo, mangia!"*

After weeks of French sangfroid, this earthy Sardinian style came as a welcome relief. In France, we couldn't even take the kids out to eat without fear of embarrassment. But in the small-town trattorias around Olbia, the children were welcomed with open arms. The moment we walked through the door, the waitresses were all over them, cooing, pinching their cheeks, and lavishing affection. We never had to worry about the kids disturbing the other diners, either. Lucas was passed around so much that his feet rarely touched the ground, and any commotion Kara and Willie might make was inevitably drowned out by the roar of the robust Sards.

Good thing, too. Because after a while, we realized we were spending approximately 40 percent of our waking hours eating. Devi's dad had made several good friends during his four years in Sardinia, and each and every one of them displayed a level of hospitality that may be unparalleled in the world. This was particularly true because one day, about a year ago, Pete showed up unexpectedly at our house in Mill Valley and announced that eight of his Sardinian friends were coming to dinner. Pete said they might like steaks, and that they had ravenous appetites. Devi and I barbecued roughly half a cow, and our guests devoured every morsel. Now we were on their turf, and they seemed determined to return the favor tenfold.

The second night we were on the island, Pete's good friends, Giancarlo and Pia, took us to an old Sardinian farmhouse that had been converted into a restaurant. It was a simple, rustic place perched high on a rocky hill. The restaurant had small windows, rough beams, and wide plank floors. One wall consisted of an enormous hearth with a whole polished juniper trunk for a mantel. There were only two tables in the entire place, but each could accommodate twenty diners.

Our table was crowded with people who knew each other from Meridiana Airlines, and when we walked into the room, the party was already in full swing. Everyone was drinking full-bodied Nepente wine, yelling, gesticulating, and dandling babies on their knees. Soon after we arrived, a violent storm kicked up. Since the old house was perched on a hillside, the whole place seemed to twitch in the wind, and the iron chandeliers flickered as bolts of lightning illuminated the sky. This didn't faze the diners at all. They just battened the wooden shutters and carried on their revelry with an air of camaraderie that held the storm at bay.

The restaurant was family-owned, and each dish was presented with a flourish by a member of the family. The first course included huge trays of salami and prosciutto accompanied by platter-sized sheets of Sardinian flat bread called *pane carasau*. The bread was drizzled with virgin green olive oil and sprinkled with rock salt. Next came *zuppa gallurese,* a delicious meat, bread, and cheese casserole that was a cross between pizza and lasagna.

Because we were guests, everyone at the table insisted we have seconds and thirds. I mistakenly thought the salami and prosciutto course was the appetizer, and the *zuppa gallurese* was the main course, so I happily complied, leaving just enough room for dessert. But we weren't anywhere within shouting distance of dessert. After everyone praised the proprietor's *zuppa gallurese,* his wife emerged from the kitchen with a huge dish of *malluredos,* small pasta shells covered with cheese and tomatoes. People kept filling our glasses with wine and shouting *"Mangia! Mangia!"* But after two helpings of pasta, I had to rub my stomach and wave my napkin in surrender.

"What are you doin'?" Giancarlo said pleasantly. "You canna stop now. The pasta dishes are only…the begeenning. You insult the owner if you don' eata the main course. Itsa delicious."

He was right. The next dish on the menu was *cinghiale,* thin slices of wild boar in a savory brown sauce. It was one of the tastiest things I've ever eaten, but it was only marginally better than the fifth course, a whole roast suckling pig, borne triumphantly from the kitchen on a coffee-table-sized cork platter garnished with myrtle branches. It took two men to carry it. The suckling pig was obviously the highlight of the feast, because it was met with lusty cries of *"Bellissimo!"* from all the diners.

By this point, it seemed evident that dining out in Sardinia was something of a gustatory marathon. No one's ever accused me of being a piker at the dinner table, but these guys were way out of my league. They ate plate after plate with boundless enthusiasm. From time to time, one of the men would glance at my ample stomach and raise an eyebrow as if to say, "You obviously know your way around a dinner plate, so how come you're just nibbling tonight?"

After a plate of suckling pig, I really was nibbling. I barely made it through the salad course and a dessert called *origliette*—fried dough drizzled with honey and dusted with powdered sugar. After that, all that was left was rich Italian coffee and three or four bottles of a 100 proof Sardinian moonshine called *filo ferro* or "iron wire." It got that name because the Sards used to hide bottles of this stuff from Italian revenuers by burying them in the dirt and marking the spot with thin iron wires attached to the bottle necks. As you might expect, *filo ferro* can take paint off a tractor.

When it looked like the orgy was winding down a bit, and a few *filo ferros* had loosened my tongue, I turned to Giancarlo and asked him, "Is this a normal night out for you guys?"

He paused thoughtfully for a moment, and said, "No, this food, itsa better than usual."

"No, that's not what I meant, Giancarlo. The food is wonderful, some of the best I've ever eaten." Giancarlo looked pleased at that. "What I meant is, do people in Sardinia normally eat this much? Where I live, in California, people take the skin off their chicken, order pizza without cheese, drink milk without fat, coffee without caffeine, and soda without sugar. Here, everyone chows down like it's their first day out of prison. Yet, compared to the average American, you guys all seem reasonably slim."

Giancarlo considered this for a while. He'd been to America several times, so he was in a good position to comment. He said very politely, so as not to hurt my feelings, "Here...I think itsa more important to cook things well. Also," he said, "there is another trick."

Oh good. Here it was. The ancient Sardinian secret for consuming massive quantities of meat and pasta without turning into a zeppelin.

"What's the trick?" I asked anxiously.

"The secret," he said, "isa to leave the ristorante before midnight."

"Interesting. Why midnight?"

"Itsa old tradition. If you stay past midnight, the owner muss bring out another pasta dish, and to be polite, you mussa eat it...Anna sometimes thatsa just too much food."

Since it was past 11:30, and the storm had passed, I figured that was our cue to leave. This was a twenty-minute process, and we nearly missed the midnight deadline. First, we thanked everyone at the table and shook hands with all the family members involved in the preparation of the meal. Then we kissed a dozen people on both cheeks and tottered out into the bracing night air. The storm had passed, and we'd just finished one of the grandest repasts I'd ever seen, read, or heard about. I thought it would be a very long time before we saw its like again.

But as things turned out, it was less than twenty-four hours. Sardinian hospitality is apparently boundless. We had dinner at Giancarlo and Pia's house. Then we ate at Gianni and Anna Maria's house. Then we ate again with Giancarlo's brother, Mino, and his wife, Birghit. Then again with Pete's neighbors, Andrea and Adriana. Nearly all of these meals included the eight traditional Italian courses: *antipasto, primo piatto, secondo piatto, contorno, formaggio, frutta, dolce,* and *caffè.**

---

*Course before the meal, first plate, second plate, vegetables (literally, trimmings), cheese, fruit, sweets, and coffee.

And it was all liberally washed down with Sardinian wine, *filo ferro,* and an aperitif called *mirtho.*

The grandest meal of all took place on our last evening in Sardinia. It was a modest seven-hour affair in a small inn called the Hotel Montenegro. Once again, this restaurant was hidden way up in the Sardinian hills, and I doubt very many tourists have ever been there. This time, it was a seafood feast. The first dish was truly memorable—mussels in a sublime garlic, wine, and olive oil sauce. It was, far and away, the best shellfish I've ever eaten, and everyone employed little pieces of bread called *scarpette*—literally, little shoes—to sop up the last of the sauce. After that came *crostino*—bread topped with chopped tomato and fresh basil. Then—in succession—octopus in olive oil, pasta with fish roe, and risotto blackened with squid ink. By then, we were pretty much ready for the main course: a platter of prawns, squid, and two types of fish called *orato* and *taglia.* We finished with roasted radicchio, cake, and coffee.

There was so much food, it was like a Bible story—or *The Flintstones.* In fact, at the end of the meal, I mentioned to Giancarlo's brother, Mino, that we had a cartoon in America called *The Flintstones,* in which the main character, Fred, ate like a Sardinian. Apparently, they also broadcast *The Flintstones* in Italy, where it's called *Gli Antenati* or "The Ancestors." Since we were well into the *filo ferro,* all the men at the table started doing Fred Flintstone imitations in Italian, bellowing *"No, no, Dino,"* and *"Wilma, dammi il bastone."**

As we walked out the door I asked Pete what a feast like this might cost. He said no more than about $25 per person.

"Are you kidding?" I asked incredulously. "All that for twenty-five bucks?"

"That's why you should stay out of Porto Cervo," said Pete, referring to the ultrachic tourist town on Sardinia's

* "Wilma, hand me my club."

nearby Costa Smeralda. "They charge you five times as much, and the food isn't nearly as good."

We actually did go to Porto Cervo twice—once for dinner with a friend of Devi's, who happened to be on the island, and once with Giancarlo's sister-in-law, Birghit, who gave us a tour of the $1,000-a-night Cala di Volpe resort where she worked. It was all very elegant, very exclusive, and very expensive—just as you'd expect. And I suppose if you had a few extra mil lying around, Porto Cervo would be as good a place as any to drop some of it. Still, Devi and I thought the entire town looked like a cross between *Lifestyles of the Rich and Famous* and Pirates of the Caribbean. We felt fortunate that Pete, Giancarlo, and their friends had shown us the real Sardinia—an earthy, gregarious place that was infinitely more comfortable.

Devi was also gratified to see her father so well settled in Sardinia. Ever since he left Bombay for an American education at age fifteen, Devi's father has been hovering somewhere between mother India and the West. Now he had finally landed in a small out-of-the-way place where everyone adored him.

One day at lunch, Pete's friend Mino told us the story of a Norwegian couple who decided to sail around the world. They left Oslo, and went port-to-port down the western coast of Europe and through the Mediterranean. When they landed in Sardinia, they only expected to stay for a week or two. But, like us, they were enchanted by the island's rugged beauty and ancient brio. According to Mino, the Norwegians' round-the-world trip ended in Sardinia and never resumed.

When Mino finished the story—which may or may not have been apocryphal—everyone at the table looked at us expectantly—like maybe we would do the only reasonable thing and linger amongst the congenial folk of Sardinia. On one level, it was tempting. Who wouldn't want to stay on a fabulous island with white beaches, crystal-clear water, and jagged mountains? And who wouldn't love a place full of exquisite food, good wine, and warm hearts? We had to move on, of course. We'd only just started our trip, and there was a whole world left to see. But as we boarded the ferry to Rome, we could hear Sardinia's siren song.

> *Ciao, amici,* from the fat
> and happy Cohens

Chapter 10

Subject: A Tough Day on the Road
Date: September 20
From: daylifers@aol.com (David Cohen)

Rome, Italy

Dear Friends:

When our happy, gluttonous week in Sardinia came to an end, it was time to head for Rome. We wedged our luggage into a rented green minivan and headed for the ferry. Devi maneuvered the van up a long metal ramp and onto the deck of a hulking old vessel called the *Gallurica*. There, a crew of rough Italian deckhands waved and whistled us into place and lashed our wheels to the deck with thick sisal ropes.

That accomplished, the entire family piled out of the van and found a spot along the stern rail where we could enjoy the maritime scene. We watched the dockworkers, far below, as they tried to load a six-car freight train into the cavernous hold of the ship. It was an impressive sight at first, and Willie and Lucas were both fascinated by the process. But as soon as the last boxcar disappeared into the hold, the entire ferry shuddered, creaked, and listed ten degrees to port. Willie yelled, "Hey, the boat's tipping over!" And Lucas fairly leapt into his mother's arms.

Down on the pier, the stevedores also looked concerned. They backed the train out of the hold, and after some animated discussion took another crack at it. This time the ferry remained more or less upright, but when we steamed out of port, we weren't as relaxed as we might have been.

As it turned out, this was the inauspicious start of our worst travel day yet. As we steamed eastward into the Tyrrhenian Sea, the skies clouded over; a cold drizzle developed; the wind kicked up whitecaps and salt spray whipped the deck. Within an hour, the *Gallurica*—freight train and all—was heaving rhythmically over leaden ten-foot swells.

For a while, Willie and I found the storm rather exhilarating, and we stayed up on deck riding the bucking ship and boldly leaning into the wind. But the novelty of playing *Captains Courageous* soon wore off, and we retreated, damp and bone-chilled, into the ferry's shabby, smoke-filled passenger cabin. We found the rest of the family huddled around a small metal table in the ship's bar shivering in their seats and complaining about the cold. I thought a good hot meal would do everyone a world of good, so I herded the kids across the rolling cabin into the ferry's pint-size cafeteria where the cooks were ladling out a hearty chili and rice dish. That seemed like just the thing to warm our bellies, and we all cleaned our plates.

That, of course, proved to be an enormous mistake, because as everyone knows (except us, apparently), *mal de mer* is a creeping affliction. As the weather grew heavier, the ferry bucked and pitched over mounting swells and the chili inevitably revolted. Betty and Lucas were the only ones who literally lost their lunch, but by the time we reached the Italian mainland six hours later, Devi was drained and nauseous and the kids were draped ashen-faced across their chairs.

When we drove off the ferry into the port of Civitavecchia, Devi and I breathed a sigh of relief. With the rough passage behind us, we thought our troubles were over. But in fact, they were only beginning. It was pitch-dark, raining harder than ever, and every window in the van fogged up like a bathroom mirror. We tried to clear the condensation in the usual ways, blasting the defogger and opening the windows in spite of the rain. When that didn't work we pulled off the road every mile or two and wiped the inside of the windshield with an old t-shirt. Eventually we found that the only effective way to clear the windshield for more than a minute at a time—other than not breathing that is—was to turn up the air-conditioner. Since it was a cold rainy night to begin with, the van quickly became a rolling freezer unit—but at least we could see where we were going.

With that problem more or less solved, Devi and I turned our attention to the road. Usually, I'm the navigator, but on this occasion Devi got detailed directions from a smooth Italian guy on the ferry. She handed me the written instructions, and said, very matter-of-factly, "Okay. This is the way we're supposed to go. Just keep your eyes on the road and tell me where to turn."

Since this was a flagrant usurpation of my navigator's role, I regarded the directions with suspicion. "How do you know these are right?" I asked.

"Because the guy who gave them to me lives here," she replied.

"That may be true," I said. "But just because he lives here doesn't mean he knows how to get to our particular hotel in Rome. Look at this map for a second. You can see right away that it's faster to use the ring road. I'm sure your friend on the ferry meant well, but he's taking us completely out of our way."

"David," said my lovely wife, "everyone is freezing cold, nauseated, and exhausted. Let's just go the way the guy said. Please."

"Trust me," I answered.

Well, I guess I don't have to tell you how that worked out. Somehow I directed Devi to an exit on the absolute wrong side of Rome. By the time we figured that out, I had no idea whatsoever how to get back on the autostrada. We drove our freezing van around some of Rome's less distinguished suburbs for more than an hour, and I have to tell you, things got a little bit tense. I was saying, "Look, I didn't try to get us lost." And Devi was beginning her sentences with phrases such as, "If you'd only just listened…" and "I don't understand why you always feel the need…"

These, my friends, are the times when world travelers such as ourselves must fall back on deep reserves of patience and humor, the times when a few kind words and a reassuring touch make all the difference. But, believe me, we were way past that, so instead we resorted to swearing, slamming things around, and silence as cold as the van.

Devi asked for help in Italian from a news agent, a flower vendor, a fruit-and-vegetable guy, and approximately ten pedestrians. Each one got us a bit closer and eventually we found our way back onto the lower left-hand corner of the "Rome Accommodations" map in our *Frommer's* guidebook. That turned out to be a partial victory because when things go wrong, they tend to go wrong all the way, and believe it or not, the map was inaccurate. To be more specific, the cartographers at *Frommer's* couldn't fit the small numbered box that indicated our hotel onto the map, so they simply moved it to the nearest available spot. It was less than an inch on the printed page, but in real life, the discrepancy was closer to a kilometer. To confuse matters further, the mapmakers—in the interest of clean graphics I suppose—deleted many of the less important side streets without mentioning that fact in any obvious way. Consequently, we spent the last two hours of a harrowing day crisscrossing our way in and around the Villa Borghese, turning down *stradas* that didn't appear on the map, and searching for an obscure hotel that was actually somewhere else.

I tried to tell Devi, somewhat timidly, that the guidebook was wrong. But by this point, I lacked all credibility. Finally, I just asked her to pull over.

"Why?" she asked.

"Because I give up."

"What do you mean, you give up?"

"I mean it's eleven o'clock at night. Everyone's frozen and exhausted and we're never going to find this hotel without some sort of divine intervention. I'm going to get out of the van, hail a cab, and pay him whatever he wants to lead us to our hotel."

Devi, who tends to be overly dogged in these matters, considered that a defeatist attitude. "Wait here," she said. "I'm going to try one more thing."

She pulled over, jumped out of the van, and ran into the lobby of a small baroque hotel. She emerged ten minutes later, clutching a detailed map of the neighborhood with our lodgings circled in red. Sure enough, we followed the map directly to our hotel. The kind English-speaking proprietor took one look at us, sized up our condition, and let us park the van right outside the front door. Devi was so enormously relieved that this day was finally over that she more or less forgave my earlier transgressions. The rain dissipated, and we carried our children, fast asleep, to their nice warm beds.

The next day, we slept late and came downstairs just in time to catch the last meager remnants of the breakfast buffet. Over coffee and toast, I announced, rather brightly, to the children that we were going to St. Peter's Basilica and the Vatican Museums. I described both in glowing terms, at which point Kara said very calmly, "No thank you. I don't like sightseeing anymore."

I considered this for a moment, and replied, "I'm sorry, Kara, but everyone else wants to go. You'll have to come, too."

"Look," she said with a preteen roll of her eyes. "We saw practically every church in France. I *get* the idea."

"This is different," I told her. "The Vatican is the headquarters of the Catholic Church, and its museums contain some of the most important artworks in the world. It'll be very interesting. I promise."

"You said all the best artworks were in Paris."

"I didn't actually say *all* the best artworks were in Paris."

"Yes you did."

"No, I said a lot of important art was in Paris, and now I'm telling you that there's more at the Vatican. Look, I'll give you an example," I said. Then I tried to intrigue her with the story of Michelangelo and the Sistine Chapel—how Pope Julius II forced him to paint the ceiling against his will, and how he had to lie on his back for four years. Kara understood how Michelangelo felt—being forced to do things by fiat. She thought the story was passably interesting, and she grudgingly agreed to go to the Vatican in return for a *gelato* afterward.

Since Devi and I vowed never to drive in Rome again, we left our van at the hotel and boarded a streetcar to the Piazza del Risorgimento. From there it was a long hike around the Vatican walls to the museum entrance. Inside, we joined a crowd of thousands and walked for what must have been miles through a labyrinth of ornate galleries.

The Vatican Museums are like a gigantic treasure house filled with a mind-numbing array of antique globes, illuminated manuscripts, classical sculpture, medieval tapestries, Renaissance oils, and Egyptian artifacts. Every inch of every wall, floor, and ceiling is covered with marble inlays, elaborate mosaics, frescoes, and trompe l'oeils. Kara trudged up and down the endless halls taking it all in, then she stopped in her tracks and said, "This Pope must be *really* rich."

"Well, it's not really the Pope who's rich," said Devi. "It's the Catholic Church."

"Why do they have so much money?" Kara asked.

"People donate things to the Church," said Devi.

"Why? Do they think it'll get them into heaven or something?"

"Not exactly. The Church has been powerful for a long time, and they acquired all these things slowly over a period of many centuries."

Kara thought about that for a moment and said, "Isn't the Church supposed to help the poor people?"

"Yes."

"Then why don't they sell all this stuff and give the money to the poor people for food and houses?"

"That's a good question," said Devi. "But believe it or not, there isn't enough here to provide homes and food for even a small portion of the world's poor. Besides, Kara, I'll tell you a story. When I was sixteen, I was an exchange student in Mexico. And I asked *my* mother how come the people there were so poor, and the Church was so rich and beautiful. She told me that the people needed one beautiful place in their lives. Someplace they could go when they were sad and tired."

"I think they'd rather have food and a house," said Kara. "Then they wouldn't be so sad and tired to begin with."

She had a point, of course. But if one goal of the Vatican's extravagant display of booty was to inspire rapture, it certainly worked for Lucas. After we ogled the Sistine Chapel with ten thousand other crick-necked tourists, we eventually found our way into the gargantuan stone nave of St. Peter's Basilica. We were all walking respectfully toward a Mass in progress, when Lucas noticed the wonderful acoustical properties of the hall. Few things in life are more inspirational to a two-and-a-half-year-old than a cavernous room with an echo. All of a sudden, Lucas took off at full speed yelling "Aaaaahhhhh" at the top of his lungs.

Hitchcock would have shot what happened next from above. From every corner of the basilica, blue-coated Vatican guards converged on little Lucas, trying to intercept him before he got to the apse of the church, where the Mass was being celebrated. This took longer than you'd expect. The nave looked larger than two football fields, and Lucas was traveling under a full head of steam. A couple of puffing guards caught up with him at approximately the same time as I did—directly under Michelangelo's 375-foot dome. Unfortunately, the guards weren't inclined to chalk this rampage up to youthful exuberance. They told me very sternly, and at some length, that St. Peter's was a sacred place of worship, and that I should take a firmer hand with my children.

Despite the obvious embarrassment, I was secretly amused by Lucas's noisy epiphany. I recalled a day—well before Lucas was born—when Kara, Willie, and their friends were rampaging around our house like little demons. Normally that wouldn't be a problem, but I happened to have Edie Turner, a well-respected anthropologist, at the house for lunch. Edie was a proper British lady of seventy or so, and as each wave of screaming children stampeded past the dining room, I grew increasingly embarrassed.

"I'm very sorry about all the noise, Edie," I said.

"My dear David," she replied, looking at me with soft, knowing eyes. "I believe this is what it must sound like in heaven."

With every day that passes, Lucas is less a baby, and more a bright little person. It's wonderful to see the world through his eyes. During our Vatican tour, Lucas found angels everywhere—in all the paintings, frescoes, and sculptures. He called them "butterfly boys," which is as good a name as any, and he considers them to be little fellows like himself. He also seemed to be particularly touched by Michelangelo's *Pietà*. While the adults were all marveling at Michelangelo's uncanny ability to sculpt Carrera marble into intricate folds, Lucas saw past technique to the subject. "The son is dead, and the mommy is crying," he said over and over. "The son is dead, and the mommy is crying."

Toward the end of our stay in Rome, I had another raucous experience with Lucas. Lucas hadn't had a haircut since we left America, and his head had exploded into a riot of curls. I asked the proprietor of our hotel where I might find a barber shop, and he directed me to Solarium Luigi across the street from the nearby national police complex. The hotel proprietor said that Luigi was an excellent barber, but since nearly all his clients were police officers, I should make sure he didn't cut the baby's hair too short.

When Lucas and I got to the barbershop, we found Luigi to be a trim, immaculately groomed man smelling of pomade and talcum powder. He had a thin mustache, wore a gray tailored suit, and he didn't speak a word of English. I indicated in sign language that I wanted him to give Lucas a haircut. He gave a slight smile and brushed off a child seat he kept in the back.

After placing Lucas in the seat, Luigi fastidiously removed his suit jacket and hung it on a wooden hanger. Then he draped Lucas in a black smock, took up his long, elegant scissors and began to clip. Lucas sat reasonably still for the first few minutes, but then he started crawling out of the chair and wandering around the shop with his little black smock dragging behind him. The first two or three times this happened, Luigi simply picked Lucas up and placed him gently back in the seat. But when Lucas wouldn't stay put, Luigi just started following him around the shop snipping here and there whenever he got the chance. As Lucas moved randomly from the sink to the magazine rack to the umbrella stand and back again, the urbane Luigi crouched behind him styling on the run. I offered to intercede several times, but Luigi assured me with signs and gestures that he had matters under control.

Luigi never once lost his composure, and despite the difficult circumstances, he gave Lucas a very good haircut. When the last curl was trimmed, Luigi brushed Lucas's little neck with talcum powder and gently slapped his cheeks with a cologne that couldn't possibly compete with his ripening diapers. Then he gave Lucas a little bottle of shampoo that he treasured for the rest of the week. As we said *"Grazie"* and *"Arrivederci,"* Luigi put his jacket back on and bowed slightly. He actually seemed to have enjoyed his encounter with Lucas, but he was no doubt relieved that his next customer would be an officer of the *carabinieri*.

It's absurd to think you can see the Eternal City in four or five days. Nevertheless, we dutifully bagged most of the requisite tourist sites, flipping coins over our shoulder into the rococo Trevi Fountain, admiring the Campidoglio, and happily paying a stiff premium to drink cappuccinos in a Via Condotti coffee shop once patronized (allegedly) by Shelley, Keats, and Byron.

In all of these places, I tried to give Kara and Willie some notion of the vast span of Roman history. In doing so, I discovered that young children don't have a natural sense of historical perspective. This was apparent when we visited the basilica of Santa Maria Maggiore near Rome's central train terminal. Most of this structure dates from the fifth century, and I was trying to convey to Willie just how old that was.

"This church is 1,500 years old," I said. "The United States is only 220 years old, so when our country was founded, this church had already been here for more than 1,000 years. Do you understand how old that is?"

"Yes," said Willie, earnestly trying to please. "It's older than Grandpa Norm."

Oh well, as we visit the progressively older cultures of Greece, India, and Africa, I'm sure he'll gain perspective. Until then, we bid you adieu from the ancient city of popes and emperors, caesars and saints, Romulus and Remus—a city even older than Grandpa Norm.

Arrivederci,
David

Chapter 11

Subject: Next Time We Take the Bus
Date: September 26
From: daylifers@aol.com (David Cohen)

Panzano-in-Chianti, Italy

Dear Friends:

After Rome, we headed north toward Panzano-in-Chianti, a small village in the famous wine-growing region between Florence and Siena. Devi rented an apartment in a restored fifteenth-century villa there, and this promised to be a highlight of our trip. The apartment wasn't supposed to be ready until late afternoon, so we decided to take a scenic loop through the rolling hills of Umbria. This proved fortuitous, because it swiftly landed us in the sublime Umbrian hill town of Spoleto.

Spoleto is best known for its superb summer arts festival, but summer had long since passed, and the town had resumed its quiet off-season routine. We wandered on foot through narrow lanes overarched with flying buttresses until we found Spoleto's small central square, its cobblestones still wet from the morning rain. The piazza was bounded by small cafés and food shops. Since it was an off-season weekend, the shops were all closed, but their windows held forth a cornucopia of Italian delicacies—towers of tinned truffles, *fagioli* and tomatoes, plump black olives in oil, red wine, pasta, and hanging salamis.

These mouthwatering displays naturally piqued our hunger so we wandered into a nearby restaurant. Inside, the walls were lined with narrow shelves holding countless *grappa* bottles of every conceivable shape and size and an ethereal aroma wafted out from the kitchen. We ordered three luncheon specials for the six of us, a carafe of house wine, and a bottle of mineral water *con gas*. Each adult shared a meal with one of the children, and there was still more than enough to go around. The *osso buco*, the pasta, the salad, and dessert were all superb. In fact, everything about Spoleto was a balm to the senses—its handsome stone buildings, the hilltop setting, the air crisp and clean after the rain, the hearty food and wine— even the tolling bells that marked the passing hours. As we drove out of Spoleto, past its hilltop castle and ancient aqueduct, we were reminded that you always encounter the best places by chance.

When we rejoined the superhighway heading north, a tollbooth attendant handed Devi a small pink ticket. Devi passed it to me, and I wedged it into a dashboard vent so it wouldn't get lost. But when it came time to exit the highway in Chianti, I reached for the ticket, fumbled and knocked it down inside the ventilation system. I didn't tell Devi right away. There was a long line of cars at the tollbooth and I thought I might be able to reach up under the dashboard and discreetly salvage the ticket before it was our turn to pay. But when we were next in line at the tollbooth, I was obliged to say, "I'm afraid we have a small problem."

"What is that?" asked Devi.

"The ticket fell down inside the dashboard."

"How could that possibly happen?"

I didn't really have a good answer for that, and the car in front of us suddenly pulled forward, which left Devi to explain, in

Italian, how her idiot husband dropped the ticket into the heating vent. The toll collector listened with a quizzical look on his face and directed Devi to the administration building. I waited in the van with Betty and the kids.

"Where's Mommy going?" asked Willie.

"She's going to explain how we lost the ticket."

"How *did* we lose the ticket?" asked Kara.

"I knocked it into the vent."

"Why did you do that?"

"I didn't mean to do it. It was an accident."

"Are they going to put Mommy in jail?" asked Willie.

"No, honey. They're not."

"You're the one who should go to jail," said Kara. "You lost the ticket."

"No one's going to jail."

"Yeah, but if anyone does go to jail, it should be you." (I made a mental note never to bring Kara along on a bank heist.)

Devi emerged half an hour later. She had managed to square things with the Italian highway authorities, and we were free to go.

"Next time, please put the ticket in your wallet," she said.

"You got it," I replied, and we were back on the road.

After that little contretemps, we navigated a series of winding roads up into the Tuscan hills until we came to the picturesque village of Panzano-in-Chianti. We arrived late in the afternoon, and the only place open was a tiny grocery. We bought a few necessities for the morning, and asked the woman behind the counter for directions to the Villa Lupinati. She said it was only about two kilometers from town and pointed us in the right direction.

The road to the villa ran past a ruined fortress and several ancient vineyards. Harvest time was nigh, and fat clusters of wet black grapes hung lush and heavy on the gnarled old vines. It took a few passes, but eventually we found the well-hidden turnoff to the villa. We bumped and jolted down a rutted track for nearly a mile until we came to a charming stone-and-stucco compound covered with ivy. It was set high on a hillside, and commanded a twenty-mile view of rolling vineyards dotted with old stone farmhouses. Thin wisps of wood smoke curled up from the farmhouse chimneys and tiny lights twinkled in the windows. I've never been to the Tuscan hills before, but the landscape looked remarkably familiar. Eventually I realized that scenes like this were depicted in the backgrounds of countless Renaissance paintings, and that remarkably little had changed in the last four hundred years.

These aesthetic considerations were largely lost on the children, but they were equally delighted with Villa Lupinati— mostly because there was a litter of calico kittens roaming the grounds. Shortly after we arrived, the children fed scraps to these little beggars, and from that point forward, there was always a coterie of tiny felines lurking outside our door. Whenever someone tried to get in or out, one or more of these infants would sneak in for a snack or a nap by the fire. I'm wildly allergic to cats, but the kittens gave the children so much pleasure I felt compelled to suffer them gladly.

When we woke up the following morning, it was raining pretty hard, but we still drove into Panzano for the weekly farmer's market. We expected a modest display of produce and rustic handicrafts, but instead we found the entire town square given over to dozens of vintners in burlap-covered booths. According to a handbill, it was the last day of the *Manifestazione Enogastronomica di Panzano-in-Chianti,* a food and wine festival that celebrated "the production of wine, oil, and food that is the envy of all the world." It was also billed as the first public gathering of all the Chianti Classico wine makers in several decades.

Devi and I love full-bodied Chianti Classico wine, so we bought tasting glasses for 10,000 lire* and sipped our way around the piazza. Despite the immodest claims on the hand-bill, the wine we sampled was still pretty rough around the edges. The vintners were pouring new wine, and Chianti takes years to mellow. Still, it was a rare experience to sample and discuss one of the world's great wines with all the local growers.

At lunchtime, we bought a bottle of Chianti Classico, a whole roast chicken, and a bag of oregano-flavored *patatine fritte*.† Then, we drove back to the villa and ate. The kids played with the kittens, and I sat by the hearth reading Jack Kerouac's *On the Road*. As the rain beat against the windowpanes and the fire crackled, I felt satisfied that our journey, like Kerouac's, was no longer a series of scheduled, predetermined events—like it was back in Costa Rica. After more than three months on the road, we finally seemed to be roaming the world freely, serendipitously finding adventure and quirky offbeat events such as the Panzano wine festival. We weren't like those pitiful hordes of busborne tourists crisscrossing Italy on scripted, predictable church-and-gallery tours. Those poor sods were missing the essence of Italy, while we seasoned world travelers were soaking up the real deal. This, of course, was pure hubris, and the next day, in Florence, I got my comeuppance.

Our day trip to Firenze began with great hope. Devi, Betty, and I had all toured Florence separately, but now we had the wonderful opportunity to show our children the glories of the Uffizi, the polychrome grandeur of the Duomo, Giotto's bell tower, Ghiberti's baptistery doors, and Michelangelo's sublime *David*. But before we did any of that good stuff, we

*About $7.
†Fried potatoes.

had to find a parking space somewhere within fifty miles of the place. For more than an hour and a half, we stalked the south bank of the Arno waiting for someone, anyone, to relinquish a spot. But our clunky van and American reticence were no match for the cunning Florentines who zipped in and snatched any open space in the blink of an eye. We were finally reduced to begging a kindly old parking lot attendant for help. Inspired by a substantial tip, he crawled behind the wheel of our van and squeezed it into a slot so narrow he actually had to crawl into the back seat and use the sliding door to get out.

With that, we broke out our umbrellas and hiked a mile or so to the Ponte Vecchio, the renowned fourteenth-century bridge now lined with dozens of tiny jewelry shops. Since we wasted half the morning parking the van, I was anxious to get to the Uffizi galleries as soon as possible. But this proved to be an unreasonable expectation, because Kara and Betty weren't about to breeze past all those jewelry shops on the Ponte Vecchio without a thorough inspection. It took us another hour just to cross the Arno.

When we did finally get to the Uffizi, we were shocked to find hundreds, if not thousands, of our fellow art lovers waiting patiently to get inside. The line, two or three abreast, stretched from one end of the building to the other, and it didn't seem to be moving at all. That, we soon learned, was because entire busloads of organized tourists—those same poor wretches I regarded with such pity the day before—were being systematically shunted to the front of the line. Apparently, the tour operators had a cozy deal with all of Firenze's art galleries, and we freelancers were left out in the cold.

After Devi and I bemoaned the rank inequity of this system, she strode to the front of the line and interrogated the guard about when we might get in. He said it could be two hours or more. There was no way on earth, short of knocking them unconscious, that our children were going to wait two hours in the rain to see an art gallery, so we had to abandon our fond plan to see Italy's greatest collection, and reluctantly move on.

Our next stop was the thirteenth-century Palazzo Vecchio—ancient home of the Medici. It was a reasonably successful visit, but when we stepped outside and tried to make our way across the Piazza della Signoria we ran into a problem. That's because a) the piazza, like every other tourist attraction in Florence, was packed with rain-soaked mobs, and b) Kara and Willie tend to hold their umbrellas at the average adult's eye level. Despite my best efforts, you could pretty well track our progress across the piazza by listening to the indignant cries of "Eh!," "Aye!," "Ow!," and "Ach!" in four different languages. I figured it would be better for Kara and Willie to get wet than to put someone's eye out, so I made them holster their weapons.

Once we made it across the piazza, we walked a kilometer or so through the rain to a particular trattoria recommended by our less-than-trusty *Frommer's Guide* as a "Family-Friendly Restaurant." I don't know whose family they were thinking of—perhaps it was the Agnellis—but when we got to the restaurant in our soaked windbreakers and muddy sneakers, we found ourselves in the sort of spot where Armani-clad executives might enjoy an elegant business lunch. The children were staring through the window at the dessert cart like starving street urchins, but Devi and I decided we'd better drag them off to someplace less refined.

We must have headed in the wrong direction, because the only restaurant we could find was a second-story cafeteria with a sign in the window that said something like "Cheap Food" in fourteen languages. The cafeteria's bare fluorescent bulbs and green Formica tables contributed to an ambience that was only slightly less charming than the average bus station. But to our surprise, the decor actually proved superior to the food. The servers at the steam counter ladled out soggy portions of what was, arguably, the worst victuals in northern

Italy. Worse yet, the cafeteria seemed to operate under a complex set of rules, and inadvertently, we kept breaking them.

The moment we sat down at the table and spread out all our dishes, the manager ran over and said in English, "Eh! You can't sit here. This area is closed."

Devi started to gather up her things, but I was too beaten down to move.

"Listen, signor," I said. "As you can see, we have three small very wet children here. It was difficult enough to get six trays to this table in the first place. Could you possibly give us a break and let us sit here, just this time?"

"Not possible," he replied. "This area is closed. You muss move."

"I really can't put all the plates back on trays and move everyone now."

"You muss move."

"Sorry," I said. "I'm not going."

At that point, the manager abruptly backed off muttering "Okay, okay, okay."

He returned a few minutes later when we committed an even more heinous offense—putting our empty trays on the table behind us.

"Eh!" he yelled. "You canna use two tables."

"Look," I said. "We have six people crammed around a table meant for four, so we don't have room for the trays. Besides, you already told us this section is closed, so obviously no one's going to use that table."

"You muss move the trays!"

"May I do it when we're done eating?"

"No. Now."

"Sorry, signor. I can't do it."

Again, he backed down abruptly, and hurried away muttering "Okay, okay, okay."

Eventually the entire meal got to be like a comedy routine. The manager watched us like a hawk. Inevitably, one of us would do something wrong, like spill some milk or use too many napkins. Then he'd run over, scold us, and scurry away.

We finally gave up and stumbled back into the rain to resume our star-crossed tour of Florence. We stopped at the Duomo and gazed at Giotto's *campanile* without too much difficulty, but despite the foul weather, we couldn't get anywhere near Ghiberti's famous baptistery doors. German and English tourists were massed thirty deep around the entire perimeter of the baptistery, and again, only organized groups were getting inside. Eventually, the whole exercise began to seem somewhat futile. I mean what's the use of shoving children through huge crowds to get a brief glimpse of art that doesn't particularly interest them in the first place? We withdrew from Firenze, wet and tired, with our tails between our legs.

I know that Florence is everyone's favorite city, so I'm sure this all sounds whiny and heretical. But between the rain, huge crowds, long lines, bad food, high prices, and rampant commercialism, our particular experience in this flower of the Renaissance was slightly worse than a bad day at Disney World. Of course, if we ever come back, we're going to do things completely differently. First of all, I'm going to book us onto one of those church-and-gallery tours I was so snotty about. That way, we'll at least see something. And we won't spend two hours trying to find a parking space or get soaked to the bone walking around. If we're really lucky, we might even get to eat someplace where the food is edible and the manager doesn't scream at you every few minutes. All aboard, fellow tourists. I am right behind you.

In a last-ditch effort to salvage the day, Devi suggested we drive sixty kilometers down the Arno Valley to Pisa. It was getting late, but I was all for it. I'd never seen the famous

Leaning Tower before, and I wanted to take the kids to see something they'd really enjoy.

We got to Pisa an hour before dusk. All the tour buses were gone, and there were only a few straggling sightseers around. Like almost every other structure of historical significance in Italy, the Leaning Tower of Pisa was being restored for Italy's upcoming millennium celebrations. This time, though, it looked serious. There were high wire-mesh fences all around the tower; huge concrete weights secured to its base; and the whole center section was girded with steel cables.

There was a good reason for these precautions. Every year since its construction in the late twelfth century, the renowned Leaning Tower has leaned just a little bit further. When the bell chamber was added in the fourteenth century, the architect had to correct the vertical by several degrees. By the late sixteenth century, when Galileo demonstrated the nature of gravity by dropping balls from the tower, the problem was very noticeable. Now the Leaning Tower is about to snap in two. Italian engineers are frantically exploring ways to stabilize the structure using hydraulics and other exotic techniques, but the prognosis isn't good. There is, of course, one easy way to save the tower—namely, to jack it straight up. But, of course, that would kill the goose that lays the golden eggs. Millions of tourists aren't likely to flock each year to the Straight Tower of Pisa. So there it stands—probably the most famous building in the Western world—propped up, lashed together, and poised to snap in half. I'm rooting hard for the Italian engineers, because in a world where every other tower stands perfectly straight, there's a palpable need for one that's off-kilter.

Anyway, the kids loved the tower, and so did the adults. After oohing and ahhing and cocking our heads, we took the usual tourist pictures where it looks like you're holding up the tower. Then Betty and the kids hit the souvenir stalls to buy Leaning Tower thermometers and pencil sharpeners. We were so taken by the cockeyed tower we practically ignored the renowned Romanesque cathedral and wedding cake baptistery that stand right next door.

When the sun set, we drove back toward the villa on winding roads through the misty gray-and-olive-tinted Tuscan hills. At one point, I devised a shortcut that got us so thoroughly lost that we actually ended up on an unlit one-lane dirt road in the middle of some woods. It was one of the darkest places I've ever been, and I was afraid a bear might jump out and attack us at any moment.

Willie looked up and said, "Where the heck are we?"

"Lost again," Kara said, very nonchalantly as if it were just a routine occurrence.

> Best wishes from the most
> inept tourists in Tuscany,
> David

Chapter 12

Subject: The Museum of Torture
Date: October 3
From: daylifers@aol.com (David Cohen)

Patras, Greece

Dear Friends:

Since our day trip to Florence was such a bust, we decided to head south to visit her ancient rival, Siena. Siena was similarly mobbed with visitors, but it was difficult not to be seduced by its crenellated walls, medieval architecture, and narrow cobblestone streets. At one point, Betty strolled off to buy souvenirs with the kids, and Devi and I found ourselves alone sipping perfect cappuccinos in Siena's sublime shell-shaped Piazza del Campo. In that moment, it was easy to ignore the shifting crush of tourists and drift back to the four-teenth-century world of St. Catherine when this same piazza was filled with farmer's stalls, nobles in sumptuous robes, and Sienese knights fresh from battle with the Florentines. But these idyllic reveries burst like a bubble when Kara ran panting back to our table.

"What's the matter, Kara?" asked Devi. "And why are you by yourself?"

Never one to squander a dramatic moment, Kara paused and replied gravely, "Betty's locked in the toilet."

"What do you mean?" asked Devi.

"I mean there's a little building over there with toilets in it. Betty went in ten minutes ago, and now she's rattling the door. I don't think she can get out."

"Where are Willie and Lucas?" asked Devi.

"They're standing outside the toilet."

With that, I frantically hailed the waiter and Devi took off with Kara. But before she got far, a visibly shaken Betty returned with the boys.

"What happened?" Devi asked.

"I went inside and the door slammed behind me, and it locked before I could find the light. Ay, it smelled awful in there."

"How did you get out?" asked Devi.

"I pushed against the door and wiggled the latch till it finally flew open. I thought I was going to suffocate."

Betty did look as if she could use some fresh air, so we decided to skip the crowded galleries in the nearby Palazzo Publico and wander the warren of streets behind the piazza. We soon stumbled across the Pinacoteca Nazionale, a rather run-down public art gallery housed in an old palazzo. There were hardly any visitors there, but the gallery was filled with wonderful paintings from the thirteenth- and fourteenth-century Sienese school. A lot of the pictures were either unframed or badly hung. The walls were stained, the pipes exposed, and the lifts were broken. But once we looked past all that, we found ourselves immersed in a fantastic medieval world that predated modern notions of perspective and temporal unity.

As in all galleries housing works from the Middle Ages, the predominant subjects were Christ, the Virgin Mary, and a supporting cast of saints and angels. Since the theme is so uniform, most adults tend to focus on stylistic differences. But children tend to see one picture after another of Christ's nativity and crucifixion. For children raised in a secular home such as ours, these tableaux raise prickly theological questions, and Kara fired them off like a Gatling gun.

"Who was Jesus' father?"

"Is he really the son of God?"

"Who killed him?"

"Why did they kill him?"

"How did he rise from the dead?"

"Where is he now?"

I was obliged to deliver an off-the-cuff New Testament exegesis that somehow reconciled our children's Jewish/Danish Lutheran/Jain* heritage. When I was growing up, my parents sent me to a Catholic prep school, which was the only decent high school in town. Consequently, I'm pretty well versed in the basic catechism, but it still required a bit of picking and choosing to tell the story in a way that was sufficiently ecumenical. I used a lot of conditionals such as, "Some people believe ..." and "Christians think..." and "Nobody knows for sure."

In the middle of this ad hoc seminar, a middle-aged American woman with a sour expression approached me and asked, "Are these children Christian?"

"Part Christian," I replied blithely.

Maybe it was because she was surrounded by so much fourteenth-century religious propaganda, but she seemed to get very upset by that. "You can't be part Christian!" she proclaimed. "You either accept Christ as your savior, or you don't."

I wasn't sure what to say to that, but I noticed the kids were listening intently, so I chose my words carefully. "By that definition, I suppose they're not Christian," I said. "But I still want them to understand various theologies, so they can shape their own spiritual life later on."

The lady shot me a look suggesting that she wouldn't mind setting me up with the Inquisition.

*The ancient Indian religion of Devi's father.

"What a way to raise children!" she mumbled, stalking away self-righteously.

"What's *her* problem?" asked Kara.

"Some people believe that there's only one right way to think about God," I replied.

"How do they know what the right way is? Does God tell 'em or something?"

"I don't think so," I said. "But believe it or not, people all over the world fight wars just because they don't worship God the same way."

"That is *so* incredibly stupid," Kara said.

I realized then that if I could teach my children only one or two basic principles, tolerance would be one of them.

Our next encounter at the Pinacoteca Nazionale was far less contentious. We were contemplating the work of the medieval master Duccio, when an effervescent young woman entered the room. She looked at Willie and did a double-take. Then she began chattering to Devi in animated Italian. Devi translated as she spoke.

"She says her son looks *exactly* like Willie...

"That he has the same face...the same eyes...the same missing front teeth...the same ears that stick out..."

Willie was now touching his ears.

"...the same skinny legs..."

Willie looked at his legs.

"...and the same big feet."

Devi didn't realize exactly what she was translating until after she said it, and poor Willie wasn't flattered by the description. After the friendly lady pinched Willie on the cheek and moved on, Willie said, "My legs aren't that skinny, are they, Dad?"

"No, they're not," I said. Then Devi and I both assured him that in our eyes he was the handsomest boy in Italy.

Our last stop in Siena was the local Duomo. At this point, it takes a great deal of persuasion to drag Kara and Willie into a church. In a way, I don't blame them. The kids have been to so many basilicas, cathedrals, churches, chapels, and sanctuaries in France and Italy, Willie thought we were calling the Sistine Chapel the "sixteenth chapel." But when it started to rain again, we trundled everyone inside—and wow, what a place it was! The nave and aisles were banded floor to ceiling in zebra stripes of black and white marble. The vault and dome were painted deep cobalt blue with gold leaf stars, and the floors were covered in mosaics. Even the thirteenth-century octagonal pulpit by Nicola Pisano was supported by a menagerie of life-size stone lions.

The Sienese Duomo isn't the most important cathedral in Italy, but it may be the gaudiest. The kids were delighted despite themselves—especially when they saw a relic purporting to be John the Baptist's arm bone along with a bronze sculpture of the saint by Donatello. (Guess which one intrigued them more.) At the end of the day, everyone agreed that Siena was a delight, and Devi and I were particularly thrilled to find both a church and a museum that the children not only abided, but enjoyed.

The next day we found another museum the children enjoyed—a little too much in fact. This time we were in the enchanting medieval hill town of San Gimignano. Known as the "Manhattan of Tuscany," San Gimignano has more than a dozen tall brick towers that give it a distinctive, picture-book skyline. But it wasn't the towers or San Gimignano's graceful squares that intrigued the children. It was the Museo di Criminologia Medievale.* Devi desperately wanted to give this place a pass, but Willie got us on a technicality.

"This is just a huge collection of torture implements," said Devi, reading the poster in the window.

To which Willie replied, "I thought you wanted us to go to museums."

"Normally I do," said Devi. "But not this museum. It's all about hurting people."

"Yeah, but it's historical," said Willie grandly. "Don't you want us to learn about history?"

"Not this kind of history," said Devi.

"History isn't only about good stuff," Willie replied.

Devi didn't have an answer for that, so with a great deal of trepidation we entered what proved to be a two-story assemblage of stocks, racks, and iron maidens. This collection was obviously assembled by a sick mind—but not nearly as sick as the folks who thought up these implements in the first place. Medieval Europeans—particularly Spaniards and Germans—apparently possessed a genius for inflicting pain. We saw spiked interrogation chairs from the Spanish Inquisition, beheading axes, and saws for cutting people in half (lengthwise). Each of these implements was accompanied by a medieval-style woodcut showing precisely how it was used, so little was left to the imagination.

Devi couldn't stand the place and she took Lucas outside after only a few minutes. That left me to explain the gruesome displays to Kara and Willie. I thought I was doing reasonably well until we got to a rusty medieval chastity belt replete with sharp iron teeth in the appropriate spot. I hoped against hope that the children would stroll by this grisly contraption without noticing it, but of course they were drawn straight to it.

"What the heck is that?" asked Kara.

*The Museum of Medieval Criminology.

"It's called a chastity belt," I said, hoping that naming it would be sufficient.

"What did they use *that* for, Daddy?"

I usually try to tell my children the truth, but frankly, there's no good way to explain a chastity belt to a nine-year-old girl unacquainted with the facts of life.

I pondered for a moment and said, "It's sort of like armor, honey."

"Ohhh," Kara said knowingly. "So your private parts don't get hurt in a battle."

"Something like that."

"It doesn't look very comfortable," she observed.

"No, it wasn't."

"Did boys wear 'em?"

"No, only girls."

"I'm glad we don't wear those anymore," she said, and blithely skipped toward the next abomination.

When we finally left this house of horrors, I had a morbid urge to ask the children which they liked better, the San Gimignano torture museum or the Louvre.

They didn't hesitate for a moment. It was the torture museum, hands down.

After six days of rain, our last afternoon in Tuscany was warm and lovely. Indian summer had set in, and at suppertime a spectacular sunset of pink and salmon lingered over the rolling vineyards for nearly an hour. The next morning, we loaded the van and headed north toward Venice. We skirted Venice proper and took the car ferry directly to the Lido, the thin oceanfront island across the lagoon from the city. Once the stomping ground of Byron, Goethe, and Evelyn Waugh, the Lido is still one of the more fashionable beach resorts in Europe. But that's during the summer. When we arrived, summer was long gone, and the Lido was practically deserted. For once, our *Frommer's Guide* was helpful, and we checked into a lovely little hotel, the Hotel Albergo Quattro Fontane, that looked like a misplaced Alpine chalet.

After Betty and the kids were settled, Devi and I took a *vaporetto** back to Venice for dinner. Even though it was so ferociously crowded that you could barely find room to put your feet, Venice was still extravagantly romantic. The silent gliding black gondolas, the lights twinkling in the Grand Canal, and the smell of moist decay all lent the city an air of melancholy passion. Couples were kissing on nearly every corner, and I soon understood why Proust wrote, "When I journeyed to Venice, my dream became my address."

The next morning, back in the hotel restaurant, we met a couple from my hometown of Erie, Pennsylvania. I'd never met the McBriers before, but my dad knew his dad, and Erie is such a small place, we inevitably had friends in common. In fact, they were joining another couple from Erie—the McLaughlins—for dinner that night. I went to high school with Sean McLaughlin, so when the McBriers invited Devi and me to come along, it sounded like fun.

I hadn't seen Sean McLaughlin for twenty years, but we recognized each other immediately. I was going to give him a hug or something, but then I remembered that he was now a federal judge, and somehow that didn't seem appropriate. We had a magnificent overpriced dinner, then strolled over to the Piazza San Marco for a nightcap. Each of the four or five cafés in the huge piazza had its own orchestra on a small raised stage, and these ensembles took turns playing songs, one after another, around the perimeter of the square. After four months of dining with the little barbarians, it felt terribly cosmopolitan to sip cognac in a Venice café while an orchestra played Nino Rota tunes.

Eventually, one of the bands struck up "Volare." It was

*The Venetian water buses.

corny, of course, but everyone in the square—patrons and waiters alike—sang and swayed with the music. A flock of pigeons, startled by the noise, fluttered up over the Palace of the Doges and sailed past the moon in silhouette.

We would have lingered in Venice for a while, but frankly, we couldn't afford it. Drinks run ten bucks a pop here and one visit to the laundromat set us back $150. (You heard me.) So after four days, we hiked over to the docks and booked a ferry to Greece.

After our rough passage from Sardinia to Rome, Devi was understandably reluctant to take another long trip on a cheap ferry. But the booking office had an illustrated brochure, and the ship looked reasonably comfortable with clean cabins and a large restaurant. There was also a picture of the ship's discotheque that looked like a Greek version of *Saturday Night Fever*. Kara was intrigued by that, and I promised to take her dancing our first night on board.

The morning of our departure, we loaded our bags onto a water taxi and sped toward the pier. The taxi couldn't tie up near the big ships, so we had to walk the last half mile. In marked contrast to our disastrous luggage convoy in Burgundy—when we all wiped out on the railroad tracks—the whole family rolled smartly toward the ferry without incident. On board, we checked in and found our cabins. They weren't exactly staterooms, but everything was clean and functional. As soon as we were settled, Kara reminded me about the disco, and I renewed my promise to chaperone her.

The disco didn't even open until 10:00 P.M., but a promise is a promise, so Betty and I took Kara inside the moment it opened. On the way up the stairs, I noticed that Kara—who isn't always a stickler for personal hygiene—had taken the trouble to put on her satin shirt and velvet jeans. She even got Betty to paint her fingernails. The three of us sat at a small table near the tiny dance floor and drank Cokes. The music pounded and a mirrored ball shot flecks of light around the room, but for the first hour or so, we were the only customers there. Eventually, a group of fifteen or twenty European teenagers lumbered in and sat down. After a few rounds of beer, one couple began to dance. Then, slowly, a few more kids, mostly girls, wandered onto the floor.

As Kara watched them, she seemed torn between intense interest and laughing out loud. I asked her if she wanted to dance with me, and she agreed reluctantly. We shuffled around a bit, but Kara quickly got embarrassed and we retreated to our chairs. Although she's very talkative once she gets to know you, Kara has always been shy in front of strangers, so I figured that was that. She wouldn't go out on the dance floor again. But a few songs later, she walked out by herself. She swayed back and forth for a few minutes, then slowly joined the rhythm of the song. During the next tune, she sloughed off her inhibitions, and danced up a storm. It was a startling transformation. One moment, she was a gawky little girl who couldn't bear to be looked at, and the next moment she was all grace and confidence. When the song ended, some of the teenage girls patted her on the back and offered her encouragement. It was a bittersweet moment for me, because I knew, in the blink of an eye, she would be one of them.

Tempus fugit, my friends,
David

Chapter 13

Subject: Autumn of the Gods
Date: October 14
From: daylifers@aol.com (David Cohen)

Kusadasi, Turkey

Dear Friends:

The next afternoon, as we steamed past the gray coast of Albania, Kara and Willie decided to go swimming in the ferry's little 15-x-20-foot pool. It was a pretty bold decision, since the pool wasn't heated, and it was only about 60 degrees outside. The ferry didn't have much in the way of on-board entertainment, so as Kara and Willie gingerly dipped their toes into the icy water, at least forty bored passengers in thick jackets and sweaters gathered around and waited for them to take the plunge. When the kids finally leapt in, the spectators all cheered enthusiastically like they were watching the sea lion show at Marine World. Willie enjoyed the attention so much he wouldn't come out of the pool until his lips turned blue. When Devi and I finally wrapped the kids in towels, several passengers came over and told them how brave they were, and for the rest of the voyage they were minor celebrities.

When the ferry finally moored in Patras, Greece, we

wheeled our bags across the docks and up a hill to a discount car rental agency. In France and Italy, we rented shiny new top-of-the-line minivans. But in Patras, Devi decided to save a few drachmas, and we ended up in a beat-up old black Mitsubishi minibus with red and orange racing stripes. This beast was roomy enough to hold a dozen people and all their luggage, but its maximum speed dropped to twenty-five miles per hour whenever we climbed a hill. Normally that wouldn't be a big problem, but we soon found out that speed and agility are critical when you drive amongst the madmen of Greece.

Officially, the highway out of Patras only had two lanes—one in each direction—but that didn't stop any of our fellow motorists from forging a third path down the middle of the road whenever they felt the need. Apparently, the preferred time to do that was while passing a semi on a blind curve. The entire drive from Patras to Olympia was an exercise in terror. Little coupes and motorcycles blew past us at ninety miles an hour. Big trucks roared straight at us from the opposite direction and swerved back into their own lane only at the last possible instant. Devi gripped the steering wheel with white knuckles. "These people are lunatics!" she cried.

"You're telling me," I screamed. "Look at that truck!"

"Whooa! He missed that little car by inches."

"Devi, Devi! Look out for that truck in the middle of the road!"

"Oh my God! He nearly took our bumper off."

Eventually, Devi decided to drive the entire way to Olympia off on the shoulder of the highway, away from the field of play. Even then, we had a few near-death experiences. By the time we limped into the hotel parking lot, Devi was shaking. "I'll never complain about Italian drivers again," she said.

"At least we're alive," I replied, and under the circumstances that seemed like an accomplishment.

After regaining our composure over gyros and beer, we set out on foot toward ancient Olympia's famous ruins. As usual, we got lost and had to ford a small stream and pass through a piney wood to get there. Eventually, though, we found ourselves in a warm, grassy valley nestled between rolling foothills studded with old cypresses and gnarled olives. Laid out before us were the tumble-down remnants of white marble temples, rich treasuries, a grand stadium, and a hippodrome. Originally dedicated to the earth goddess, Gaea, and later to Zeus, this sanctuary was the site of the first Olympic games more than 2,500 years ago. All that remain are stone paths and wide fields, piles of carved limestone, a stairway or two, and some platforms where temples once stood. Still, the valley was a deeply serene, almost mystical place, and I wanted Kara and Willie to imagine the days when Plato and Aristotle came here from Athens to watch the footraces and Herodotus read his *History* to cheering crowds.

"Imagine you lived in ancient Greece," I said. "And you were the fastest kid in your town." Willie, who's fleet of foot like his mother, liked that idea. "Once every four years, you would come here to race against all the best runners in Greece."

"How would I get here?" asked Willie.

"Well, there weren't any buses or cars, so you'd have to ride in a horse-drawn chariot or walk—sometimes for hundreds of miles."

"I'd take a chariot," said Willie.

"When you finally arrived, you'd train for several weeks at the gymnasium. Then you'd pray for victory here at the Temple of Zeus."

Kara looked around and said, "There's no temple here."

"Not now, but if you put together all those stone wheels over there, they'd form columns that supported the roof of a magnificent temple."

"Who knocked it down?" asked Kara.

"I'll get to that in a minute. Anyway, on the day of the big race, you'd pour oil all over your body and walk naked through that passageway into the stadium."

"Naked!" screamed Kara and Willie. I knew that would get their attention.

"Yep, all the boys had to run naked—except for warriors who ran in full armor."

"How 'bout the girls?" asked Kara. "Did they run naked?"

"No, they wore tunics—which are like short dresses."

"I don't think I'd run naked in front of girls," said Willie.

"Girls and boys had their own separate Olympics," I replied. "And no girls were allowed in the stadium when the boys were running."

"Okay. Then I'd do it."

"Finally, you'd run from one end of the stadium to the other. And if you won the race, you'd get a crown of olive branches from one of those trees up on the hill."

"That's it?" exclaimed Willie. "Olive branches?" He wanted something more substantial—like a bag of gold.

"That was the beauty of it," I replied. "The ancient Greeks, as Herodotus wrote, competed, 'not for money, but for virtue.' Of course, if you won a crown of olives, everyone had to be nice to you for the rest of your life, and they'd even tear down a section of the city walls so you could return triumphantly in a four-horse chariot."

"That's better," said Willie.

"Okay, but what the heck happened to this place?" Kara repeated. "It looks like there was an earthquake or something."

"Well, they held the Olympics here in the sanctuary of Zeus, on and off, for more than a thousand years. Then the Byzantine emperors became Christians and they didn't want anyone praying to the old Greek gods. So they banned the Olympics and burned the temple. And yes, Kara, you're right. There were two big earthquakes here about fifteen hundred years ago. After that, people carted away most of the stones to make walls and other buildings."

I knew Kara and Willie would probably forget everything I told them about ancient Olympia, so I came up with a way to help them remember. "Listen, you guys, do you want to run the same race as the ancient Greeks did?"

They thought that was a good idea.

"Okay, then let's go over to the stadium, and have our own family Olympics."

"This time, the boys and the girls can run together," said Willie, confident of victory.

We walked through a long arched entryway called the Krypt onto the floor of the huge rectangular stadium. The grassy slopes where spectators once sat were still intact. At the sound of "Go," Kara, Willie, and even Lucas ran the Dialous or 400-meter race first held on this very spot in 724 B.C. Only Devi and I were there to cheer, but we yelled more or less the same cries of encouragement that echoed through this same stadium more than 2,500 years ago. Willie won as expected. We didn't have a crown of olive branches or a four-horse chariot for him, so he had to settle for a donkey ride from a grizzled old vendor outside the ruins.

"Everyone has to be nice to me for the rest of my life," Willie declared from astride his humble mount.

"Well, maybe not for the rest of your life," I said. "But at least for the rest of the day." Willie agreed that was fair enough.

The next morning we left for Athens. Again, the drive was terrifying, and by the end of it Devi didn't feel like wandering around the city in search of our small hotel. We hailed a taxi and offered the driver 2,500 drachmas (about ten bucks) to lead us in. Good thing, too, because the hotel was a small well-hidden building on a back street in Syntagma.

Up until this point in the trip, I've been a staunch advocate of cheap hotels. When you're traveling as long as we are, even moderately priced accommodations begin to add up. But in Athens, we proved you could go too far down-market. The hotel was well located, within walking distance of the Acropolis and the festive Pláka district, but half the lights in the room didn't work, the bathrooms were dicey, and, believe me, you wouldn't want to eat off the floor. Worse yet, the hotel was patronized almost entirely by college students—notably, a group of Danish party boys who drank heavily and sang in the stairwells every night till three in the morning. I thought about complaining to the management, but at the price we were paying, I figured we didn't have much of a case.

Anyway, because of the late night revelry, we weren't particularly vigorous when we set about to climb the Acropolis. "Acropolis" means "High City" in Greek, but I never realized just how high it was until we stood in its shadow. Kara, in particular, seemed unimpressed by the notion of climbing a fifty-story mountain to see—and I quote—"a buncha broken-down temples."

I said, "At least we haven't taken you to any churches or art galleries lately."

"Yeah," she replied, "now you're taking us to buildings that aren't even standing anymore." In retrospect, St. Peter's and the Louvre were starting to look good to her. Despite all the grumbling, Kara and Willie were, by this point in the trip, first-rate hikers, and with Lucas strapped in his stroller, we breezed right past the ambulance they keep near the top for coronary-prone tourists.

Outside the Propylaia, the grand entrance to the Acropolis complex, we were approached by a crusty old guide in a Chicago Bulls cap who offered to show us the marvels of the High City for twenty bucks. Yourgos had been an Acropolis guide for more than thirty years, and he knew the place like the back of his hand. He showed us the siege tunnels used to smuggle in food and water. He explained how the lines of the Parthenon were ingeniously curved to correct for optical illusions, and he recalled the sad day in 1687 when the Venetian army scored a direct hit on the Parthenon, detonating a store of Turkish gunpowder and blowing off the roof.

Yourgos didn't have too many kind words for the Turks, who've been the Greeks' mortal enemies for centuries, but he saved his most trenchant remarks for members of his own government. After a short while, our tour of the Acropolis was roughly 50 percent historical analysis and 50 percent vehement jeremiads about corrupt Greek politicians. Some of Yourgos's remarks were pretty colorful, and it was lucky that the kids couldn't fully decipher his accent.

A simple discussion of something like the siege tunnels would start out innocuously with, "This is how the ancient Greeks sneaked spies into the enemy camp." But it always ended up with, "Of course, in the old days, you could only bribe and steal to save your city. Nowadays these thieving politicians bribe and steal just to line their own filthy pockets!"

When we innocently asked about the conspicuous restoration projects under way at the Parthenon and the Temple of Diana, we were treated to a ten-minute harangue about the late culture minister, Melina Mercouri, and her band of thieves, and how they stole all the funding and gave lucrative contracts to their friends and yadda, yadda, yadda.

Eventually, we had to cut Yourgos loose and make our own way around the Acropolis with only a guidebook. Not only was the temple complex magnificent, but the views from the high plateau were breathtaking. You could look directly down into the Theater of Dionysus, a 17,000-seat arena where the plays of Sophocles, Aeschylus, and Aristophanes first debuted, and far below you could see the Ancient Agora, where Socrates cross-examined his students. But most of all you could just see Athens, sprawling to the Saronic Gulf in the south, and off to the north and west as far as the eye could see. It was hard to imagine that, as late as the mid-nineteenth century, this cradle of civilization was a forgotten Ottoman backwater with only a few thousand inhabitants. Now—despite Yourgos's complaints—Athens was a spirited metropolis, full of classical wonders, bustling squares, wonderful restaurants, and artsy neighborhoods.

Devi and I had one very stimulating moment in Athens. We were walking down a crowded thoroughfare when we saw five or six policemen waving every motorcycle on the road over to the curb. The cops had nabbed at least twenty-five or thirty drivers, and they were giving them all traffic tickets. For some reason, this struck Devi as a colorful scene, and she decided I should photograph it.

"I don't think that's a good idea," I said.

"Go ahead. It'll make a great picture."

"Believe me, Devi, policemen do not like to be photographed."

"Oh, it's only the traffic police. They won't care."

"All right," I said, acquiescing against my better judgment. "But just one quick shot."

I leaned over to get a good angle, snapped the picture, and looked up to find a rather large Greek policeman standing in my personal space.

He started screaming at me—and even though it was all Greek to me, I quickly caught his drift. He wanted my camera, or at least, the film inside it. The roll in question had all our Acropolis pictures on it, and I didn't want to lose it. So purely by instinct, I put the camera back over my shoulder, held up both hands in the universal sign of surrender, and slowly backed away. The policeman was barely satisfied with this ostentatious display of submission and grudgingly let me go.

"That was a little more excitement than I needed," I said to Devi.

"Oh, he wasn't going to do anything to you. He just wanted to scare you."

"Well, in that case, he was successful," I said, my heart still beating like a drum.

Our last morning in Athens, we rose before dawn and went down to the port of Piraeus to catch the 6:00 A.M. ferry to Mykonos. The ferry, which made interim stops at the islands of Siros and Tinos, was bursting with life. A bouzouki band played traditional Greek music for coins. Passengers conversed loudly, and all sorts of peddlers passed amongst the passengers loudly hawking food, souvenirs, and worry beads (or "worry beans," as Lucas calls them).

After six hours skirting tiny islands on a gorgeous turquoise sea, we made port on the fabled isle of Mykonos. We found a taxi and rode three or four kilometers to our hotel. The road was rough and narrow; the hills, barren and rocky; but every time we rounded a bend, there was another fabulous view of the wide blue Aegean. Furthermore, every house, church, and store on the island was white stucco with doors and windows in brilliant shades of red, blue, orange, yellow, and green.

We stayed in a condominium complex consisting of several hundred of these small white houses. Taken together, they could have easily accommodated a thousand guests. But except for the caretaker and one group of three rather large ladies from Athens, the place was entirely empty. In fact, we soon realized we had most of the island to ourselves. There was little sign of Mykonos's famous gay scene—or its renowned nightlife—and except for the two afternoons when a cruise ship steamed into port, even the main village was devoid of tourists. Apparently, Mykonos is strictly a summer resort, and nearly no one—except a few misinformed numskulls like ourselves—shows up in mid-October. The reason for this quickly became evident: Except for a few hours in the middle of the day, Mykonos in autumn is a rather cold and windy place.

That's not to say we had an unpleasant time. We drove a tiny rented 4 x 4 all over the island visiting charming tavernas, where, more often than not, we were the only patrons. Devi and the kids rode horses in the barren hills above the sea, and the children loved the ubiquitous cats and donkeys and the famous four-foot pink pelicans that wander at will through Mykonos's portside restaurants.

We even spent a passably warm afternoon at Paradise—one of Mykonos's famed nude beaches. I was worried at first that the kids would point and giggle when they saw a bunch of naked grown-ups frolicking on the sand. But first of all, there weren't that many nature-lovers around, and second, the beach was pretty well segregated. The center section was reserved for families and other patrons who found it too embarrassing (or too cold) to go *au naturel*. The far ends of the beach were for full-on nudists, and the areas in between were essentially topless. Every so often, a nudist would stroll past the family section, but the kids hardly noticed.

I'm afraid the same can't be said for the busload of Asian tourists that pulled up midway through the afternoon. The men in the group were neatly dressed in khaki shorts and polo shirts. Initially, they settled in the conservative center section of the beach with their wives and girlfriends. But one by one, they all decided to take a walk on the wild side. They left at regular intervals so they wouldn't look like one huge group of Peeping Toms, but by the time these guys hit the nudist area, they looked like spectators at a tennis match. You could sort of tell that the nude beaches of Mykonos were a big selling point for the tour. After about forty-five minutes, the whole group abruptly packed up and left—probably off to Super-paradise, an even more licentious beach up the coast.

One day, near the end of our stay in Mykonos, we all piled into our little rental car and took off in search of a particular taverna on the island's north shore. The mountain road was only one lane wide, and after a while we found ourselves stuck behind a big old truck loaded with telephone poles. The truck stopped every twenty meters or so, and each time it did, two guys jumped out of the cab, pulled a telephone pole from the back of the truck, rolled it to the side of the road, and climbed in again. Then they drove another twenty meters and did it all over again.

I watched the pole crew repeat this procedure about ten times before I realized something was different—namely, I wasn't going berserk. I mean here we were stuck behind a truck going five miles an hour and stopping every thirty seconds. There was no way to pass it, no way to turn around, and no end in sight. Four months ago, this same situation would have driven me crazy, but now I wasn't particularly bothered.

Another time, we booked a day trip to the nearby island of Delos. The boat wasn't leaving for an hour, so we took the ticket clerk's advice and went to a nearby café for a quick breakfast. The waiter took forever to bring our food, and eventually we had to choose between eating the meal we ordered and missing our boat. Before we left, I would have found this situation very stressful, but in Mykonos, I just strolled back to the booking office and calmly asked the agent if we could go the next day instead. "No problem," she said, examining the tickets. "I forgot to date them anyway."

I think these incidents signify that I've finally completed the transition from one way of life characterized by constant overscheduling, impatience, and mindless rushing around to a different way of life. where I'm more likely to live in the moment and accept things as they come. This is a very welcome change, and a much more healthy, sensible MO, but I have to tell you, it didn't require any great resolution or effort on my part. When you travel with three small children for any length of time, you eventually learn that speed and efficiency aren't part of the plan and schedules are meant to be broken. When Kara or Willie have to go to the bathroom or Lucas gets hungry, that's it. The whole expedition grinds implacably to a halt. If I couldn't accept that, I'd be in for a lot of self-imposed aggravation. And if I can accept it, then I can also learn to live with all manner of mishap and delay—canceled planes, hotels that lose reservations, even getting stuck behind a truck for several hours on a small mountain road in Mykonos. I know this new laid-back attitude wouldn't be too useful in the business world, but it's wonderful for traveling, and probably pretty good for life in general.

Of course, Mykonos isn't the worst place in the world to develop a relaxed attitude toward life. I don't know if our experience here was typical, or because it was off-season, but we found virtually everyone on the island to be wonderfully relaxed, generous, kind, and trusting. When we had trouble booking our passage from Mykonos to Sámos, the caretaker of our condominium complex told us we could stay an extra day without charge. When we forgot to refill the gas tank in our rental car, the owner said, "It's okay. Just come back and see us again." And once, when I thought I didn't have enough Greek currency to pay the lunch bill, the proprietor of the restaurant said, "Just bring it by tomorrow, when you have time." In short, we found Mykonos to be the perfect tonic for the stress of modern life, and we vowed to return someday—preferably when it's warmer!

Maybe it was because of all the bad blood between the Greeks and the Turks, or maybe it was just because we were traveling on the cheap. But there didn't seem to be any way to book a ferry from Mykonos to the Turkish port of Kusadasi. Travel agents in Mykonos didn't know very much about Turkey, and the maps posted in Greek booking offices all depicted the country as a big tan void. Finally, Devi suggested we take a midnight ferry to Sámos—just off the Turkish coast—and try it from there. As she predicted, Sámos had a harborside office that booked small boats to Kusadasi. Almost as an afterthought, I asked the booking agent whether Betty's

Guatemalan passport would pose a problem at Turkish immigration.

"Not at all," he said confidently. "You just pay your money, and everyone gets in."

"Are you sure?" I asked. "Because we tried calling the Turkish embassy in Athens several times, and we couldn't get through."

"I've been doing this for ten years," he said, "and I assure you it won't be a problem."

The booking agent seemed like a reasonable, experienced man, and his words provided great comfort right up to the point where the Turkish border guard seized Betty's passport and told her she was being deported. But I'll tell you about that in my next letter.

> Best wishes till then,
> David

Chapter 14

Subject: Your Wife Doesn't Love You
Date: October 19
From: daylifers@aol.com (David Cohen)

Istanbul, Turkey

Dear Friends:

The moment we stepped off the boat in Kusadasi, Turkey, I knew it would be a bad scene. The other passengers were aggressively jostling for position at passport control. Touts were steering credulous tourists toward fleabag hotels, and some guy in civvies was selling everyone visas for twenty bucks—U.S. money only—even though the guidebook said they should cost half that much.

As usual, we were last in line at passport control, and when we finally reached the front of the queue, we found ourselves face-to-face with a very stern-looking mustachioed Turkish soldier who spoke only a smattering of English. I handed him our small stack of passports. He stamped the five American documents in a perfunctory fashion, but when he got to Betty's Guatemalan passport, a quizzical look crossed his face.

"Was dees?" he asked, holding up the red passport like a smelly fish.

"Our friend is a citizen of Guatemala, but she's also a permanent resident of the United States," I said, pointing to Betty's green card inside the passport. I honestly don't think this guy had ever seen a Guatemalan passport before and the green card didn't mean anything to him.

"She no come in," he said firmly.

"The boat has already gone back to Sámos," I replied as calmly as possible. "There's nowhere else for her to go."

"She no come in," he repeated.

Unfamiliar with local custom, I asked an assertive young tout who was enthusiastically trying to adopt us whether this was the sort of problem that could be settled with a crisp $50 bill.

"I am afraid not, my friend," he said, and he advised me not to try it.

"Then would you please ask the officer if I could speak to his boss."

The tout and the soldier exchanged a few words in Turkish, and I was escorted to another counter, where I met a young female officer who spoke nearly fluent English. I explained our problem—and she seemed sympathetic—but she said there was nothing she could do until the head office in Ankara reopened in the morning. Meanwhile, Betty would have to return to Greece. I didn't even want to think about what might happen if there were no more boats back to Sámos that evening, but a night in the local hoosegow didn't seem like an attractive prospect.

"I have an idea," I said to the officer. "Betty can't go anywhere without that passport, right? So why don't you hold on to it. We'll stay at a hotel here in town, and you can call Ankara in the morning. That way, we won't have to split up our party or all go back to Greece."

Incredibly, she agreed, and Betty was permitted to enter Turkey—at least until ten o'clock the following morning. I quickly hustled everyone out of passport control before the officer could change her mind. On the way out, Betty asked, "What's going to happen to me?"

"Have you ever seen that movie, *Midnight Express?*" I said, referring to the '70s film about an American thrown into a Turkish prison.

"That's not funny," said Betty, hitting me on the arm and laughing in spite of herself.

"Seriously," I said. "Either the head office in Ankara will tell these guys to let you in. Or we'll buy you an air ticket to Zurich, and meet you there at the end of the week. Either way, you'll be fine."

Betty looked hugely relieved. In fact, we were all so happy to get out of passport control we weren't really paying that much attention when our dogged tout set us up with a suspicious-looking driver in a decrepit Chevy station wagon. The driver took us to the Hotel Kismet, as we requested, but Devi had some trouble deciphering the tab. As he drove off, I asked her how much she paid.

"Two million lire," she replied.

"Two *million* lire? How much is that in American money?"

"I'm not sure. Let me see. There are 97,000 Turkish lire to the dollar."

"Really? *Ninety-seven thousand?*"

"So two million divided by 97,000 is...just over twenty dollars."

"That's a bit stiff for a four-minute ride," I said.

"Yeah, you're right. I'll ask the doorman what it should've cost."

The doorman confirmed that we paid approximately five times the going rate. What's more, the Kismet didn't have any vacancies, so we had to take a second taxi ride to another nearby hotel. The driver only charged us 400,000 lire, and the hotel was a mere eight million lire per night.*

---

*About eighty-five bucks.

The next morning, I dug out my only sport jacket and tie from the bottom of my suitcase and dusted off an article about our trip that I wrote for the *San Francisco Chronicle*. I wasn't sure just how much pull the *San Francisco Chronicle* would have with Turkish passport control, but I figured it couldn't hurt.

At the portside immigration office, I waited at the counter for the officer I met the previous evening to finish a phone call. As she walked toward me, she said, "I called Ankara, and sent them a fax, but I haven't received a response."

Oh no, I thought. Now we'll either be stuck in Kusadasi for days or Betty will be kicked out of Turkey.

"So I suppose that's their problem," she continued, and she stamped Betty's passport with a *kerchunk* and handed it back to me.

"*Çok tesekkür ederim,*" I replied, butchering the Turkish phrase for "Thank you very much."

She laughed and said, "You're welcome, and give my regards to your friend from Guatemala."

Devi blamed herself for getting fleeced by the larcenous Kusadasi taxi driver. I told her not to worry about it—that it was only a matter of fifteen bucks—but she was determined not to be duped again, so she drove a very hard bargain with the poor guy who drove us north to the ruined city of Ephesus.

In the first century, Ephesus, or Efes as the Turks call it, was the crossroads of Asia Minor—a cosmopolitan outpost of the Roman Empire with a diverse population of Ionian Greeks, Jews, Romans, and Egyptians. St. Paul preached his new religion here and later wrote his epistle to the Ephesians. Some religious authorities—notably the Catholic Church—believe that the Virgin Mary spent her last days in a small house in the hills above the city. Ephesus is also considered one of the best-preserved Roman cities in the world, and with even a bit of imagination, a stroll down its Sacred Way is like a trip through the mists of time to the glory days of the Roman Empire.

Of course, after two weeks in Greece and Turkey, Kara and Willie felt roughly the same way about classical ruins as they did about medieval cathedrals at the end of our Italian tour. Still, Ephesus held marvels that piqued even their imagination. They loved the Great Theater, a huge 2,000-year-old, 25,000-seat arena that's still used for concerts today. Our guide, a retired professor of antiquities named Ayhan Guçet, told us about the theater's renowned acoustics, and we decided to try them for ourselves. Kara and Willie clambered up to the seventieth row of the amphitheater, and sure enough, they could hear us whisper on the stage several hundred feet below.

But Kara and Willie's favorite spot in Ephesus was undoubtedly the first-century public latrine. This ancient father of men's rooms could accommodate fifty patrons at a time, and most of the marble toilet seats (shaped remarkably like the modern variety) were still in place. The adults, on the other hand, were more amused by the secret underground tunnel that linked Ephesus's renowned Celsus Library with the city's public brothel. It gave "lust for knowledge" a whole new meaning.

As dusk fell, we found ourselves at the eastern end of the Arcadian Way, a broad marble boulevard that once ran from the Great Theater to Ephesus's bustling port. Professor Guçet told us that Antony and Cleopatra trod these very stones when they stopped off in Ephesus on their journey from Alexandria to Rome, and it was easy to imagine the pomp and splendor that would have marked their procession into the city.

As usual, Kara wanted to know what could have possibly happened to reduce such a great metropolis to ruins. "Was it an earthquake, like in Olympia?" she asked.

"Not this time," I told her. "In Ephesus, the city was ruined by neglect."

"What do you mean, Daddy?"

"Over the centuries, the channel that connected Ephesus to

the sea slowly filled with silt, and no one dredged it out. Eventually, the harbor was choked with dirt, and the coastline gradually moved away from the city. Ships couldn't get their cargo into port, and Ephesus lost most of its trade."

"Yeah, but that didn't wreck the buildings," said Kara.

"True. Something else happened here sixteen hundred years ago."

"What was that?"

"As the Roman Empire weakened, it could no longer defend outposts like Ephesus. Eventually, a band of warriors called the Goths marched south from the Black Sea. They sacked the city and destroyed its magnificent temple—one of the Seven Wonders of the Ancient World. After that, the citizens of Ephesus gradually drifted away, and the city was buried under shifting sands."

"Who dug it up?" asked Willie.

"People called archaeologists. They excavate old cities and look for clues that tell them how people lived in ancient times."

"Do they look for treasure?"

"Some do, but mostly they search for knowledge."

Willie looked a bit disappointed at that, but I'd still have to say that this ancient town on the Turkish coast was the best place we found to introduce our children to the wonders of the classical world.

On the way out of Ephesus, Devi and Betty followed the kids into a souvenir stand, and I popped into one of the many Turkish rug shops situated strategically near the entrance to exploit gullible tourists. I suppose everyone has their particular souvenir weakness. With Devi, it's hand-painted crockery and any place she goes she usually picks up some sort of pot, crock, or serving dish. With me, it's oriental rugs. All you have to do is show me a hand-woven tribal motif in red and black, and the money practically leaps from my pocket. The middle-aged woman who owned the rug shop was obviously a hard-ened veteran of her trade, and she knew a patsy when she saw one. By the time Devi came to retrieve me, she'd pretty much sold me on an overpriced 3 x 5 Afghan carpet.

"What do you think of this one?" I asked Devi.

"It's fine," she said. "But I think we have three very similar ones sitting in storage at home. Plus, you don't want to carry that rug all the way to Istanbul, do you?"

"No, I guess not," I replied. Then I turned to the proprietor and said, "Sorry, I'm not going to buy the rug after all."

The proprietor, deprived of her prey at the last possible moment, immediately flew into a rage. "What's wrong with this rug? Why don't you want it?"

"Look," I said, "my wife says we don't need it, so that's that."

But that wasn't that. The woman kept screaming at me, and as Devi and I retreated from her shop, she chased us out into the street where Betty and the children were waiting.

"Your wife doesn't love you," she yelled at me.

"What?" I said, noting the kids were taking this all in.

"Your wife doesn't love you. She only wants your money. She doesn't want you to spend money on a rug so she can have it all for herself."

"What's she talking about, Daddy?" asked Willie.

"She's just a crazy lady, honey. She's mad because I didn't buy her rug."

"She doesn't love you!" the woman kept screaming. "She doesn't love you, and she has another lover!"

Kara and Willie looked somewhat taken aback by that accusation.

"She doesn't," I said to them.

"I know," Kara said.

I thought it might be futile to explain to this harpy that Devi had actually been with me twenty-four hours a day, seven days a week for the last four months, making it, at the very least, problematic for her to have another lover. So instead I just said, "You know, lady, you really need to work on your sales technique."

That only incensed her further, and we could still hear her screaming as we trotted toward the car.

After that unpleasant exchange, we drove north to the city of Izmir. Once a cosmopolitan trading post, Izmir was burned to the ground by the Greek army as it retreated before the Turkish hero, Atatürk, in 1923. As a result, Izmir is a modern, somewhat sterile, city with wide streets, office towers, and little in the way of historical interest. Still, it was the best place to catch the express bus to Istanbul, and better yet, Devi had a 50 percent off coupon for the Izmir Hilton.

As we dragged our ragged entourage into the Hilton's opulent marble lobby, an expression of pure delight played across Kara's face. During our travels through Greece and Turkey, our accommodations have been pretty basic, and apparently Kara has been yearning for some good old American luxury. Her elation was so touching that we abandoned our usual practice of dining in a cheap neighborhood restaurant and let her do her favorite thing in the world—order room service.

The next morning we got up before dawn and caught the bus to Istanbul. You might think a nine-hour bus trip through Turkey would be a pretty grueling ordeal, but the bus had reclining seats, plenty of leg room, air-conditioning, and a hostess who served coffee and snacks at regular intervals. By my reckoning, the kids knocked back enough cookies, crackers, and sodas to pay for their tickets. If it weren't for the television set blaring Turkish soap operas at the front of the bus, the trip would have been nearly perfect.

Fortunately, we didn't take the highway all the way into Istanbul. Near the end of the day, the bus squeezed onto a small ferry that chugged across the Sea of Marmara and into the Bosporus—the narrow strait separating Europe from Asia. This brief waterborne leg allowed us to "sail to Byzantium," and a few miles out we were treated to the dreamlike vision of Istanbul's domes and minarets rising weightless from the mist. This same approach has stirred the hearts of travelers for more than a thousand years, and it frankly took my breath away.

It also elicited a strong sense of déjà vu, and I realized that a stylized version of this same vista graced the cover of a book I owned when I was a boy of nine or ten. Entitled *Richard Halliburton's Complete Book of Marvels,* it was a child's tour of the world with simple descriptions and grainy black-and-white photos of all the most wonderful places on earth. When I was a boy reading in bed in Erie, Pennsylvania, I never dreamed I would ever get to see all these places myself. They all seemed so remote and romantic. Thirty years later, with my own children in tow, the reality exceeded the dream.

The bus made several stops in Istanbul, and when the hostess asked us where in particular we were getting off, we realized we didn't have the slightest idea. Fortunately, there was a friendly young Turkish-American woman on the bus. We showed her the name and address of our hotel, and she organized our transfer to a couple of taxis that took us across the Atatürk Bridge into the ancient district of Sultanahmet.

The taxis pulled up in front of the most remarkable hotel of our trip thus far. The Ayasofya Pansiyonlari consisted of seven or eight nineteenth-century row houses lodged into a narrow cobblestone alley between the Topkapi Palace and Aya Sophia—Emperor Justinian's magnificent sixth-century church. In short, we were wedged between the two seats of power—Byzantine and Ottoman—that made Istanbul the most powerful and influential city in the Western world for more than a thousand years.

Once we settled into our old-fashioned rooms—done up with period brass, glass lamps, and Turkish carpets—we decided to wander into the night. Aya Sophia was dramatically lit by floodlights that accentuated its graceful form and picked out seagulls wheeling gracefully among its domes and minarets. Across from Aya Sophia was a huge lighted fountain framed by the massive Blue Mosque. After a while, Betty and the kids went back to the hotel, and Devi and I strolled alone down dark, narrow streets to the spot where the Golden Horn enters the Bosporus. There, fishermen grilled their catch in the shadow of the Galata Bridge, and passengers scurried to and fro among Istanbul's ubiquitous ferries.

Devi and I climbed onto the Galata Bridge to get a better view of the old district. We turned in time to see a crescent moon rise above the sixteenth-century Mosque of Süleyman the Magnificent. For one perfect instant, we stood under the stars at the crossroads of Asia and Europe, Islam and Christendom—a place of great deeds, deep intrigues, and grand illusions. If there is a more fascinating, more romantic spot on earth, we've yet to find it.

Resting in the shadow of Aya Sophia had its advantages, but sleeping late wasn't one of them. Each morning, at the crack of dawn, the muezzin's call-to-prayer exploded from a loud-speaker right outside our window like the voice of Allah himself. This holy wake-up call meant that we always got an early start on the day—and each day we spent in Istanbul, we were rewarded with a rich mélange of sights, sounds, and smells.

Though it's not terribly original, my favorite place in Istanbul was Aya Sophia itself. Once inside its courtyard, I was amazed to find the 1,500-year-old church ringed with a bewildering accretion of buttresses, kiosks, tombs, and outbuildings that stuck to its sides like barnacles. Once we got past these layers, we found ourselves standing inside a grand narthex decorated from floor to ceiling with polychrome marble slabs. At this point, we definitely had a feel for ancient Byzantium, but it wasn't until we passed through a second narthex and into the nave itself that we understood the vast splendor of the place. There, in a space the size of a modern sports arena, we were encompassed by an improbable admixture of stained glass, somber-faced Byzantine mosaics, and thirty-foot golden shields inscribed with assertive black Islamic calligraphy.

Hundreds of feet above us were two half domes and, ultimately, the huge central dome of the church. When it was first constructed in 537, Aya Sophia's dome was considered an impossible engineering feat and, in fact, it has collapsed four times over the centuries. But it was rebuilt each time, and today it remains an awe-inspiring metaphor for heaven. The contemporary author Procopius wrote that this dome seemed to be "founded not on solid masonry but suspended from heaven by a golden chain," and Justinian himself, upon entering his church for the first time, fell to his knees and cried, "Oh, Solomon, I have outdone you!"

Anyway, if there's such a thing as a spectacularly funky old church, Aya Sophia is it. Between its Ottoman chandeliers, dour Byzantine icons, and its countless architectural curiosities layered on bit-by-bit over the centuries, there's a surprise around every corner. By comparison, St. Peter's in Rome feels like Christian corporate headquarters.

But Aya Sophia was by no means the only fascinating site within walking distance of our hotel. The Blue Mosque, Sultan Ahmet's failed attempt to rival Justinian, is still a remarkable accomplishment. The Topkapi Palace, with its manicured courtyards, elaborate harem, and fabulous porcelain collections is, by itself, worth a trip to Istanbul. And of course, you can only imagine our children's rampant delight when we ventured into Istanbul's Grand Bazaar—the fifteenth-century mother of all shopping malls with more than four thousand jewelry, rug, and tchotchke shops.

All that's not to say that Istanbul is perfect. The food, while generally cheap, is also generally awful, and every tourist attraction in the city is plagued by aggressive touts who pester you incessantly with little toys and other assorted crap. I also noted, with some irony, that this is conceivably the worst place on earth to buy a Turkish rug or any other fakeable item of value. Plus, it's impossible to wander the streets of this city without that damned song "Istanbul (Not Constantinople)" rattling around in your head all day.

Those quibbles aside, no city we visited thus far has been so thoroughly engrossing as Istanbul. It was a joy to stand on the banks of the Golden Horn and tell the children how the last Byzantine emperor ran a massive chain across the Golden Horn in a futile attempt to stave off the gunboats of Mehmet the Conqueror. And the Topkapi Palace was the perfect setting to recount how the Ottomans conquered the world from Mesopotamia to the ramparts of Vienna. We had great expectations for Istanbul, but the city exceeded them all. Even Betty agreed it was worth her trouble getting here.

> As they say in Turkey,
> *Hoşça kalin* (Stay happy),
> David

Chapter 15

Subject: Kara's Shangri-la
Date: October 30
From: daylifers@aol.com (David Cohen)

Victoria Falls, Zimbabwe

Dear Friends:

If Istanbul was cheap, funky, and romantic, then Zurich, Switzerland, was its cosmic opposite. We came to Zurich to catch a South African Airways flight to Johannesburg, and as long as we were there, we decided to stay a few days and see a bit of Switzerland (or "Switcher Land," as Willie calls it).

We began to question the wisdom of that decision shortly after we landed. Devi, who speaks near-native Japanese, struck up a conversation with some friendly JAL flight attendants on the airport shuttle bus, and all they could do was complain how expensive Zurich was.

"Where do you live?" Devi asked in Japanese.

"Tokyo," replied one of the flight attendants.

"And you find Zurich expensive compared to Tokyo?"

"Oh, yes, much more costly."

Since Tokyo was the most expensive city we'd ever been to, we naturally began to worry. These fears were well founded, because the prices in Zurich were simply breathtaking. A t-shirt in the hotel gift shop ran $45. A ten-minute train ride into town cost the family more than $50, and a McDonald's Happy Meal was more than $9. In short, everything in Zurich was three times as expensive as America and about five times as much as Turkey.

This compelled us to adopt some drastic cost-cutting measures—one of which backfired badly. After spending more than $100 for a run-of-the-mill pizza dinner, we decided to prepare some of our meals in the hotel room—like Devi's mom did during her round-the-world trip thirty years ago. Consequently Devi and I hiked over to the local supermarket to procure some sandwich supplies. As we pushed our cart up and down the immaculate aisles, we encountered a well-dressed middle-aged woman, dispensing samples of chicken ravioli in cream sauce. I said, *"Guten Tag,"* to her in a friendly fashion, and before I knew it, she'd thrust a small paper plate full of chicken ravioli into my hands.

"Try it," she said with a heavy German inflection. "Iss gut."

I ate the ravioli and said, *"Danke.* That was very good."

"Now you buy zome," she replied. It was more a command than an invitation, and I found her German accent intimidating.

I almost told her that we were staying in a hotel and didn't have any way to cook ravioli, but that seemed too complicated, so I took the coward's way out and accepted a small plastic bag containing eight squares of pasta.

"Why did you take that?" Devi asked when we got out of earshot. "It cost nearly ten dollars, and we don't have any way to cook it."

"Don't worry," I said. "I'm going to take the package around the corner and dump it in the dairy case. That way I don't have to get into an argument."

Devi looked at me as if I'd lost my marbles.

When we got to the dairy case, I glanced furtively over my shoulder to make sure the ravioli lady wasn't looking. Much to my surprise, she was peering at me like a hawk. When our eyes met, I knew I looked guilty, but a few seconds later, I was hidden from sight, and I quickly flipped the ravioli into the dairy case.

I thought I'd made a clean escape, but halfway through checkout, I heard the voice of doom behind me. "I tink maybe you forgot *zis.*"

It was the evil ravioli lady. She'd recovered the package of ravioli and she was standing right behind me.

"Thank you again," I said, and before that sentence was out of my mouth, the cashier snatched the bag and dragged it over the scanner.

"You really are an idiot," Devi said, as we walked out of the supermarket.

"Don't worry," I vowed. "We're going to eat that ravioli if it's the last thing we do."

Back in the room, I made several feebleminded attempts to boil water that included, among other things, mounting a hotel water glass on top of our travel iron. Needless to say, that didn't work. So the next day I tried to give the ravioli to one of the hotel porters as a tip.

"It's excellent ravioli," I said. "It cost more than ten Swiss francs." The porter just said, *"Nein, danke,"* and looked at me as if I were trying to poison him.

The chicken ravioli became an albatross around my neck the whole three days we were in Zurich. Even on the way to the airport, I made one last-ditch attempt to foist it off on our Indian shuttle bus driver—who was probably a vegetarian, anyway.

"No, I am very sorry," he said, "but I cannot accept this gift."

"Oh, go ahead," I said. "It's great ravioli, and I can't take it with me on the airplane."

He shook his head vigorously, then studiously kept his eyes on the road.

As we got out of the bus, Devi said, "Please do me a favor. Don't try to give that ravioli to anyone at the airport."

At that point, I knew the jig was up, and I dumped the bag into a trash bin.

If that story seems like an odd way to sum up three days in Zurich, let me just add the following: Zurich is a lovely, prosperous city of stately buildings and meticulous streets set on a picturesque Alpine lake. It is surrounded by tidy farms, emerald-green meadows, and snow-capped mountain peaks. The trains run on time. The museums are impressive, and everything else generally seems to function perfectly. If you happen to have excess funds, I'm sure you'd enjoy shopping for Fabergé eggs, Mont Blanc pens, and other fabulously expensive gewgaws in the posh Bahnhofstrasse shops. And you can certainly get a superb meal here for the price of a used car. Still, it's easy to see why Lenin, while living in Zurich, dedicated his life to toppling the capitalist system. And I have to say that this is the only city in the world where we were cheered to see graffiti. If your family is on any kind of budget whatsoever—or if you prefer vacationing someplace that isn't defined by money and decorum—you might want to give Zurich a pass. Believe me, no one here will miss you.

When we boarded the plane in Switzerland, it was cold and gray with a light dusting of snow on the ground. Eleven hours later we disembarked in Johannesburg, South Africa, where we were greeted by a glorious spring day. The skies were an electric blue; the air was fresh and warm; and the streets were lined with jacaranda trees ablaze in a riot of orange and purple. Our brains were addled by the long, brutally crowded flight and the radical change of climate, but nothing could quell our excitement. We were finally in Africa—the segment of the trip that everyone in the family looked forward to the most.

We stayed overnight in a Johannesburg suburb, then headed straight back to the airport for a short flight north to Victoria

Falls. We were met at Victoria Falls Airport by a compact, reserved young woman in khaki named Susan. Susan was a white Zimbabwean whose family has lived here for generations. Devi had phoned ahead and hired Susan to take us a hundred kilometers across the Botswana border to Chobe National Park, reputedly the best place on earth to watch elephants.

Susan's vehicle was an enormous four-wheel-drive Land Rover, so I figured the drive from Vic Falls to Botswana might be pretty rough. But the road turned out to be a smooth strip of tarmac that cut through the flat dusty bush of western Zimbabwe like a black ribbon. It was burning hot as we barreled down the road, and I was astonished how desiccated everything looked. I knew October was the end of the dry season, but the foliage—what little there was of it—seemed dead, and nearly every tree had either been charred black by fire or completely reduced to white ash.

"Is it normally this…burnt?" I asked Susan.

"Yes, it's usually pretty well parched by October," she said in a quiet Rhodesian accent. "But in the last few years, it's been a lot worse than usual. All of Southern Africa's been hit by a drought, and this particular area has suffered several major bush fires."

As Susan described the water shortage, Kara suddenly shrieked—as only a nine-year-old girl can. "Oh my God! Oh my God! Oh my God!"

"What is it?" I asked with alarm.

But Kara couldn't talk, only point.

I pivoted around to see what she was pointing at and spotted an eighteen-foot giraffe loping gracefully down the shoulder of the road.

"Did you see that?" Kara cried breathlessly. "It was just running around free."

"I did, honey. It was wonderful."

"I'm going to like Africa a lot," Kara said, and her face was lit with wonder.

Shortly after the giraffe sighting, we pulled up to a small cinder block shack with a blue and white flag that housed the Botswana border control. If you think the Turkish border guards were baffled by Betty's Guatemalan passport, you should have seen the Batswana.*

"I've been at this post for five years," observed the inspector, "and I have never seen anything like this. Where in blazes is Guatemala?"

Betty was slightly offended by that remark, but I pointed out to her that the passport inspectors in Guatemala probably didn't know where Botswana was either.

"I know," she said, "but Guatemala is an important country."

Anyway, when it looked as if we might be headed toward another sticky visa predicament, Susan motioned the rest of us to step outside and discreetly intervened. Five minutes later she emerged from the shack with all our visas in order.

"Any trouble?" I asked.

"A little," she replied, "but we have a good arrangement with these fellows."

"Do you have to pay them or something?"

"Oh, no, nothing like that. They just don't have any place to get lunch around here," she said, sweeping her hand across the wide panorama of desolate bush, "so we bring them a loaf of bread from time to time."

"I'm glad we didn't try to do this without you," I said.

"No, your friend would have probably been turned back."

Once we crossed the border, we detoured a few miles off the main road and drove our vehicle through what looked like a long, shallow concrete mud puddle.

*Citizens of Botswana are referred to as Batswana. The singular is Motswana.

"I'm afraid you'll all have to get out and walk through this," said Susan. The kids thought that was a wonderful idea and immediately splashed in.

"What is this stuff?" asked Devi.

"Oh, the water is supposed to contain chemicals that kill any hoof-and-mouth disease you might carry in from Zimbabwe on your shoes or on the tires of the vehicle."

"You mean this is full of chemicals?" Devi asked, as she watched the kids cavorting in the brown soup.

"Ostensibly. But I wouldn't worry too much," replied Susan. "It's unlikely that anyone's actually put the chemicals in."

After that, we skirted the border town of Kasane and eventually came to a small turnoff marked "Chobe Game Lodge." At this point, Susan shifted into low gear and said, "You better hang on. This may be a little rough."

Now I understood why we needed the big Land Rover. The road to the lodge was little more than a sandy track, and the vehicle fishtailed back and forth in the soft dry earth. When we were about a mile up the path, Kara yelled, "Elephant! Elephant!" and we all turned to see a young male stripping leaves from a tree.

"Do you mind if we stop here for a moment?" asked Devi.

"Not at all," said Susan. "I'll just find some solid ground." She pulled the Land Rover forward and switched off the engine.

"He's so beautiful," Kara said, watching the young elephant intently.

"Everyone be very quiet," Devi said to the kids. "We don't want to scare him off."

"I wouldn't worry about that," said Susan. "That young fellow weighs around four thousand kilos, and he isn't the least bit afraid of us."

Susan then directed our attention to the other side of the car where there was a break in the bush. Through the gap, we could see the broad floodplain of the Chobe River, which forms the border between Botswana and Namibia's Caprivi

Strip. The river was at its lowest level of the year, and its wide grassy banks were teeming with wildlife. There were herds of sleek black waterbuck and muscular kudu, several herds of elephant—many with young calves—and a pod of rotund hippos grazing at the water's edge.

Up until that point I thought that an African wildlife safari involved driving around in the bush all day trying to spot a few stray animals. And apparently it can be like that during the wet season when the bush leafs out. But in October, the water holes were dry, the foliage was almost completely gone, and every beast within two hundred miles was gathered by the banks of the Chobe, the only perennial water source in these parts. This meant, among other things, that thirty thousand elephants—one out of every twenty in Africa—were rummaging around in the immediate neighborhood.

"Look at that," I said, gazing out over the Chobe floodplain. "There must be seven or eight different species down there."

"I know," Kara said, almost reverently. "This is the best place you ever took us."

By the time we got to the lodge, the children were in a frenetic state. They wanted to get out and see the animals, and they didn't want to waste one extra minute loitering in the room. While it did our hearts good to see the kids so enthusiastic, we had to tell them that we couldn't go game watching in the middle of the day.

"Why not?" asked Kara indignantly. "There are animals all over the place."

"I'm sorry," Devi replied. "But it's more than 100 degrees outside. You're not used to the heat yet, and you can get sunburned or heatstroke. Besides, according to the guidebook, a lot of the animals, like lions and hyenas, are either nocturnal or crepuscular."

"Crep...what?" asked Willie.

"Crepuscular. It means they're only active at dawn and dusk—so we'll see a lot more species once it cools down a bit."

The kids were naturally disappointed but they found it easier to be patient once they found out that the animals would come in to see them. Apparently, the only thing they had in the way of a fence around the lodge was a low barrier along the river that was supposed to keep crocs out. Otherwise, the bountiful African wildlife had free access to the grounds. We soon got used to seeing the vervet monkeys and baboons cavorting on the lawn outside our room. But the kids were slightly taken aback when they stumbled across a mother warthog and her baby rooting around next to the pool. And you should have seen their faces when a fifteen-foot elephant crashed out of the bush and strolled casually down a hotel path.

"Do you think this place is safe?" Devi asked when the elephant passed.

"I don't know," I replied. "It's sort of like letting the kids play inside the enclosures at the zoo."

"Maybe they shouldn't go outside without an adult."

I agreed, and after a big baboon leapt from the roof of the hotel and landed directly behind them, Kara and Willie did, too.

When four o'clock rolled around, the kids were waiting by the door with their hats on and their cameras ready. We trooped to the front door of the lodge, where we met a thin, muscular Motswana game ranger named Steve. A quiet friendly fellow of about thirty, Steve was our game guide for the day. As we pulled away in an open four-wheel-drive vehicle, Willie asked him if we would see a lot of elephants.

"I promise you," Steve said in a thick African accent, "you'll see more ellies today than you have ever seen in your life."

That was no exaggeration. While elephants may be an endangered species in other parts of Africa, there was clearly a population explosion in northeastern Botswana. The minute we pulled onto the track alongside the Chobe River, we saw herd after herd of the lumbering beasts. There were breeding herds of mothers and babies, bachelor herds of adolescent males, and old rogue bulls roaming around by themselves. There were so many elephants, in fact, that they'd thoroughly ravaged the landscape, stripping bushes of whatever little greenery they had and toppling large trees just so they could reach the leaves at the top. The entire area looked like some sort of combat zone.

"They sure do a lot of damage," commented Devi.

"Oh, yes," replied Steve. "The farmers across the river in Namibia hate these beasts. They rip down fences and eat their crops. And if a farmer is foolish enough to leave some sugarcane or a bag of oranges on the seat of his car, the ellies roll the car over and over until the windows break. Then they fish out the bag with their trunks."

"You're kidding!" Devi said.

"Not at all. They can be very aggressive."

Not to mention stubborn. We soon learned that there's no way to move an African elephant that doesn't care to be moved. Several times during the drive, we had to wait patiently while twenty recalcitrant pachyderms milled about in the road for no discernible reason. In fact, the elephants had a lot more luck moving us. At one point, a young bull trumpeted a warning, flared his impressive ears, and charged our vehicle. That got everyone's attention—especially Steve's. He blasted down the road in reverse.

"He wasn't serious, was he?" I asked Steve.

"Probably not," Steve replied. "He was probably just showing off for the other ellies. But it is best not to take chances." Everyone agreed that was good policy.

Elephants weren't the only game in abundance. Within a three-hour period we saw herds of kudu and sable grazing by the riverbank, timid impala darting through the bush, and a colony of several hundred four-foot-high meerkats migrating en masse across the plain. The kids also witnessed a lurid tableau when we stumbled across an eviscerated elephant carcass being picked apart by more than a dozen ugly vultures. And they learned how perilous the bush can be when we drove around a bend and found ourselves smack in the middle of a herd of Cape buffalo, considered one of the most dangerously aggressive species in Africa.

As we carefully picked our way through the Cape buffalo, Steve's radio crackled to life and another ranger alerted him that there was a pride of lions in the area. Steve advised us to hold on tight, and we bumped and jolted several miles down a rutted track until we spotted five lions sauntering away from a gnawed giraffe carcass. The lions settled beneath a tree by the side of the track. Then they yawned and stretched gracefully. We pulled within ten yards, and Kara and Willie breathlessly snapped a dozen photos each. Devi kept a taut grip on Lucas—just to make sure he didn't become dessert.

By the time we returned to the lodge, Kara was, without doubt, the happiest child on earth. As far as she was concerned, you could keep every cathedral, museum, and ruin in Europe. For that matter, you could keep all the amusement parks, video arcades, and television sets in the world. Just give her the plains of Africa with its elephant herds and lion prides, because that's where her happiness lay.

The next morning, we took a small motor launch out on the Chobe River to get a close-up view of the crocs, hippos, and other riverine animals that dwelled along its muddy shores. Our guide was another young Motswana ranger named Thomas. Thomas surprised us when he said hippos were the most dangerous creature in Africa.

"More dangerous than lions or crocodiles?" asked Kara.

"Certainly," replied Thomas. "More people are killed by hippos each year than any other animal."

"I thought they were vegetarians," Kara replied.

"They are, but the males are very protective. They circle around the females underwater, and try to capsize any boat that comes too close to the pod. Sometimes they capsize boats for no apparent reason. Then they pick up the swimmers in their powerful jaws and crush them or they hold them underwater until they drown.

"The most important thing," continued Thomas, "is never to get between a bull hippo and his females. That's when he feels threatened. Also remember that a hippo is most dangerous when he dives. If he dives, it means he's trying to come up under the boat and roll it."

This ad hoc seminar gave me a whole new respect for the ungainly hippopotamus. Even though they look clumsy and harmless on land, they're apparently very aggressive and lightning-quick in the water. Five minutes later, we found ourselves circling a pod of females. After shooting some videos of the ladies, I looked around through my viewfinder to see where the male was. About fifty yards off I noticed a small gray object in the water. I zoomed in. It was him, and only his eyes and ears were above the water line.

"Hey Thomas," I said. "I thought we weren't supposed to get between the male and his pod."

At that moment, Thomas also spotted the male, and he suddenly gunned the engine. Through my lens, I saw the beast drop beneath the water. At that moment, I knew this four-ton behemoth was headed for our little twelve-foot motorboat.

"He's diving!" I yelled at Thomas. "He's diving! We better get out of here!"

But Thomas already had the engine going full bore. "Hang on," he yelled. The kids all grabbed the nearest adult as the boat thrust forward, and after that, it was only a question of relative speed.

More in the next installment,
David

Chapter 16

Subject: "In the Jungle, the Mighty Jungle…"

Date: November 2

From: daylifers@aol.com (David Cohen)

Johannesburg, South Africa

Dear Friends:

My video camera was running when the hippo attacked, so I captured the entire incident on tape. While it was happening the ambush seemed to last forever, but the tape shows that the whole affair took less than ten seconds. The first thing you see is a male hippo with only his tiny porcine ears and beady little eyes above the waterline. Then the beast slips underwater, and you hear me shrieking words of warning along with a few choice expletives. The boat's engine roars to life, and as I stumble backward, there are some inelegant shots of the river and sky. When the camera steadies, you see a hostile four-ton hippo lunge from the water with his powerful jaws flung open like a car trunk. He's less than ten feet behind the boat, so you get a pretty good view of his huge peglike teeth and the pink gullet beyond. The leviathan's design seems clear: to capsize our little boat, grab us with his jaws, and shake us like rag dolls. Providentially, the boat has reached full speed at this point, and the behemoth's lunge falls short. All he can do is snort and glare as we beat a hasty retreat. The tape ends with some trifling profanity from the cameraman and several anxious questions from the children. Even Thomas, our game guide, looks slightly shaken.

I tell you all this somewhat casually, but after the hippo attack, I guarantee you that we all viewed the exuberant African wildlife in an entirely new light. The pretty beasties no longer seemed like tourist attractions set upon the plain for our amusement. They now seemed like what they were— eminently dangerous and cunning adversaries. Several species, like elephants, Cape buffalo, even some types of antelope, will attack if they feel threatened. Others, like lions, hyenas, and crocs, wouldn't mind having you for lunch. Most game guides try to convey these facts to wide-eyed tourists the moment they set foot in Africa, but take my word for it, the lesson's far more vivid once you've stared down the throat of a lunging eight-thousand-pound hippo.

This practical wisdom was impressed upon us further when we left Chobe and drove back to Victoria Falls. We stayed in a hotel compound out on the edge of town for five days in an African-style bungalow with a high thatched roof. On the night table was a handbook that itemized the particular perils posed by each of the neighborhood species. After the creature-by-creature rundown, the author offered the following common-sense admonition: "Basically, it is incredibly stupid to feed or taunt any wild animal." Hotel residents were then advised not to venture outside their huts after dark without an escort.

The hotel compound had a locally renowned restaurant, and we were anxious to sample its Zimbabwean cuisine. Since we were now convinced that we could become dinner walking to dinner, we phoned for an escort. The guard—a small, wiry Ndebele man with a nightstick—escorted us to a traditional open-air *boma** replete with African drummers and a buffet stocked with dishes you won't find at your neighborhood Sizzler.

Devi and I began our meal with crêpes stuffed with ostrich (not bad), kudu paté (better), and curried crocodile that tasted more like curried rubber. After that, we sampled warthog steaks, taro root, and impala cutlets. We wanted to set an adventurous example for the children, but neither Devi nor I could muster the courage to try the boiled millipedes in red sauce. The children, by the way, were thoroughly disgusted by the entire spectacle and refused to have any part of it.

Willie, who'd been subsisting primarily on rice, pasta, pizza, and potatoes for the past four months, objected on general principle, and Kara objected on ethical grounds.

"How can you eat endangered species?" she demanded in high dudgeon.

"I don't think warthogs are an endangered species," I replied.

"Still, I don't see how you can go out and watch beautiful animals all day, and then come back and eat them for dinner."

"Did you get a good look at the warthogs, Kara?"

"Yeah?"

"Believe me, they taste better than they look."

Kara sighed in disgust, and would only eat vegetables and rice. But after dinner, she and the boys were mesmerized by a dozen lithe African dancers in leopard-skin loincloths. While the kids watched the dancers, Betty and I strolled outside to a small hut near the entrance of the restaurant to have our fortunes told. The soothsayer's hut was the size of a chicken coop and was lit by a single candle. Betty told me to go first, so I stooped inside, and a very serious young shaman motioned me to sit down. Then he chanted impressively and threw what looked like small mammal vertebrae onto the dirt floor. He tossed the bones several times, then proceeded to

*A circular open-air dining pavilion enclosed by a fence made from sticks.

augur. I think common sense and a glance inside the restaurant might have informed his first two observations: "You have three children and are traveling far from home." But after that he went out on a limb, confidently proclaiming that I would return safely to my home village, that I would never get divorced, and that I would live to see the birth of five grandchildren. Despite his excellent showmanship, I wasn't convinced this particular soothsayer had any special prognosticative powers. Still, I hoped he was right on all three counts. Betty refused to tell us what the shaman divined for her, but for the rest of the evening she smiled more than usual.

Before we left California, Devi made several attempts to arrange an overnight safari with the kids in Zimbabwe's Hwange National Park—one of Southern Africa's best-stocked, least-crowded game reserves. She faxed several professional safari companies, but they all wrote back saying they wouldn't take children younger than twelve out overnight. They worried that small children might wander into the bush, where their small size made them attractive to hyenas.

When Devi persisted, one of the safari outfits put her in touch with a professional hunter named Jane Bettenay. Jane was raising two young children of her own, so she felt more comfortable taking kids out into the bush. Devi assured Jane that Kara and Willie would follow all her rules, and we agreed to leave Lucas back at the hut with Betty.

The morning of our safari, Jane roared up in a gigantic utility vehicle with a game-viewing platform mounted above the cab. She was a tall, raw-boned woman in her mid- to late thirties with sun-weathered skin and well-worn khakis. Jane wasn't very talkative, but once we got to Hwange, she proved an excellent game spotter. She located several species we hadn't seen at Chobe, including a herd of zebra, some wildebeest, and much to the kids' delight, a hyena with suckling cubs.

By mid-morning, Willie and I got into the spirit of things and climbed up on the game-viewing platform. We jolted down the sandy red track with the hot wind whipping our hair. Every few minutes or so, a hornbill with an enormous yellow beak darted out from a tree ahead of us, and herds of impala, startled by our approach, would bound into the bush.

We enjoyed the panoramic views from Sinamatella Camp, then headed south toward Masuma Dam, our campground for the night. The Masuma Dam camp was located next to a perennial water hole. It had a long, low blind with a thatched roof for game viewing, a small water tank, a barbecue pit, and a clearing for tents. The camp was surrounded by a rickety fence, but as Jane and a posted sign confirmed, it would be fairly useless in the face of a charging elephant or a determined lion.

While Jane prepared dinner, we sat quietly in the blind observing life at the water hole. During the last daylight hours, herds of antelope timidly approached the water's edge to slake their thirst. They stood back as far as they could to avoid being taken by a crocodile. At dusk, six or seven hippos laboriously hoisted themselves from the pond and lumbered off across the plain to graze. Then a dozen elephants approached and stood in noble silhouette against the setting sun. The sky went blood red, then ebony, then a billion stars exploded into life. Finally, a full moon rose from the east and obscured all but the most brilliant constellations.

By that time, dinner was ready, and much to the children's relief, it turned out to be glazed chicken rather than braised kudu or curried Cape buffalo. Over coffee, the campfire conversation turned, as it often does in these parts, to stupid-tourist stories. It seems that foreign visitors to Africa routinely underestimate the danger lurking all around them, so the guides responsible for their safety have honed a well-rehearsed repertoire of cautionary tales. The first of these concerns a Taiwanese tourist who, against all better advice, hopped out of his Land Rover in order to kneel beside a pride of lions. He evidently thought this would be a great photo opportunity for his family, but the lions saw it more as room service. He was promptly killed and eaten at leisure.

Second on the list of Darwin Award winners was the macho German tourist in Namibia who snuck out of camp late at night so he could sleep next to the water hole. Apparently, he wanted to take some close-up photos of the elephants as they shambled down to the pond at first light. But when dawn broke, only a well-masticated sleeping bag was found at the water's edge. Since we, too, were sleeping near a water hole, we found this tale particularly poignant.

Finally, we heard about some canoers on the Zambezi River above Victoria Falls who repeatedly slapped the water with paddles in order to frighten away a hippo lurking under the water. As we've already determined, hippos aren't easily intimidated, and certainly not by canoe paddles. When the beast attacked, the guide managed to wound it with his pistol, but the hippo retaliated by amputating his arm above the elbow.

Needless to say, these gruesome tales put the fear of God into us, and before we all turned in for the night, Devi and I read Kara and Willie the riot act.

"Kara will sleep in Mommy's tent, and Willie will sleep with me," I said. "And under no circumstances will either one of you set foot outside your tent until morning. Is that clear?"

"What if I have to go to the bathroom?" asked Kara.

"Then wake up Mommy, and she'll go with you."

"I'm not going anywhere outside that tent," said Devi, "so you better go before you fall asleep."

"But what if I have to go in the middle of the night?" asked Kara, pushing the envelope as usual.

"Then go in your pants," I said. "Are we clear?"

"Yes, Daddy," said Kara.

"Willie?"

"Yes, Daddy."

"If you stay inside the tent, there's no reason to be frightened. We'll be right beside you, and no animals will come inside."

I actually had no evidence whatsover that this last statement was true. Happily, our children still have excessive faith in us, and neither of them asked what we might do if an animal did happen to turn up. Personally, I planned to keep my Leatherman knife drawn by the side of my cot, and I entertained a fantasy or two about plunging it into the throat of a crazed hyena. But in my heart of hearts, I knew that sort of thing only worked in Tarzan movies.

Anyway, the kids were exhausted, and they quickly dropped off to sleep without any apparent worries. Consequently, only Devi and I heard what happened next. Let me put it this way: Whoever wrote that song, "In the jungle, the mighty jungle, the lion sleeps tonight," has obviously never been in the mighty jungle, because:

a. Lions don't live in the jungle; they live on the savanna;

b. They hunt at night; and

c. The African bush—once the nocturnal sonata gets cracking—is far too noisy for sleep.

You know how small noises are amplified at night—even in quiet suburbs. Well, imagine the worst possible case of that—then quadruple it. As I lay in my sleeping bag I heard cicadas hissing, crickets chirping, bullfrogs croaking, lions roaring, elephants groaning, and God knows what rummaging around in the underbrush right next to the tent. About the time I managed to convince myself that most of this was normal run-of-the-mill African bush noise, the most blood-curdling cacophony I ever heard came rolling through the camp.

First, a large animal—Jane later said it was a Cape buffalo—came crashing through the underbrush just outside our camp. Then a pride of lions followed in pursuit, growling and roaring. The buffalo screamed. (This, by the way, is a particularly unsettling noise.) Then the lions dragged the beast down through the snapping brush and apparently ripped its throat out. The buffalo died a very long and excruciating, blood-gurgling death that left me lying in my cot with my eyes bulging and my pulse pounding like timpani.

During the entire twenty-minute kill and for several hours afterward, I grasped the hilt of my knife with white knuckles ready to eviscerate any beast that might come crashing through our tent. Eventually I fell asleep, but it was a fitful slumber. I woke up every fifteen minutes or so, and each time I did, I thought to myself, "What sort of an idiot would bring his children on a sleepover in the African bush surrounded by lions?" The kids, by the way, never heard a thing.

As if all that weren't excitement enough, the next day, Devi and I were scheduled to shoot the rapids on the Zambezi River below Victoria Falls. We'd done some white-water rafting in Costa Rica at the very beginning of the trip, but those were level two rapids, the white-water equivalent of a stroll in the park. The stretch of the Zambezi we were going to tackle was rated level five, the most difficult rapids you could traverse with a reasonable expectation of survival. To make matters worse, the river was at its lowest level of the year, which meant there were more exposed rocks than usual. Still, I think the most intimidating part of the whole deal—aside from the two-page waiver we signed—was the fact that each one of the seventeen rapids on this part of the river had a charming moniker such as "The Devil's Toilet Bowl," "The Muncher," "Gnashing Jaws," "The Terminator," "The Washing Machine," and my personal favorite, "Commercial Suicide." (Kind of makes you wonder how that last one got its name, doesn't it?)

When we arrived at the staging area, Devi and I couldn't help notice that we were ten to fifteen years older than all the other assembled adrenaline junkies. One married couple our age showed up at the last minute, but the husband fell and broke his finger on the steep path down to the river, so they had to drop out. (His wife was wearing nail polish, gold jewelry, and designer clothes, which suggested she didn't fully grasp the program in the first place.)

Our big yellow raft, one of five in the fleet, was crewed by a pleasant young couple from Holland, a compact red-haired Irishman named Steven; our African helmsman, Gordon; plus Devi and me. I was assigned to the port bow on the theory it might be useful to have a few extra kilos up front if the raft began to flip over backward. I was joined in the front by Steven, the Irishman, whose chief qualification for the bow position was that he was a complete raging lunatic.

I've never skydived or bungee-jumped, so the first few rapids of the Zambezi will have to qualify as the most adrenaline-soaked half hour of my life. The first cascade of the day, Morning Glory, looked more like a small waterfall. We could hear it roaring a hundred yards ahead of us. Gordon, the helmsman, picked out the best course. Then everyone followed his orders to paddle like demons. The raft was sucked into the torrent and *whooosh*, down we went. Our stomachs dropped from under us, and we were suddenly paddling air. Then *bash!*, the front end of the raft hit the river, and Steven and I were submerged beneath the raging water. Then the stern of the raft crashed down behind us, and we popped back up into the air. That's when our real work began. Steven and I had to throw our weight forward immediately to prevent the raft from flipping backward into the drink. Then we had to get our paddles up to fend off the boulders flying toward us at twenty miles an hour.

There were two reasons why Steven and I were determined to keep the boat upright and not end up as what the guides drolly called "swimmers." First of all, once you're out of the boat the swirling rapids can pin you underwater for thirty seconds to a minute before spitting you out downstream—not a pleasant prospect. Secondly, the Zambezi is absolutely teeming with crocodiles. The guides assured us that the crocs avoided the white water in favor of the languid pools by the river's edge. But, honestly, who wants to count on that?

Anyway, I'm proud to tell you that between Gordon's helmsmanship, the crew's esprit de corps, Steven's frightening zealotry, and my sheer avoirdupois, ours was the only raft in the fleet that navigated all seventeen rapids in an upright position. Some of our crew, including Devi, fell out a few times, but that was nothing. One of the other rafts capsized so often its crew became known as "the swim team." When we completed the run, I crumpled ashore, bruised and bone-tired but proud that I could keep up with the youngsters.

In that brief halcyon moment when I felt like a young warrior, I didn't imagine that the worst was yet to come. You see, the fact that we kept descending a series of rapids for twenty-five miles should have tipped me off to the fact that the climb back up to the rim was becoming progressively more daunting. By the time we concluded our kamikaze run, we were nearly a thousand feet below the plain. And since there was no incline, cable car, or other *deus ex machina* to spirit us out of the gorge, our only means of egress was to trudge up a steep path consisting of more than 750 hand-cut steps. That, if you're counting, is the equivalent of seventy-five flights of stairs—which may not have been a big deal for all the 150-pound twenty-year-olds on the expedition, but my battered forty-one-year-old carcass wasn't exactly fine-tuned for the task.

Devi, of course, skipped ahead of me like a happy mountain goat. Then all the guys passed me. Then some of the girls. Finally, I was overtaken by the African bearers who were hauling deflated hundred-pound rafts on their shoulders. I can't tell you how relieved I was that there were three or four chubby young women on the expedition who were actually in worse shape than I was. Still, it was manifestly humiliating to arrive at the top fifteen minutes after the front-runners. Even more so that Gordon, our African helmsman, felt compelled to lag behind to make sure I made it without suffering a coronary.

When we were ten steps from the rim, I used the last wisp of breath in my burning lungs to tell Gordon to jump on my back.

"Why ya wahnt me to do dat?" he asked, looking at me like I was some sort of foreign pervert.

"Just as a joke."

Gordon shrugged and jumped on my back. I emerged over the top of the rim into a crowd of thirty people sitting around drinking beer and swapping war stories.

"Sorry I'm late," I said, "but Gordon here couldn't quite make it up the steps." Of course, Gordon had a washboard stomach, rippling leg muscles, and looked like a poster boy for steroids. So no one really bought it, but at least I'd salvaged my middle-aged pride—which is more than I can say for my middle-aged legs, because for the next five days I could barely walk.

> Best wishes from your ("ow!
> ow! ow!") decrepit old friend,
> David

Chapter 17

Subject: Flight of the Damned
Date: November 14
From: daylifers@aol.com (David Cohen)

Cape Town, South Africa

Dear Friends:

It wouldn't be right to bid adieu to Victoria Falls, Zimbabwe, without mentioning the falls themselves. Three hundred feet high and more than a mile wide, Victoria Falls are exquisitely dramatic—a bona fide wonder of the world. In the Kololo language, the falls are called *Mosi-Oa-Tunya*—The Smoke That Thunders—and most of the year, thick veils of mist rise from the gorge in such quantities that the falls themselves are obscured. But in the dry season, the vista was spectacular.

I might also add that our view was unimpeded by anything so pragmatic as guardrails. Had we been so inclined, we could have sauntered to the brink of the chasm and dangled our feet over the edge. This, of course, was not the ideal arrangement for small children. Even with Lucas on the baby leash, we had our hands full keeping all three of our progeny from tumbling into the rainbowed mist. As we slouched back to town, Devi and I agreed that this one wonder of the world we might have skipped until the children were older.

After eight exhilarating days in the wilds of Botswana and Zimbabwe, we boarded a flight south to Johannesburg, South Africa. The plane was four hours late—not unusual for Africa—and by the time we set down, it was early evening. Our hotel was in a well-heeled white suburb called Rosebank. According to Moses, our African cabbie, Rosebank and nearby Sandton were the only neighborhoods left in Johannesburg where you could still safely walk the streets at night. He said Soweto and downtown Johannesburg were practically off-limits to white people. And when we told him we planned to rent a van and drive ourselves to a game reserve in the Eastern Transvaal, he burst into a hearty laugh and roared, "Don't make any wrong turns on the way out of town."

Devi and I had no way to know whether Moses was exaggerating or not, but we couldn't help noticing that every house we passed had high cinder block walls topped with glistening razor wire. Once we settled into our hotel room, and the kids were asleep, Devi said, "What do you think? Should we still try to drive ourselves across South Africa?"

"I don't know," I replied. "Maybe it's not as bad as he says. When foreign tourists come to New York, I'm sure the cabbies try to frighten them, too."

"Yeah, but in New York, we know where it's safe and where it isn't. We don't have the same advantage here."

It was a good point—so we fished out our guidebook to see what the author had to say on the subject.

"Look at this," said Devi. "He actually recommends a visit to Soweto and downtown Johannesburg. He says these areas offer a 'glimpse of the country's future.'" But further down the page, Devi found a more sobering passage: "Of course, there is a good chance of being mugged, or worse."

The author went on to suggest that tourists travel in groups or hire a professional bodyguard, and he warned that carjacking and highway banditry were dramatically on the rise. Those caveats alone might have dissuaded us from a South African motor tour, but the following day we met someone who'd been shot through the thigh during a carjacking, and that pretty much settled the issue. We canceled our rental car and hired an armed driver to take us to the game reserve.

The driver, recommended by the hotel, was a burly blond young half-English, half-Afrikaner* man named Walter. He had a pleasant demeanor, a weapon under his seat, and radically right-wing views on the ANC, race relations, and gun control. As we rolled out of Jo'burg, he fired off a fusillade of reactionary opinion that made everyone else in the van cringe. But by the time we reached the green hills of Eastern Transvaal, his demeanor mellowed, and he regaled the children with tales of Jock of the Bushveldt, a famous Transvaaler dog that rescued his master from all manner of wild animals.

South Africa is a huge country—twice the size of France—and during our seven-hour drive east we encountered stark contrasts between regions. First we passed through the bleak gold-mining district surrounding Johannesburg, full of slag heaps and scarred earth. Then we found ourselves in farm country that, except for the iron-red dirt, could have been anywhere in the American Midwest. Eventually, the crops gave way to sheep and cattle ranches that spread across rolling hills reminiscent of Northern California. Just when we thought we couldn't be in Africa anymore, we rolled into Lydenburg, a medium-sized market town where Swazi women in colorful garb carried babies on their backs and impossible loads on their heads. After that, we climbed into the Drakensberg, a rugged mountain range that delineates South Africa's mile-high interior plateau. There we beheld stunning

---

*Afrikaners are descended from the mostly Dutch settlers who came to the Cape Colony in the late seventeenth century.

mountain vistas, verdant gorges, and dozens of feathery waterfalls. Finally, we dropped onto a flat, sun-beaten scrubland
called the lowveldt.

Our particular destination in the lowveldt was Makalali,
one of several private game reserves clustered around the
periphery of Kruger National Park. Our three-day stay at
Makalali was, hands down, the biggest splurge of our entire
round-the-world trip, but the brochure promised an up-close
game experience for the kids so we decided to bite the bullet.

We were met at the gates of Makalali by a polite, earnest
young South African naturalist named Werner Smith. Werner
had short hair, black horn-rimmed glasses, and a khaki uniform
that looked like it just came back from the dry-cleaners. He
drove us ten miles through the bush to a riverside camp that was
a whimsical fusion of tribal architecture and Western luxury.
There was an open air dining *boma,* a small swimming pool,
and six spacious sleeping huts. The camp was embarrassingly
well staffed with three nature guides, two cooks, several
Shangaan game trackers, and a fellow called a *muchinda,* who
was more or less our butler.

The kids wanted to get out into the bush as soon as possible, so we all piled into an open Land Rover equipped with a
two-way radio, a spotlight, and a formidable Czech elephant
gun. Werner drove, and Jeffrey, our Shangaan tracker, perched
on a seat mounted above the front bumper.

Jeffrey immediately demonstrated his tracking prowess by
locating a herd of twelve giraffe. Then, as dusk approached,
we followed a trail of fresh excrement to the first herd of rhinos we'd seen in Africa. The rhinos were prehistorically regal,
and one of the beasts had a cute (if you can use that word for
a rhinoceros) three-foot calf that mesmerized the children.
Even Lucas sat perfectly still as we inched our way toward the
edge of the herd.

When darkness fell, Werner told us it was time to track lions.
Public game reserves in Southern Africa don't usually allow

tourists to wander around outside after dark, but Makalali was privately owned, so we were free to explore. Jeffrey pulled out a powerful handheld spotlight. Werner rechecked his gun. Then we jolted over miles of rough tracks reconnoitering the pitch-black bushveldt. We finally zeroed in on a dry river gulch. Werner slid the Land Rover down a steep embankment while Jeffrey scanned the riverbed with his searchlight.

Just crashing through the bush at night hunting for lions was a wonderful adventure for the children, but when Jeffrey finally picked out a sleek lioness nursing a pair of cubs, the kids were beyond ecstatic. The lioness squinted in the bright light, but apparently considered it too much trouble to move her cubs, so the kids got to sit in the Land Rover ten yards off "oohing" and "awing" for more than fifteen minutes. Finally, the mother and cubs wandered off, and we moved on to the next nocturnal wonder, a cute little bush baby with gleaming bug-eyes sitting in a tree.

When we finally got back to camp, we washed off the dust in an open-air shower and made our way toward the *boma* for a magnificent dinner of Indian-spiced beef with chutney, barbecued guinea fowl, grits, Ethiopian sweet potatoes, and oranges in mint sauce. We were also introduced to our camp mates: an American wine magnate and his wife, a down-to-earth Irish couple from Cape Town who won their trip to Makalali in a magazine contest, and a well-dressed Parisian honeymoon couple—Alain and Muriel—who excused them-selves right after dessert. Twenty minutes after they departed, while the rest of us were sipping coffee and cognac, we heard a disturbing shriek emanate from the honeymoon cottage. At first, we couldn't make out what the young bride was scream-ing, but we quickly realized it was, " 'Elp! 'Elp me, please!"

This posed something of a dilemma for the three fresh-faced game guides at the table. On the one hand, it was the first night of Alain and Muriel's honeymoon, and the guides really had no way to assess Muriel's savoir faire in matters marital. On the other hand, we were in the middle of the African bush, and the dewy French couple might be besieged by a troop of baboons.

"What do you think?" Werner said to Chris, one of the other guides. "Should we check it out?"

"I don't know, Werner," Chris replied uncomfortably. "It might be a bit...indiscreet."

But then another scream pierced the night air, and the guides forsook discretion for gallantry. As they charged to the rescue, the rest of us made no pretense whatsoever of resuming our dinner conversation. The first thing we heard was Werner, shouting, "Wake up, Thomas! Wake up!"

Thomas was the armed guard who was supposed to protect us from the neighborhood wildlife, and the fact that he could sleep undisturbed through five minutes of bloodcurdling shrieks did little to buttress our sense of security. Next, we heard some muffled cries, some male voices murmuring, then silence.

Ten minutes later—which seemed like an eternity—Werner and Chris returned to the *boma*.

"What was it, man?" demanded Dermot, the Irishman. "Baboons? Hyenas? Or just her brutish husband?"

Werner smiled. "None of the above," he replied. "It was only a mouse."

With that, the entire table collapsed in hysterics.

The next morning at dawn, we joined Werner for a bushcraft lesson. Up until this point, I'd have to admit that all the scruffy desiccated shrubs on the lowveldt looked remarkably similar to me. But as we strolled through the bush, Werner supplied a name and practical use for nearly every plant we encountered.

"If you find yourself in the bush without a toilet kit," said Werner, "there's no need to worry, because everything is right here."

"Where?" asked Willie, surveying the parched landscape.

"Right here," said Werner, cracking a twig off a bush. "This is from a magic guary bush. You can fray the end of a twig, and use it as a toothbrush." He demonstrated. "Over here is a leadwood tree. Its wood contains fluoride. You burn it and mix the ash with water to make toothpaste. And if you need toilet paper, you can peel the bark off this wattle tree. See," he said, handing Willie a piece. "It's soft."

Werner taught the children how to use anise seed for deodorant, sicklebush leaves as a toothache poultice, and common spikethorn as a diarrhea remedy. He showed them big black dung beetles rolling balls of elephant feces down the trail and thousands of communal spiders working together to construct a gigantic web. But I think Werner made his greatest impression during his discussion of poisonous snakes.

"There are three venomous snakes indigenous to this region," he said, "and they strike in three completely different ways. The puff adder never flees. He coils like a rock. If you're very still, and you're careful not to step on him, he'll pretty much leave you alone. The black mambo, on the other hand, is lightning-quick. He springs up and strikes you high on the body. If you see a black mambo, it's best to run away."

"Don't worry," said Willie. "I will."

"Either of those can kill you," continued Werner. "But the most deadly by far is the vine snake. Its venom will stop your heart in half an hour."

"How do you get away from that one?" asked Willie.

"Ahh, that's a bit of a problem," replied Werner, "because vine snakes attack by dropping out of tree branches. There's really not too much you can do about it."

The kids began to nervously scan the branches above them. While they were doing that, Werner took a few steps forward and kicked a two-inch scorpion across the dust. The scorpion curled its spiked tail over its head, poised to strike.

"Hey, be careful," yelled Willie. "Scorpions are poisonous."

"I know," said Werner, smiling. "But this little guy doesn't have a big enough stinger to penetrate my boot."

"But what if he did sting you?" asked Willie.

"Ah, well, in that case, I'd walk to that tree over there, sit down, and enjoy my last minutes on earth."

Willie was duly impressed with Werner's bravado, but after that last demonstration, neither he nor Kara would wear sandals until we left Makalali.

All this talk of poisonous creatures brings up an important point. Devi and I are both aware that we took certain risks by bringing our children on an African safari. We tried to ameliorate those risks by learning the rules and following them conscientiously. But the risks were there, nonetheless, and anyone who's thinking of bringing small children on a safari should consider them very carefully. That being said, I would have to characterize our forays into the African bush as the most wondrous, adventurous, and captivating segment of our trip to date. The African wildlife engaged the children's imagination—and intellect—far more than anything they saw in Europe, and their genuine enthusiasm and thirst for knowledge made these safaris far more enjoyable for Devi and me. In fact, I couldn't even imagine coming here without the children. The whole time we would have been saying, "Oh Kara would've loved this" and "Willie would have been amazed by that." So if you asked us, at this point, to name the most thrilling place in the world to take a seven- to twelve-year-old child, I'd have to say nothing beats a wildlife safari. We'd also tell you, by the way, to leave your three-year-old at home.

After three days at Makalali, Walter recovered us at the front gate and drove us back to Jo'burg. At one point, hailstones the size of grapes pelted our van, but eventually we made it back to our Rosebank hotel safe and sound. The next morning, we drove to the airport to catch a flight to Port Elizabeth on South Africa's southern coast. When we arrived at the airport, we were pleased to learn that our Com Air flight was actually on time—a rarity for Africa. That joy was short-lived, though, because what should have been a run-of-the-mill two-hour flight from Johannesburg to Port Elizabeth somehow turned into a ghastly twenty-four-hour voyage of the damned.

The flight began routinely enough, but as we approached Port Elizabeth, we encountered high winds, rocky turbulence, and dense fog. The pilot tried to land, but when we were about a hundred feet above the runway, he pulled up sharply and retracted the landing gear.

"Due to leck of visibility, we cahn't lend at Port Elizabeth at this time," he announced. "So we're going to Bloemfontein to refuel. Then we'll try it again." The passengers issued a collective groan, and Devi and I pulled out a map to see exactly where Bloemfontein was.

Forty-five minutes later, we set down in a sunny farm town in the heart of the Orange Free State. We lolled around the airport lounge while the plane refueled. Then, as we were about to reboard, a Com Air employee announced on the loudspeaker that Port Elizabeth was still socked in, and that we were returning to Johannesburg instead. A dozen frustrated passengers pulled out their cell phones, and we heard the first murmurs of insurrection.

By the time we reached Jo'burg it was three in the afternoon. Four and a half hours into the trip, and we were right back where we started. The gate attendant said we'd take another crack at 3:30, but when 3:30 came and went, she sent us to the cafeteria for a complimentary lunch. When about half the passengers had their food, Com Air suddenly announced that they were reboarding the plane, and that everyone should return to the gate immediately. Those who were lucky enough to have gotten some food shoved it into their mouths as quickly as they could. The rest protested bitterly, but we all scuttled back to the gate like the pathetic lemmings we were. Somehow, we lost two passengers in the process—which meant that every single suitcase had to be pulled off the plane and identified by its owner. This forty-five-minute process was supposed to prevent someone from leaving a bomb on the plane—a plan several passengers were actively considering.

As we settled into our seats for the third time that day, the pilot made another announcement. In America, the cabin crew tend to report delays and problems—no matter how dire—with a flat Chuck Yeager–type calm, but the Com Air pilot made no such concessions to decorum. "We're goin' beck to Port Elizabeth," he said in an irritated tone, "but I'll till you people this. If I cahn't see the runway, I'm not going to lahnd this plen, and I don't care whet anyone has to say about it." The social contract between the passengers and crew was clearly beginning to fray.

The pilot's ultimatum proved prophetic. We flew to Port Elizabeth, and circled the airport several times. Once again, the pilot engaged the landing gear, but just above the runway, he had to pull up and beat another bumpy retreat. "No way I'm going to lend in that fog," the captain announced. "We're going bawck to Bloemfontein."

At that point, several passengers, including the young linguistics professor directly in front of me, became openly mutinous. "Why the hill cahn't we lawnd in East London or George?" he screamed, naming two nearby airports. "This is the most pathitic airline I've ever been on. We could have walked to Port Elizabeth by now."

A frazzled flight attendant rushed over and screamed at him. "The seat belt sign is on! You hahf to sit down...now!"

He did so, grumbling, but then a larger than average Afrikaner—which is to say very large indeed—rose defiantly from his seat and yanked a bottle of cheap brandy from the overhead bin. He stood in the aisle ostentatiously swilling his grog straight from the jar. The flight attendants had the good sense not to challenge him, and after a while he started stumbling up and down the aisles striking up drunken conversations with the other passengers.

I don't know if you've ever heard drunken Afrikaans, but the closest approximation is the Klingon language on *Star Trek*. It gives a whole new meaning to the word "guttural." At one point, this inebriated behemoth stumbled up to Lucas, who was sitting in Devi's lap, and said, "Till your Deddy ah said you hev a beautifil Mommy."

"Tell him yourself," I said from across the aisle.

"Ah shit, ah'm sorry," he said, breathing warm brandy in my face. "Ah didn't mean a thing by it. I really didn't." After that, I had a new best friend.

At 7:00 P.M.—nine hours into the flight—we landed in Bloemfontein for the second time that day. At that point, Devi and I made a good-faith attempt to bail out and drive ourselves to Port Elizabeth. We figured we might have better luck with carjackers and highwaymen than with Com Air. But, unfortunately, there was no way to retrieve our luggage and no rental cars available. So an hour later, we slumped back onto our Sisyphian plane, which for some undisclosed reason returned once again to our point of origin in Johannesburg.

The children, I'm proud to say, comported themselves angelically during the entire prolonged fiasco, and by the end of the day, even two-and-a-half-year-old Lucas knew how to buckle his own seat belt. When we finally stumbled off the plane in Jo'burg, he looked up brightly and said, "That was a really long trip, Mommy."

Devi didn't have the heart to tell him that six flights and twelve hours later, we were exactly where we started.

> We're going nowhere fast,
> David

C h a p t e r   1 8

Subject: The Most Beautiful Place on Earth
Date: November 18
From: daylifers@aol.com (David Cohen)

Mumbai, India

Dear Friends:

After a few fitful hours' sleep at the Johannesburg Airport
Holiday Inn, we staggered back to the gate at 5:00 A.M. and
took one more crack at flying to Port Elizabeth. The third try
was the charm, and nearly twenty-four hours after our first attempt we finally set down in the somewhat unlovely Indian
Ocean port. We rented a van and drove straight out of town
onto the four-hundred-mile coastal road to Cape Town. This
two-lane highway is called the Garden Route—and although
that name conjures up prim country flower patches, it's actually
a wild winding road slung between the mountains and the sea.

Most Americans, when asked to name the most stunning
stretch of coastline in the world, will chauvinistically invoke
Big Sur or the rockbound coast of Maine, but for sheer drama,
neither compares with South Africa's southern coast. Here,
the Tsitsikamma Mountains cast towering shadows over
breathtaking precipices, white beaches, and pristine tidal pools.
Dolphins, sea otters, and sei whales abound, and long stretches

of virgin seashore are unsullied by the hand of man. After seeing rugged Storms River, sweeping Plettenberg Bay, and a stunning four-acre field of blooming lavender, Devi and I concluded that this craggy southern nub of Africa is probably the most magnificent spot on the face of the earth.

About halfway to Cape Town, we wandered off the coast road and drove into a dry grassy valley known as the Little Karoo. This valley has long been the best place in the world to raise ostriches. In the decades prior to World War I, when ostrich feathers were *tout le rage* amongst fashionable European women, the Little Karoo enjoyed a remarkable prosperity, and huge mansions known as "feather palaces" sprung up on the streets of its largest town, Oudtshoorn. When fashions changed, the region slumped, but lately there's been renewed international demand for ostrich leather and lean ostrich meat, so the Little Karoo is experiencing something of a renaissance.

Every pasture on the road to Oudtshoorn was occupied by flocks of gawky six-foot birds. Every restaurant in town featured ostrich salad, ostrich burgers, and ostrich stew, and all the souvenir shops along Hoog Street hawked ostrich-skin wallets, purses, and belts—not to mention huge, decorated ostrich eggs.

Although Oudtshoorn seemed nearly deserted, we had the good fortune to meet a handsome family of commercial ostrich farmers who had three dozen newly hatched chicks in the back of their Land Rover. The father let Kara, Willie, and Lucas pet and cuddle the spotted foot-high birds to their hearts' content. Then we drove out to the Highgate Ostrich Show Farm, where we learned everything we wanted to know, and then some, about ostrich farming. (No, they don't actually stick their heads in the sand.) Kara held an ostrich egg fresh from the nest. Willie stood on top of another egg to demonstrate its strength, and both kids mustered the courage to ride a big skittish bird around an ostrich corral.

When we looped back to the Garden Route, we drove

past pin-neat Dutch colonial farms at the foot of the sweeping Langeberg range and stopped in at the gorgeous coastal villages of Mossel Bay and Hermanos, where pods of dolphins surfed the waves and spouting whales migrated to the west one after another. Few things on earth could command Kara's attention like surfing dolphins. In fact, the scene was so spellbinding that we lost all track of the time. When I finally glanced at my watch, I noticed how late it was.

"Hey, Devi," I said. "Aren't we supposed to be off the road by sunset because of the bandits?"

"Yeah?"

"Well it's close to five now, and we're still more than a hundred kilometers from Cape Town. We better get going."

"We'll get there in time," said Devi. "As long as we don't end up in downtown Cape Town after dark, there's really nothing to worry about."

An hour later, the sun was setting in a blood red sky, and we still weren't anywhere near Cape Town. We had less than a quarter tank of gas left, and it seemed clear that we wouldn't make it to our hotel by nightfall. At that point, the minutes turned into hours, and we clenched our teeth every time a car full of young men passed us. The only precaution we had left to us was to make sure we skirted central Cape Town, and headed straight for our suburban hotel. Needless to say, I managed to lead us off the highway smack into the middle of downtown. By that time, it was completely dark; the streets were nearly deserted; and we had only a limited conception of where we were and how to get to our hotel. At least, the children were asleep.

"We better pull over and look at the map," said Devi.

"Bad idea," I replied. "We already look like complete tourists. If we turn on the light, and spread out the map, we'll attract too much attention."

"So what are we supposed to do?" asked Devi, nervously raking her eyes across the shadowy streets. "Just drive around till we find the hotel by accident?"

"Try to look like you know where you're going," I said, "and leave some room between us and the car in front of us in case we run into carjackers. In the meantime, I'll use this little penlight to look at the map under the dashboard."

That proved difficult, and we wandered the dark streets of central Cape Town for nearly twenty minutes. In those moments, fear begot fear. We recalled every gruesome crime story we'd heard in the last few weeks. Our pulse quickened every time a car pulled up behind us, and we framed every group of men loitering on a street corner as potential carjackers and rapists. Eventually, we stumbled into the residential Sea Point district. There, behind the usual high walls and iron gates, we found our hotel. We identified ourselves to the guard and pulled into the parking lot with a huge sense of relief.

The fact of the matter is we never really knew whether we were in danger or not. Practically everyone we met in South Africa—black and white—told us, in no uncertain terms, to stay out of the city centers at night. For the children's sake, at least, we felt compelled to follow that advice. But no one in central Cape Town actually threatened us in any way. I'm sorry to report that after only two weeks in this country, we've heard so many lurid crime tales that we're nearly as fearful (and race conscious) as the South Africans themselves. Devi says getting lost in a South African city at night was the most frightening aspect of our trip to date. Given our paranoid state of mind, I would tend to agree, but I have no idea whether that paranoia was justified or not.

By now, you're probably sick of hearing about how beautiful the landscape is in South Africa. So just add Cape Town and environs to the list. Towering Table Mountain, lovely Camps Bay, glorious sunsets over the convergence of two oceans, an endless convoy of ships rounding the Cape of Good Hope: the wild, natural Cape itself, the gorgeous eighteenth-century wineries of the Stellenbosch, the tastefully developed Victoria and Alfred Waterfront—the entire area is sublime.

Well, not the entire area. The cultured pulchritude of Cape Town and its pristine white suburbs pose a stark contrast to the squatter camps that line the N2 highway beyond Table Mountain. As we drove out of Cape Town one day on our way to a spectacular country estate,* we passed the black townships of Crossroads and Khayelitsha. These destitute black communities encompass thousands upon thousands of tiny cardboard and corrugated-metal shacks that line the highway for nearly twenty kilometers. The Cape Town guidebooks only mention these neighborhoods in passing, but it would take a great deal of steely determination to ignore them.

"Look at that," I said to Kara and Willie as we drove past the endless succession of pitiful hovels. "Look carefully, and remember how some people have to live in this world."

Kara and Willie did gaze out the window for a while, but after several miles of monotonous squalor, their eyes glazed over, and their minds wandered. When I called their attention back to the slums, Kara said, "Why do we have to keep look-ing at *that*. It's just a buncha run-down shacks."

"Because," I replied, "unless you really see these squatter camps and realize that children your age live there without any electricity, heat, or running water—sometimes without any food—then you'll never understand that most of the world isn't like Marin County. And if you *can* imagine what it's like to live in one of these metal shacks, then you'll be thankful for your blessings, and maybe you'll try to help peo-ple who aren't as lucky as you are."

"I appreciate what I have," Kara said defensively, "and I

*This horse property, called Broadlands, was owned by a wonderful local character named Patricia O'Neill. The Hon. Mrs. O'Neill, legendary for her kindness and generosity, adopts orphaned and injured animals. She practi-cally floored the children when she came to the door with a baby baboon on her hip—wearing diapers!

don't really see what I can do to help all the people who live in those shacks."

"There isn't much you can do now," I replied. "But sometime in the future, you might be able to help—with the way you vote, or the way you give money to charity, or the way you live your life, generally."

Kara looked at me skeptically. "So what do *you* do to help the poor people?"

"Well, we give money to charity, and I volunteer at the food bank, but basically, we could do a lot more. I hope you'll do better when you grow up."

Kara didn't really buy into the whole sermon at that particular moment, and she only showed a passing interest in our subsequent discussion of apartheid. But I don't think that anyone of her impressionable age could see all those brutally poor shantytowns without some lasting effect. I'm glad we didn't leave South Africa without showing Kara and Willie these sprawling slums—even if it was only from the highway. For five months, we've trotted the kids through some of the loveliest places on earth, and it was good for them to finally see the other side of the coin.

As things turned out, it wasn't really necessary to hammer the kids over the head with the South African squatter camps. That's because twenty-four hours later, we'd left Southern Africa behind, flown across the Indian Ocean, and set down in Mumbai, India. Mumbai—formerly known as Bombay—may be the best place on earth to show children the chasm between poverty and wealth. As anyone who's been there will tell you, India doesn't maintain the same serviceable separation of rich and poor we have in the West. And the moment we stepped off the plane, we were thrust into a world where the haves and have-nots lived cheek-by-jowl in pitiless gut-wrenching contrast.

To our complete delight, and totally without warning, Devi's father, Pete, flew all the way from Sardinia to greet us at Mumbai Airport. Being Indian, he wanted to make sure we had a pleasant stay in his native land, and being a proud *bopuji,* he wanted to show off his grandchildren to the Bombay clan. Pete and his gracious brother, Dipu—a longtime Mumbai resident—brought two cars to the airport to pick us up. As we walked through the car park, we enjoyed a wonderful family reunion. In fact, we were so busy catching up, we didn't realize that Kara and Willie were lagging far behind us.

When I finally looked back, I saw Kara dragging her suitcase thirty yards back. Suddenly, she was accosted by a tiny dark-skinned beggar girl dressed in rags. The girl was probably six or seven years old, but she was so small from malnutrition that she looked much younger. On her hip she held her little brother—an emaciated boy of two or three with a dirty face, and open sores. Between them, they couldn't have weighed forty pounds.

The girl held her shriveled brown hand out toward nine-year-old Kara, mutely begging with enormous black eyes. Kara, who's invariably generous, was all alone, and she didn't know what to do. She didn't have any money to give, but she didn't want to ignore the little girl, or turn away. They stood face-to-face for several seconds—two feet and an entire world between them. Still, they seemed to recognize each other as little girls. Finally, Dipu, who undoubtedly sees a thousand beggars a day, walked over and gently shooed the little mendicants away. When we climbed into the car, I was prepared to discuss the incident with Kara, but from the look on her face, I knew anything I said would be superfluous.

More from India in the
next dispatch,
David

Lucas in the lava fields surrounding Costa Rica's Arenal Volcano. Bringing a two-year-old on a three-mile hike up an active volcano wasn't the brightest thing we did on this trip. *(Devyani Kamdar)*

Devi and Kara at the Monteverde Cloud Forest Preserve in Costa Rica. *(David Elliot Cohen)*

Willie was our first mate as we navigated our houseboat through the Burgundy canals. *(Devyani Kamdar)*

Devi and Lucas on the Lido ferry with Venice in the background.
(David Elliot Cohen)

When our trip to Firenze went bust, we assuaged the kids with some Italian *gelato*. As you can see, this ploy worked well with Lucas.
(Devyani Kamdar)

Willie in front of the famous windmills on Mykonos. It was October, and we were practically the only tourists on the island. *(Devyani Kamdar)*

Kara and Willie silhouetted by the fountain in front of Istanbul's Blue Mosque. Funky, romantic Istanbul was one of our best stops.
(David Elliot Cohen)

At the original Olympic stadium in Greece, Willie handily wins our family's version of the Dialous, or 400-meter race, first held on this spot in 724 B.C. *(Devyani Kamdar)*

Kara points out lion tracks at Hwange National Park in Zimbabwe. *(Devyani Kamdar)*

In the bushveldt at the Makalali Game Reserve in South Africa. With so many lions and hyenas around, I wouldn't have looked nearly so brave without the gun and the Land Rover. *(Werner Smith)*

Kara and Willie in front of our tents at Hwange National Park in Zimbabwe. That night a pride of lions killed a buffalo right outside our camp. *(Devyani Kamdar)*

Some of the thirty thousand elephants in Chobe National Park. We didn't have much in the way of a telephoto lens (only 90 mm), so at this point we were pretty close to the wildlife. *(Devyani Kamdar)*

At Makalali, our game guide, Werner Smith, shows the children how dung beetles roll balls of elephant feces into nests. *(David Elliot Cohen)*

On the main street of Oudtshoorn, in South Africa's Little Karoo, we met an ostrich farmer who let Lucas hold some newly hatched chicks.
(Devyani Kamdar)

Professional hunter and game guide Jane Bettenay shows Kara a tortoise at Hwange National Park in Zimbabwe. *(Devyani Kamdar)*

The view from our lodge outside Victoria Falls, Zimbabwe. Those are Cape buffalo in the water hole. *(Devyani Kamdar)*

During most of our journey we stayed in very modest accommodations. But in India, we splurged at Jodhpur's Umaid Bhawan Palace Hotel, ancestral home of the local maharaja. *(David Elliot Cohen)*

The children ride the luggage cart—pulled by a camel—to our tent at the Pushkar camel *mehla* in Rajasthan. *(Devyani Kamdar)*

ABOVE: Kara rides a camel at the Pushkar *mehla* in Rajasthan. Each year during the full moon in the month of Karttika, Thar Desert nomads bring fifty thousand camels to Pushkar to sell and trade. *(David Elliot Cohen)*

LEFT: The fifteenth-century Jain temple at Ranakpur. Its twenty-nine halls are supported by 1,444 intricately carved pillars—no two exactly alike. The yellow dots on the children's foreheads were placed by the head priest. *(Devyani Kamdar)*

ABOVE: The Eyre Highway on Australia's vast Nullarbor Plain. *(David Elliot Cohen)*

RIGHT: Willie with a new friend, one of dozens of tame kangaroos at an animal park in the Margaret River region of Western Australia. Don't try this with a wild kangaroo, by the way. *(Devyani Kamdar)*

A road sign on Australia's Eyre Highway warns motorists to watch for wild camels, wombats, and kangaroos. *(David Elliot Cohen)*

Australia's Nullarbor Plain meets the Great Australia Bight.
(David Elliot Cohen)

As we climbed aboard this raft near Chiang Mai, Thailand, Devi mentioned that a similar raft once fell apart, dumping her into a muddy Thai river.

Lucas was delighted to find an elephant even smaller than he was at Elephant Nature Park near Chiang Mai, Thailand. *(Devyani Kamdar)*

Kara at Ta Prohm temple, one of Cambodia's fabulous Angkor ruins.
(Devyani Kamdar)

After visiting the Buddha caves at Pak Ou, Laos, we returned to our creaky old longboat for the trip back to Luang Prabang.
(David Elliot Cohen)

LEFT: In front of the Taj Mahal in Agra. I look all right here, but I'm actually sick as a dog with some sort of crud I caught at the Pushkar camel festival. *(Beatriz Oliva)*

BOTTOM: Willie poses with some local characters at Yoyogi Park in Tokyo. Most of these kids go to school or work in buttoned-down Japanese offices during the week. But on the weekend, they pursue an active fantasy life. *(David Elliot Cohen)*

Chapter 19

Subject: Another Planet
Date: December 2
From: daylifers@aol.com (David Cohen)

Bangkok, Thailand

Dear Friends:

Our three days in Mumbai were a whirlwind of social calls with some sightseeing on the side. There were aunts, uncles, cousins, and family friends to meet, and these joyous reunions invariably took place over elaborate multicourse meals. Since everyone involved was a member of the strictly vegetarian Jain faith, you might imagine that these repasts were bland. But nothing could be further from the truth. We ate a bewildering array of chickpeas, lentils, mung beans, *naan, chapattis,* and *puris* spiced with cunning combinations of chili, turmeric, mustard seed, fenugreek, cumin, and coriander (to name the few I recognized). These feasts always ended with a sweet dessert and a soothing glass of *masala chai*—tea leaves boiled in milk and flavored with secret family mélanges of clove, cinnamon, pepper, and ginger.

When Devi's father loaded us onto the plane to Udaipur, our foreheads were dotted in blessing. We were well fed and content and only regretted that we'd scheduled such a short stay in Mumbai. We hadn't encountered such gracious hospitality since we left Sardinia two months earlier, and we added Mumbai to the list of places we hoped to revisit soon.

In Udaipur, Devi wanted to stay in the renowned Jagmandir Palace Hotel—the so-called floating palace built in the middle of Lake Pichola. Unfortunately, the hotel was completely booked months in advance, so we settled for a converted hunting lodge called the Shikarbadi. The Shikarbadi, set on the edge of a dry lake, wasn't nearly as luxurious as the Jagmandir Palace (or a Holiday Inn, for that matter), but it did boast excellent riding stables, and spacious grounds abundant with spotted Indian deer and feral pigs. The kids loved this place, and we spent our three days in Udaipur riding horses around the hotel grounds and visiting tourist attractions in town.

Foremost among these was the City Palace—a truly massive agglomeration of royal *mahals* erected by a succession of Rajput maharanas over the course of several centuries. Although the City Palace had obviously seen better days, its faded opulence still evoked the bygone glory of the local kings. We also enjoyed a serene afternoon at the Sahelion-ki-Bari—a luxurious formal garden built for the ladies of the royal court in 1734. The gardens featured life-size marble elephants, graceful pavilions, broad lotus ponds, and a fascinating array of gravity-flow fountains that operated without pumps. But without doubt, the most fascinating thing we did in Udaipur was simply walk the city streets. In Mumbai, Devi's dad whisked us around in private cars, so we didn't get the chance to wrap ourselves in the sensuous fabric of Indian street life. But in Udaipur, we witnessed the kaleidoscopic spectacle at close range. The narrow lanes of the old quarter teemed with mustachioed men in red turbans and women in dazzling Day-Glo saris. Sacred cattle, affectionately decorated for *dewali** with pink and gold polka

---

*The Hindu festival of lights.

dots, wandered the streets, and mangy pigs rooted through noxious garbage heaps. Men urinated on walls; deformed, mutilated beggars vied for our attention (and our change); and all manner of motorbikes, cars, trucks, buses, and rickshaws honked and beeped incessantly as they tried to coerce a path through the milling crowds. All in all, it was an unremitting torrent of exotic sights, sounds, and smells.

On our last day in Udaipur, Devi and I decided we should see the Rajasthani countryside in this same intimate fashion. So we canceled all our air tickets and reorganized our journey from Udaipur to Delhi as a thousand-kilometer drive through the heart of Rajasthan. We couldn't find any one driver who would take us the whole way, but the hotel organized a minibus that would go as far as to Jodhpur, two hundred miles to the north. As we climbed aboard the bus, Devi and I speculated that this road trip would be one of the more adventurous legs of our round-the-world voyage. In that respect, we weren't disappointed.

Our first stop on the road to Delhi was the famous Jain temple in Ranakpur. The roof of this fifteenth-century architectural wonder is supported by 1,444 intricately carved pillars. No two are alike, and they're staggered so that you can always see dozens at a time. Jains don't worship a deity, per se. Instead, they revere twenty-four *tirthamkaras** who set forth the precepts of the faith several thousand years ago. The most important of these precepts is *ahimsa* or nonviolence, and observant Jains take great pains not to injure any life, no matter how seemingly insignificant. In practice, this means most Jains are strict vegetarians. But Jain monks go so far as to sweep the road in front of them so they don't inadvertently step on any mites or other tiny insects as they walk. Jains don't

*Literally "ford-makers."

proselytize, and their faith is rigorous, which is probably why there are only 4 million left in a nation of 900 million people. As Devi's Jain father says, it's a lot easier being Hindu.

Devi urged me to make a contribution toward the upkeep of this magnificent shrine, so I sought out the head priest and gave him the equivalent of about $50 in rupees. He must have considered that a generous gift because, from that point forward, he became our personal guide. The priest blessed our family elaborately, chanting at length and placing yellow dots of paint on our foreheads with a long brown finger. He helped us make a *puja** before a four-faced statue of the *tirthamkara* Adinath. Then he benevolently patted the children on the head and directed us toward the roof of the temple, where there were spectacular views of the nearby Aravalli Mountains.

The roof also held countless domes, parapets, nooks, crannies, towers, and covert little rooms to explore. Willie and I climbed a long stone staircase with no guardrail on either side, opened a door and found ourselves inside a cramped tower chamber that held a serene *tirthamkara* image and a young Scandinavian-looking fellow who was deep in meditation. The young man opened one eye to look at us, and Willie and I quickly retreated.

There was so much to investigate on the roof that we lost track of time, and after a while no one noticed that we were the only ones there. Apparently the rooftop is closed to visitors near the end of the afternoon, and when we tried to get down, we found the only staircase locked off at the top by an iron gate. Since the temple was a place of sacred reflection, we didn't really think it would be appropriate to scream for help. So we waited ten minutes until a monk passed by the foot of the staircase. Then we all whispered "Psst, psst, psst" to attract his attention and held the bars like prisoners to indicate our plight. The monk ran off to find a key, and before long we were liberated. We figured that was our cue to

*An act of propitiation or atoning sacrifice.

leave, so we found our shoes and returned to the minibus, delighted that we could show the children such a glorious manifestation of their Jain heritage.

The drive northwest from Ranakpur to Jodhpur was unforgettable. The narrow blacktop was plied by trucks meticulously decorated with painted murals. Countless herds of goats, sheep, and camels crowded the berm. Painted oxen turned waterwheels and pulled plows as they have for centuries, and women working in the fields wore saris in brilliant shades of red, orange, and fuchsia, forming streaks of luminous color on the dusty landscape. In the smaller roadside villages, everyone looked up from their work and waved as we passed, flashing bright teeth in gentle brown faces.

Indian highways are not for the faint of heart—or even the sane of mind. The road was rarely wide enough for two trucks to pass each other, and the question of which truck would give way was often settled at the last possible moment. While not as outwardly flamboyant as the manic Greek and Turkish drivers we encountered earlier in our trip, the Indian drivers still seemed to get into some truly spectacular auto accidents. In the space of a single day, we saw a bus lying on its side, two trucks knocked right off their axles, and a flipped gasoline tanker. I later read that more than 150 people die in auto accidents in India every day—a staggering number considering fewer than 1 percent of the population own cars. Our Lonely Planet guidebook suggested renting a car and driving ourselves around India, but after viewing the carnage firsthand, I'm glad we didn't try.

We arrived in Jodhpur after sunset, and from the edge of town we could see an immense hilltop edifice illuminated by floodlights. This was the Umaid Bhawan Palace, ancestral home of the local maharaja and our hotel for the next two nights. It took several thousand serfs fourteen years to build the hundred-room palace and its formal gardens, but by the time they finished, India was on the verge of independence, and the thousand-year Rajput regime was breathing its last gasp. As a result, the palace quickly became a costly anachronism and the royal family—like obsolete aristocrats everywhere—were obliged to take in paying guests to make ends meet.

The palace was built on a spectacular scale. The lobby ceilings were at least a hundred feet high, and our room was six times the size of a normal hotel suite. There was a huge indoor pool in a muraled hall, a private cinema, and a garden gazebo the size of a house. The floors of the palace were marble, the ceilings were carved from rare woods, and some of the furniture was actually crafted from solid sterling silver. The service was impeccable, and for two days we lived the life of Rajput royalty—all for the price of an average New York hotel room. Everyone in the family enjoyed the amenities, but Kara, in particular, took to the royal life like a fish to water. Given the chance, I believe she would have settled here permanently.

From Jodhpur, we drove more than a hundred miles east to the holy town of Pushkar. Eleven months of the year Pushkar is a quiet way station on the Hindu pilgrimage trek. But for twelve days in the month of Karttika (October–November), the town attracts nearly a million people. They come for several different reasons. First, Hindu pilgrims gather to bathe in Pushkar Lake, a large pond said to have sprung up miraculously when a lotus fell from the hand of Lord Brahma. At the same time, thousands of desert nomads ride in from the Thar Desert to trade their camels and other livestock. Then tourists like us come from around the world (mostly Europe) to witness the whole vivid spectacle. And finally, merchants, hawkers, and traders of every stripe swoop in to sell their wares to the gathered multitude. The resulting *mehla** is one of the largest, most exotic and colorful festivals on the face of the earth.

---

*Indian religious festival.

We knew we were approaching Pushkar when we saw more and more camels on the narrow road. At first, there were just a few small herds of ten or twelve. But closer to town, the road was choked with hundreds upon hundreds of the loping ten-foot beasts. The children's faces were glued to the windows as our driver tried to blaze a trail through the camel herds.

While a few hundred decorated camels sauntering down the road is undoubtedly a colorful sight, nothing could prepare us for what we found near the edge of town. There, we were amazed to see a three-hundred-acre field of sandy dunes filled with thousands of desert nomads—the men in bright red turbans, the women in colorful saris. And with them—grunting, groaning, gurgling, hauling carts, running, lying down, drinking from troughs, snorting, pissing, and spitting—were more than fifty thousand camels decorated with black spots, stripes, and mysterious signs, tinkling bells, and embroidered harnesses. The children's jaws just dropped, and Lucas, with his beguiling grasp of the obvious, exclaimed, "There are a lot of camels here, Mommy!"

After a wide-eyed survey of the nomad camps, we crossed the road to find our own accommodations. These turned out to be two old saffron-colored tents—numbers K40 and K41—in a gigantic tent village erected by the Rajasthani Tourist Board. Each of these tents held three army field cots made up with grayish sheets and thin well-worn olive blankets. Toilet and bathing facilities were located in a large and rather odoriferous tent, where attendants heated water for the showers in a huge black iron pot over a wood fire.

Just that morning, we'd been living like courtiers in a fairy-tale palace, and now we found ourselves pretty much at the other end of the spectrum. The boys didn't mind the new digs at all, but Kara, who had savored her languid afternoons sipping Cokes on the palace veranda, was manifestly unimpressed by her change of fortune.

"Are we supposed to sleep in here?" she sniffed.

"Think of it as camping," said Devi.

"I don't like camping," said Kara. "I like the palace."

"You'll like this, too," said Devi. "Just give it a chance. Right, David?"

"Absolutely," I said. And Kara shot me one of her "get real" looks.

We ate a passably good vegetarian lunch with several hundred other people in a huge communal dining tent, then we wandered across the road—past dozens of souvenir stands—to the nomad camps. We rambled around the dunes all afternoon, snapping pictures and shooting video until the sun slipped behind Nag Pahar, the Snake Mountain. The lingering sunset shimmered through the dust kicked up by fifty thousand camels, suffusing the field in a dusky golden glow.

I flagged down one of the many camel carts that serve as provisional taxis during the *mehla* and asked the driver—a handsome thirty-year-old man with an enormous handlebar mustache and a rakish red-and-black scarf—to take us on a tour. The driver, whose name was Kelas, sat on the open front edge of the rough cart deftly guiding his camel. Occasionally, he passed the reins to his nine-year-old son, Skaloo, who held them with enormous pride.

We loped rhythmically across the dunes to a nearby road where various amenities were set up for the sojourning nomads. There was a fairground with two decrepit Ferris wheels and a long row of makeshift stalls that sold fancy camel harnesses, rope, textiles, silver jewelry, bootleg music cassettes, homemade candy, and tall burlap sacks full of rice and beans. As we rolled slowly past the crowded stalls, I felt a great vital surge of human activity. Tailors measured nomads for suits. Barbers shaved their customers with straight razors, and Rajasthani women wrapped head-to-toe in gauzy pink and orange saris sifted through equally colorful piles of yellow curry powder and red chili peppers. Above it all, tinny Indian pop music wailed relentlessly from a dozen loudspeakers.

The road eventually led to the town of Pushkar itself. By then, it was dark, and as our camel clopped down the pavement past rows of small houses, we could peer into lighted windows and doorways. In some houses, large families sat in a circle eating dinner on the floor. In others, ten or twelve children crowded around a flickering television set.

We passed through the town and circled to the other side of Lake Pushkar. Kelas reined the camel to a halt at the water's edge, and we all climbed down off the wooden cart. Gazing across the water, I could see a dozen lakeside pavilions decked out with strings of twinkling lights. Each of the pavilions had a set of wide stairs—called a bathing ghat—that led down into the inky lake. On this festival night, the ghats were jammed with thousands of ecstatic chanting pilgrims who were floating countless little oil lamps out onto the lake. These pinpoints of light formed constellations on the surface of the pond, and since it was a starless night, the firmament looked as if it had been turned upside down.

The stirring undertone of the pilgrims blended with the high Indian pop music from the fairgrounds and the distant murmur of a million people gathered on the plains around Pushkar to form a strange, otherworldly din. In fact, everything about this scene—the eerie discord, the shadowy forms, the pungent smells—seemed profoundly alien.

Willie nuzzled against me, shivering in the cold night air, and I picked him up, glad to feel his familiar weight in my arms. Devi came close by, too, and I wondered whether this Indian scene evoked any old, unconscious memories in her, or whether she, too, found it a wholly foreign spectacle.

"Well, Toto," I said with a strained insouciance, "I don't think we're in Kansas anymore."

"No," Devi said, shaking her head in astonishment. "We're as far from home as possible."

On the way back to the tent village, Kelas skirted the town completely and steered the camel cart down deserted paths under a black, moonless sky. After a while I became completely disoriented, and I wondered whether Kelas would ever bring us back to our tents. But in time, we rolled to the edge of a hillock above the camel fields. It seemed like a completely different place at night. The camels were pegged and hobbled and nomads were warming their hands around dozens of campfires scattered randomly across the dunes. As we passed each circle of nomads, I could hear them swapping stories in an unfamiliar tongue.

When we finally bid Kelas and Skaloo good night, Devi, Betty, and I carried the children back to the tents and laid them in their cots. By then it was bitterly cold, and we spread every jacket and sweater we had on top of them. Finally I collapsed into my own astonishingly uncomfortable cot with all my clothes on. As the temperature dropped toward freezing, I clutched the thin old blanket to my breast, grateful for whatever little warmth it could provide.

Unfortunately, it wasn't enough, because the next morning I woke up with a hacking cough. Devi, Betty, and the kids made it through the frigid night and the one that followed without any ill effects, but for me, it was the beginning of a very unpleasant period. As I became progressively sicker, our last four days in India melted into a foggy-headed blur. It was a great shame because during that time we stayed in Jaipur's fabulous Rambagh Palace, ascended to the Amber Fort on elephant back, and toured the sublime Taj Mahal. It's not that I don't remember those things. No one who's ever seen the Taj Mahal—under any circumstances—will ever forget it. It's just that my body shut down a few more defenses with each passing day, and India—already a very foreign place—began to feel completely surreal.

By the time we got to Jaipur, I had a cold, diarrhea, and some sort of skin rash. By Delhi, the cold had transmuted into bronchitis, and I could barely stand up. Finally I retreated to my bed and spent my hours deconstructing Hindi music videos on Indian MTV (an activity best undertaken in a delirious state). When the rest of the family returned from their day of sightseeing, I lay in bed and groaned ostentatiously.

"Do you want me to get you a doctor?" asked Devi, who's well used to my sickbed martyrdoms.

"No need for that," I said with a well-crafted blend of courage and pathos. "Just wheel me onto the plane to Bangkok and I'll make it somehow."

The midnight flight from Delhi to Bangkok took eight hours. That didn't help my bronchitis much, but it gave me time to think about our two weeks in India, and what the children may have learned there. For the most part, India was sort of a shocker—loud, crowded, filthy, bureaucratic, disorganized, prehistorically sexist, and wildly inhumane in its distribution of wealth. The cities were so polluted that it literally made me sick, and even the Taj Mahal—possibly the most glorious edifice ever built—was set next to a stream so putrid that Kara gagged as she walked by. (There was, among other things, a rotting cow carcass in there.)

Nevertheless, I'm glad we came here, and happier still that we brought our children. Even though I dragged my own fat carcass off the subcontinent weak and decimated, I can say with some pride that we managed to get three small children across India without so much as a tummy ache. And while they were there, Kara and Willie had some rare opportunities. They met many of their Indian relatives and learned something about their family history and their Jain heritage firsthand. They also saw in unremitting detail what life is like at the bottom of the heap—a memory that should make it difficult for them ever to take their advantages in life for granted. And they saw true wonders of the world here—the camel *mehla*, the palaces of the maharajas, the Mehrangarh Fort, the markets of Jaipur, the Palace of the Winds, the Amber Fort, the Taj Mahal, even tribal girls dancing in the night with pots of fire balanced on their heads. These are all purely Indian things that will be forever etched on their souls and mine.

Namaste,
David

Chapter 20

Subject: The Middle of Nowhere
Date: January 14
From: daylifers@aol.com (David Cohen)

Ceduna, South Australia

Dear Friends:

Everything's relative, and after two weeks in funky old Rajasthan, Bangkok—with its elevated highways and forty-story office towers—looked every bit the First World city. My body was still wracked by bronchitis and some sort of Indian crud, so as soon as we checked into our hotel room, I slung out the "Do Not Disturb" sign and put myself in quarantine for forty-eight hours. After that, I felt practically human again, but the moment I was back on my feet, Devi and I had to contend with the first serious injury of the trip.

Initially, it didn't seem like much. Kara and Willie were chasing each other around the hotel room, and Willie slammed two of Kara's fingers in a heavy wooden door. Devi and I repeatedly assured Kara—who tends to suffer theatrically—that she'd eventually recover. But the third day after the accident, her fingernails were black and the tips of her fingers were a disturbing shade of green. At that point, I trotted Kara over to the hotel nurse. She took one glance at Kara's fingers and immediately dispatched us to nearby Bumrungrad Hospital.

As Kara and I rode through the muggy, crowded streets of Bangkok toward the hospital, I didn't know what to expect. But the taxi dropped us in front of a large, modern facility that would have looked right at home in any American suburb. Inside, a nurse directed us to a pediatric waiting room decorated in bright primary colors. We filled out a simple form, and ten minutes later we were introduced to Dr. Chiraporn, a prim professional woman in a white coat who spoke English with a cultured accent. Dr. Chiraporn cut the bandages from Kara's fingers and promptly made her diagnosis.

"Abscessed subungual hematomas," she said.

"I told you it was serious," Kara said, vindicated that her injury had such a grave moniker.

"So what do we do?" I asked.

"The fingernails must be removed to relieve the pressure," replied Dr. Chiraporn. "Then she'll need a course of antibiotics."

"They have to cut off my fingernails!" wailed Kara. "Ohh, noo!"

"Is that something you can do, doctor?"

"No, it's a surgical procedure. But, if you like, I can arrange a surgeon here at the hospital."

"I'd really appreciate that," I said, only trying to imagine what sort of bureaucracy we'd face trying to organize an operation in a foreign hospital.

Dr. Chiraporn talked on the telephone for a few minutes, then directed us to the emergency room. "When you get there, ask for Dr. Wongsrisoontorn," she said.

"Could you repeat that?" I said, demonstrating the *ferang*'s* usual lack of facility with the long Thai names.

---

*Thai slang for foreigners, literally Frenchman.

"Wongsrisoontorn," she replied. "Amnauy Wongsrisoontorn. Don't worry. They're expecting you."

Dr. Wongsrisoontorn turned out to be a rather elegant USC Med School grad in his mid-thirties. He confirmed Dr. Chiraporn's diagnosis and said, "I can remove those fingernails now."

"Right now?" I asked, amazed that everything was so easy and efficient here.

"If you like."

Kara was quickly laid on a gurney and wheeled into the operating room. She was utterly terrified, so I stayed by her side, comforting her as the surgeon injected anesthesia into her fingers. When it took effect, the doctor deftly sliced two fingernails off with a scalpel and drained the accumulated blood and pus. It was a gory procedure—painful even to watch. When the surgeon finally wrapped Kara's fingers in gauze, I held her in my arms, and asked if she was all right.

"I told you it was serious," she said, tears running down her cheeks. "I told everyone it was serious, but no one would listen to me."

"You were right, Kara. We should have listened to you," I said, stroking her hair and wiping away her tears. "Are you feeling better now?"

"I guess so," she said, gazing at her bandaged fingers. "But I couldn't even watch while they were doing it. Was it really gross?"

"*Really* gross," I said. "I thought I was going to throw up."

She laughed and said, "Stop it, Daddy."

Of course, our medical insurance wasn't going to cover any of this, so as we walked toward the discharge desk, I wondered how much the whole fandango was going to cost. The cashier called out something vaguely resembling Kara's name, and handed me a bill addressed to "Girl Kara Cohen." It was for 1,927 baht—slightly less than $78—and that was for everything—two consultations, the surgery, anesthesia, nurses, the operating room, supplies, dressings, antibiotics, the works. Any American hospital would have taken three times as long and charged ten times as much to achieve the same result. Obviously, the cost of living is lower in Thailand, but not that much lower.

"Are you sure this is right?" I asked the clerk. "It doesn't seem like it's enough." He looked at me quizzically and reconfirmed the figures. Then he ran my MasterCard and sent us on our way.

Needless to say, I'm sorry that Kara got hurt, and I feel bad that she had to go to the hospital and have a minor operation. But, in one sense, it was good to get this out of the way. Before we left San Francisco, our deepest fear was that one of our children would get sick or injured someplace that was either too remote or too impoverished to provide competent medical care. Those fears may have been justified in Botswana, or India—fortunately we didn't find out—but in Thailand, we received more efficient, more courteous, and far less expensive health care than we could have ever gotten back home in Marin County. I would take my kids back to Bumrungrad Hospital without hesitation—though in the future that might prove inconvenient.

The next day, we flew four hundred miles north to Chiang Mai. I've never been to Chiang Mai before, but Devi spent several weeks here shortly before we were married. That was eleven years ago, back when Chiang Mai was a quaint provincial capital marked by serene Buddhist temples and laid-back handicraft markets. The temples and markets are still here, but now they form little oases in a bustling, polluted city full of hotels, shopping malls, American fast food outlets, and swarms of buzzing *tuk-tuks.** Still, we enjoyed a placid day touring the city's shrines and temples. Devi and I attempted a

*Thailand's ubiquitous three-wheeled taxi.

Thai cookery course, and the whole family enjoyed a nearly perfect day on, of all things, an organized bus tour.

As you know by now, we're not really big on tours—especially really touristy ones like this one was, but it turned out brilliantly. The bus left the hotel in the cool early morning and rolled thirty or forty miles through gorgeous tropical countryside to Elephant Nature Park—a retraining facility for elephants formerly employed by Thailand's logging industry. The park was set beside a muddy stream that ran between acres of rice paddies on one side and some thickly wooded hills on the other. It had ten or twelve trained elephants, some nice bamboo paddocks, and a primitive little reviewing stand where visitors could watch the animals do their tricks. The best thing about Elephant Nature Park, though, was its utter lack of rules and regulations. Obviously unconcerned by lawsuits, the mahouts let Kara, Willie, and Lucas mingle with the pachyderms to their hearts' content. After spending so much time observing African elephants from a respectful distance, they had a wonderful time playing with their domesticated Asian cousins.

There were two baby elephants at the park—playful three-foot-high creatures with stubby little trunks. The kids patted their heads and fed them bananas for more than an hour. I thought Lucas would burst with delight. The mahouts showed the children how to wash elephants in the river with a bucket and brush. Then we took a long elephant trek through miles of brilliant green rice paddies up into the wooded hills. We finished the day with a river trip on a raft consisting of a dozen bamboo poles roughly bound together.

As we gingerly climbed aboard, Devi recalled a similar raft the last time she was in northern Thailand. She told us it broke apart, dumping everyone aboard and all their backpacks into a shallow, muddy river. With that in mind, Devi slapped a pair of water wings on Lucas. (Only a mother would have a deflated pair of water wings in her purse.) Fortunately, that precaution wasn't necessary. The raft stayed intact, and the whole family floated lazily past tiny riverside villages and gorgeous jungle scenery.

I realize that the whole shebang—the elephants, the bamboo raft, the rustic ox carts, and everything else we saw that day—was a setup for tourists, but it was still a memorable day in the splendid Thai countryside and a sweet parting image of Asia.

After a week in Chiang Mai, we flew back to Bangkok airport and boarded a three-thousand-mile flight south to Perth, Western Australia. This gleaming metropolis set on the shores of the Indian Ocean is a long way from anywhere else. It's separated from Australia's East Coast population centers by more than two thousand miles of bleak desert, and the closest major city, Jakarta, Indonesia, is four or five hours by air. Blessed with vast mineral resources, a balmy Mediterranean climate, crystal waters, and miles of clean white beach, Perth's one million inhabitants live their lives in splendid isolation.

Our hosts in Perth were friends of friends named Rick and Bettina Cullen. Both were lawyers with some old family vineyards and a fine wine shop on the side. Rick's family has lived in Perth for generations, and he and Bettina were the best possible people to show us around. The nice thing about visiting people at the far ends of the earth is that they're usually happy to see you. Even so, Rick and Bettina raised Australian hospitality to a rarefied level by foolishly taking all six of us into their oceanfront home, on and off, for three weeks.

I'm not sure I'd want one house guest for three weeks, let alone an entire family, but the Cullens, who had three young children—including a newborn—accepted us with an easy grace. We celebrated Christmas and New Year's Eve with their many friends and close-knit family, and when Devi's brother showed up, they ignored our feeble protests and took him in, too.

It wasn't too hard to get into the W.A.* swing of things. We enjoyed the traditional Christmas morning champagne on Cottesloe Beach. We packed an esky full of stubbies, grabbed our sunnies, and floated out to Rotto for the day.† We strolled through grocery stores barefoot, like almost everyone else in town, went to an outdoor film festival, and showed up for dinner parties bearing the requisite two bottles of wine and two six-packs of beer. ("I hope you're not one of those Americans who doesn't touch the stuff," said one concerned party guest.)

Using Perth as a base, we flew a thousand miles north to the remote pearling town of Broome and south to Eagle Bay, where we enjoyed fine wine and water sports while battling swarms of demon flies intent on burrowing their way into every orifice in our heads. Insects aside, we somehow got used to perfect days on perfect beaches, five-hour lunches at bucolic wineries, body-boarding sweet four-foot ocean curls, and swimming with curious dolphins near the mouth of the Swan River. (You should have seen Kara's face when that happened.)

I hesitate to say this, because word might spread, but Perth's hundred-mile beaches, pristine streets, crystal-clean air, mild weather, cheap rents, and general joie de vivre may combine to make it the most livable city on the face of the earth. (And as the comedian Dame Edna says, it's only thirty hours from anywhere.) As a matter of fact, I wasn't particularly anxious to leave W.A., and if I had my way, we might have rented an oceanside cottage and settled here indefinitely. But Devi convinced me to stick to the original plan, which was to settle in Sydney for a few months in order to get the children some formal schooling. Finally, the sad day

---

*Western Australia, the name of the state that covers the western third of the country.

†Translation from Australian: We packed a coolerful of beer bottles, grabbed our sunglasses, and took a boat out to Rottnest Island for the day.

came when we bought a clunky old Mitsubishi Starwagon and prepared to drive ourselves across the wide Australian desert.

The only road traversing the southern half of Australia is a lonely, two-lane affair called the Eyre Highway. It begins in the small town of Norseman (named after a famous horse who kicked up a gold nugget) and runs 1,500 miles along the Great Australian Bight. Most of this stretch is a wide arid plain called the Nullarbor.* Although the highway has been paved from one end to the other since the mid-1970s, only a tiny percentage of Australians have ever driven it. First of all not that many East Coast Australians (or anyone else for that matter) ever go to Perth, and those who do invariably choose a comfortable five-hour flight over a grueling seven-day drive.

When we told the dozen or so friends and acquaintances we made in Perth that we were preparing to "cross the Nullarbor," as this journey is commonly known, we invariably got one of two reactions. The most common, by far, was, "Why on earth would you want to do that?" The other was a macho account of the listener's own Nullarbor passage.

"Ah, yeah," said one fellow. "The time I drove 'cross the Nullarbor, it was so hot, the birds were falling dead by the side of the road."

"I made it 'cross the Nullarbor in a beat-up old ute"† said the mechanic who inspected our van. "It had four bald tires and a bad carbo‡—and that was before the road was even paved. Miracle I made it."

Despite these colorful tales, we followed our usual MO of taking all reasonable precautions—but going nonetheless. We

---

*Latin for "no trees."
†A pickup truck, short for utility vehicle.
‡Carburetor.

loaded ten-gallon cans of water and gasoline into the back of the van along with an extra fan belt, four quarts of motor oil, flashlights, flares, jumper cables, and a spare tire. Then we bid a fond farewell to the incredibly hospitable Cullens and drove east into Australia's empty heart.

It was an extraordinary seven-day journey. We didn't hit the desert right away. Initially, the cool southwestern landscape was marked by picturesque coastal towns and towering old gum trees called karris and jarrahs. After that, we whisked past mile after mile of yellow wheat fields where literally hundreds of pink and gray parrots stood by the shoulder of the road and took flight, one after another, as the van approached. Further on, there were expansive sheep ranches that gradually gave way to scrubland, unsuitable even for grazing. The scrub eventually got shorter and sparser until there was only a level plain in dusty tones of gray and lilac beneath an immense ultrablue sky.

At that point, there were practically no hills or curves in the road, and the black line of the highway ran endlessly to the horizon. In the dead center of the Nullarbor it was nearly impossible to drive for more than an hour at a time. With no trees, telephone poles, road signs, or even any large rocks to break the monotony, my eyes were inexorably drawn to the white dashes that ran down the middle of the road. These had a strong hypnotic effect, and even though it was the middle of a sunny day and I wasn't particularly tired, I inevitably fell into a daze. At that point, there was nothing to do but pull over, slide out of the van, and switch drivers.

And those were the magic moments—when we all piled out of the van and stood by the side of the road in the vacant heart of the Nullarbor. The lucent air and crisp, white light made the landscape look like a hyperrealist painting. The wind blew from west to east rustling the low gray spinifex and hardy blue bush as it went. And wisps of cloud, borne on the wind, cast mercurial shadows that flew down the road one after another.

There was no other living soul for twenty miles, and nothing aside from the highway itself to suggest that anyone else had ever been here.

"Well," I said to Devi, putting an arm around her shoulders, "this has got to be the middle of nowhere."

> Best wishes for a joyful
> new year,
> David

Chapter 21

Subject: Heads or Tails
Date: June 8
From: daylifers@aol.com (David Cohen)

Sydney, Australia

Dear Friends:

I can't believe it's been five months since my last message. I apologize for the long hiatus, but time has flown since we settled into reasonably normal, everyday urban life here in Sydney. My last dispatch trailed off in a very obscure place: the middle of Australia's 1,500-mile Nullarbor Plain. Everyone should drive across the Nullarbor once in their life just to experience its pure desolate beauty. Once is enough, though. Not only is the highway monotonous to the point of hallucination, but the facilities along the way are basic, to say the least. Our map promised a little town with a colorful name like Balladonia or Cocklebiddy every 200 kilometers or so. Somehow I pictured these places as frontier settlements with quaint pubs and general stores, but they all turned out to be nothing more than cinder block compounds with a few gas pumps, a dingy diner, and a primitive ten-room motel. The only "inhabitants" of these towns were employees ferried in by van to work two-week shifts.

You wouldn't patronize these places by choice, but of course, there was no choice. You could either eat, drink, and fill your tank in these godforsaken way stations or perish by the side of the road. The food made McDonald's look like *cordon bleu,* and the service was amusing even by Australia's lax standards. Once a very pleasant young waitress completely screwed up our order despite the fact we were her only customers. By way of excuse, she said, "Awww, Ah'm really sorry, but Ah haven't gotten much sleep laitely."

"Why's that?" I asked, thinking maybe a pack of obstreperous dingoes had been baying outside her window all night.

With no hint of irony, she replied, "Ah, there's just been too many pahties to go to."

Now, remember, there weren't more than a dozen living souls within a hundred-mile radius. So either she had a Bell Ranger helicopter parked out back, or the local social scene consisted of a very small crowd mustered around a very large keg. I suspect it was the latter, but you do have to admire the Aussie instinct for revelry, which flourishes even in this unbearing wasteland.

Anyway, it was with some sense of accomplishment that we crossed the Nullarbor (hey, we got the bumper sticker) and rejoined civilization on South Australia's Eyre Peninsula. We sampled Ceduna's famous plump oysters, toured Port Augusta, and discovered a large lake full of bright pink water— apparently due to some sort of algae infestation. I guess the locals had grown used to this phenomenon, because when I asked a waitress if the lake was always so pink, she replied, rather indifferently, "Naw, sometimes it's orange."

We arrived in Sydney—surely one of the fairest cities on earth— on a bright, summery January morning. We knew we were going to settle here for a while because it had now become imperative to get Kara and Willie some proper schooling. Before we left home, Devi and I were fully confident that we could home-school our children on the road. It didn't even occur to us that we'd fail in this area—but fail we did, and dismally. First of all, Kara and Willie were endlessly creative in weaseling out of their lessons. The slightest excuse—a knock on the door, a bug on the ceiling, a piece of lint on the carpet—and off they went. Even when we did manage to focus their attention, albeit briefly, on math or phonics, Devi and I simply didn't have the patience to do the job right. I don't know how the many people who home-school their children manage it, but the third time I stopped just short of calling one of the children an idiot, I knew in my heart of hearts that real schools and professional teachers existed for a reason. We decided that we didn't want to ruin our once-in-a-lifetime trip with two hours of pure hell each day, so we packed up the books and resolved to put the kids in school for three or four months when we got to Sydney.

With the help of some old publishing friends we found a well-regarded public school and a furnished sublet nearby.* We even found a cute nursery called Little Branches for Lucas, and one day, Devi and I faced the bittersweet moment when our last little cub toddled off to school. Lucas wore a parti-colored surfer hat and carried his blankie and stuffed bear in a yellow "Bananas in Pajamas"† backpack he got for Christmas in Perth. After spending twenty-four hours a day with his family for eight months straight, Lucas looked slightly stunned when we abandoned him amid the blocks and finger paints. Fortunately he didn't cry—which is more than I can say for Devi.

Kara and Willie were also stunned by their new school, but for different reasons. After eight months of freedom, they were suddenly dropped into a no-nonsense regime where

---

*Tourists can enroll their children in Australian public schools, free of charge, for up to three months. We stretched it to four and no one seemed to mind.
†Stars of Australian children's television.

discipline was a serious matter and lessons were imparted with a firm hand. To make matters worse, they had to wear admittedly nerdy yellow and blue uniforms.

"No way I'm wearing that," announced Kara, when she saw her new blue culottes and sun hat.

"You better take that up with the school," I replied, delighted that someone else was laying down the law for a change. And lay down the law they did. In Australia, the school year starts in early February, and the opening assembly for new children and their parents was a real eye-opener. Back home in Marin, educators spend a lot of time talking about "nurturing our children" and "giving kids freedom to be creative," but in Sydney, a stern headmistress stood under an equally stern portrait of Queen Elizabeth and set her young charges straight.

"When I get up in the morning," she declared, "I groom myself carefully and put on clean, neat clothing. This is my uniform, and it indicates my intention to work. You, too, will wear clean, neat uniforms. You will bring your assignments and textbooks to class every day without fail, and you will mind your teachers to the letter."

She even made me a little nervous, but this boot-camp approach worked particularly well for Willie, who had slumped back into functional illiteracy during his long sabbatical. And guess what? After only a few months at North Sydney Demonstration School, our previously shy Kara was self-assured enough to emcee a school assembly. Of course her confidence was bolstered when everyone kept telling her how cute her accent was. Still, it was amazing to watch her lead the entire school in the singing of the Australian national anthem!

The Dem School, as it was called by the relentlessly abbreviating Australians, also offered an after-hours sex-education class. So one evening Devi and I bit the bullet and finally trundled Kara and Willie off to learn about the birds and the bees. At one point, the teacher asked several people to stand up and hold large signs bearing the names of various sexual organs on them so the kids could differentiate the male and female components. Since I was so obviously embarrassed by the whole discussion, she naturally chose me to be a sign-bearer. "Would you mind being the scrotum?" she asked politely. Now, what could I say to that? Still I defy any one of you to stand before a group of thirty people—including your spouse and children—and maintain any semblance of dignity while holding a huge sign with the word "SCROTUM" scrawled across it.

Anyway, Kara and Willie seemed to be completely nonchalant—practically uninterested in the whole grand revelation. They didn't ask one question on the way home, and when we questioned them about what they learned, they answered monosyllabically. Still, I think they got the big picture, and I only pray that the image of their father standing in front of a large group of people with the word "SCROTUM" brandished across his chest doesn't linger.

One day, on the way home from Sydney's wholesale fish market, I struck up a conversation with our cab driver, a recent émigré from Poland. "How do you like living in Sydney?" I asked.

"Everyone here is very happy," replied the cabbie in heavily accented English, "and if they're not, they're stupid."

That summed it up for us as well. We found Sydney to be a clean, civilized city ensconced in a gorgeous natural setting with wonderful restaurants and shops, superb beaches, and dozens of distinctive neighborhoods. The surrounding countryside also had its share of attractions. When visitors like my parents or Devi's mother showed up for a few weeks, we toured the rugged Blue Mountains, Hunter Valley wineries, and the posh horse farms around Scone. We even flew up to Port Douglas for some unforgettable scuba-diving amidst the delicate coral formations and fabulous Day-Glo fish of the Great Barrier Reef.

It was on one of these expeditions, and a rather routine one at that, where we faced the most terrifying ordeal of our entire round-the-world trip. After all the outlandish places we've been, you wouldn't think we'd court trouble in homey old Oz. But I suppose that was just it. In Africa and India, Devi and I were constantly on alert—always checking and double-checking that the kids were safe. But in Australia, everything seemed so familiar, I guess I let my guard down.

It all began pleasantly enough. The kids were on Easter break, and a friend of mine from Melbourne graciously offered us the use of her family's oceanfront condo in Surfer's Paradise—a resort town on Queensland's sunny Gold Coast. It was too good an invitation to pass up, so the whole family, including Devi's mom, piled into our old Mitsubishi Starwagon and drove five hundred miles north.

When we got to Surfer's Paradise—the Miami Beach of Australia—we found it mobbed with tens of thousands of auto racing fans who had come to see an Indy Car race that was run through the streets of the city. Most of these people were far more interested in the big race and the bacchanalian street parties surrounding it than they were in the sand and the surf. So on the windy, overcast morning when Kara and I went out to ride the waves, we had the beach entirely to ourselves.

I'd already taken the fearless Willie out body-boarding several times, but Kara was far more cautious, and it wasn't until our third day at Surfer's that she worked up the nerve. That morning, she surprised me over breakfast by saying, "You always take Willie out boogie-boarding. Today, I want you to take me out—just us."

"Are you sure?" I asked, glancing out the window at the choppy gray ocean. "It looks a lot windier than it was yesterday."

"I'm sure," Kara said confidently. "Let's go."

Our first few rides, close to the beach, went pretty well. So after a while I took Kara out past the sandbar where we could catch some decent waves. When the first set rolled in, I said, "Okay, Kara, get ready. We'll jump on the next big one."

"Okay," she said, shivering on her board. "I'm ready."

When the wave closed in, I kicked hard with my flippers and caught it right in the curl. I rode the foam all the way back to the beach, and when I rolled up on the sand I looked around to see how Kara had fared. But she wasn't there. In fact, she hadn't caught the wave at all, and she was still bobbing around on her board out by the sandbar. That happened a few times with Willie, so I figured it was no big deal, but then I noticed that Kara wasn't where I left her. She was about a hundred yards downwind and a good deal further out to sea. Furthermore, she seemed to be drifting away from the beach at a 45-degree angle. Kara was obviously caught in some sort of current or riptide, but she didn't know it. She was just lying on her board waiting for me to come out and get her. Unfortunately that was beginning to look difficult because Kara was gathering speed rapidly.

I grabbed my board and stumbled clumsily through the shallow water in my flippers. Then I worked my way out through the breakers. I used to swim competitively as a kid, and I was kicking as hard as I could, but even with my flippers on I couldn't seem to close the distance. After five minutes, my thigh muscles began to burn, and I was gasping for breath. By that point Kara had drifted a quarter mile down the beach, and was further than ever from shore.

"Damn," I thought. "This isn't fooling around anymore."

I glanced back at the beach to see if there was anyone who could help us, but there wasn't another soul on the sand. At that moment, I realized that Kara could easily be washed out to sea.

"Okay. That's it," I said to myself. "I'll be damned if I'm going to lose her this way." I put my head down and kicked with everything I had.

I don't know if I ever mentioned this, but Kara was born with a congenital birth defect. When she was two months old, a pediatrician held a stethoscope to her little chest and heard a telltale whooshing sound. It was blood rushing through a hole between the chambers of her heart—what they call an atrial septal defect. The doctors said they could fix this anomaly with "garden variety" heart surgery, but even the garden variety involved sawing through Kara's breastbone, stopping her heart, and sewing up the hole.

There are so many harrowing moments when your child needs a serious operation—the body blow when you first hear the diagnosis, the cruel practice of informed consent, the long hours in the waiting room—but for me, the most difficult part of the process, the part I'll remember for the rest of my life, came just before surgery. That's when Devi and I carried our baby into the scrub room adjacent to the operating theater. There were seven or eight doctors and nurses there, washing up and milling around. Suddenly, one of the nurses walked up to me and tried to take Kara from my arms.

"Wait. Just one minute," I said, a little too loudly, and I began to choke up. Then Devi, who was pregnant with Willie at the time, said, "Look, if you're not going to hold it together, neither can I." I swallowed hard and handed Kara, kicking and thrashing, over to the nurse. That was the single worst moment in my life.

Four hours later, Kara was wheeled out of the operating room. She was unconscious and ghostly pale with tubes and electrodes running all over her body and a red-stained patch of gauze over her heart. She looked so tiny and frail. In the end, though, she was fine. Everything went smoothly. Her heart was stitched up like new, and her only souvenir from the whole affair was the zipper scar that runs down her chest.

Now, eight and a half years later, my baby was in danger again. I felt a wild surge of adrenaline and kicked like a maniac. I could close some of the distance while I was kicking hard, but if I let up even for a second Kara slipped further away. So I kicked without relief, and when I thought I couldn't go another inch, I found the same current that Kara was in and closed the last hundred meters. I caught her board breathlessly.

"Hi, Daddy," Kara said casually. "What took you so long? I've been out here for ten minutes." She still had no concept she was in danger, and I figured there was no use telling her.

"Listen, honey," I said as calmly as possible. "We've drifted pretty far from shore."

"Oh, yeah. We have," she said, looking up.

"Do me a favor. Put your board on top of mine. Jump up, and I'll swim us in."

"Okay," she said. "I want to go in anyway. I'm getting cold."

At least I knew enough not to fight the current. I kicked parallel to the beach at an easy pace until we finally slipped out of the current. Then I headed toward the beach at an angle so I wouldn't have to fight the wind. It took an unbearably long time, but eventually we made it back to the beach. When I finally felt sand under my feet, the adrenaline receded. My legs wobbled and I could barely stand up. The waves kept knocking me over.

"These damned flippers," I said to Kara. "I can't walk through the surf with these things on." I stopped and pulled one of the flippers off, and then it struck me. I didn't usually wear both flippers for just this reason. It was too hard slogging through the shallow water. I usually wore one flipper when I body-boarded like the Hawaiian kids do, so I could swim *and* walk.

But today, for some reason, I put both flippers on, and because of that insignificant twist of fate, I was able to kick hard enough to catch Kara and pluck her from the current. Isn't it funny what the course of your life turns on? A crummy $20 piece of rubber. Wear it. Don't wear it. Save your kid or lose her. Heads or tails. It tends to make you value every moment.

Best wishes from Down Under,
David

Chapter 22

Subject: Land Mines and Temples
Date: June 16
From: daylifers@aol.com (David Cohen)

Phnom Penh, Cambodia

Dear Friends:

The most disturbing aspect of the whole Surfer's Paradise incident was the fact I endangered Kara's life in the first place. But beyond that, what bothered me most was how insidious it was. One moment Kara was happily bobbing in the surf. The next moment, she was heading out to sea. I didn't expect dramatic music or a guy in black robes with a sickle, but the line between a happy day at the beach and profound tragedy was so fine that Kara never even knew she was in danger.

Anyway, after that I had infinitely more respect for ocean currents and riptides, and whenever we went to the beach I watched the kids like a hawk. Of course, the moment I mastered that particular facet of child safety, Willie decided to leap recklessly down a flight of stairs and break his ankle. That gave me an opportunity to survey various aspects of the Australian medical system (radiology, orthopedics, and physical therapy), and once again, I was amazed how much cheaper and more efficient health care is overseas than it is in America.

By the time Willie was off his crutches, we were obliged to consider our next move. It was hard to believe, but we'd been in Australia for nearly six months. Our visas were about to expire and the school term was winding down, so we had to decide whether to renew our visas and settle in Sydney for the rest of the year, prolong our world tour, or just go home—wherever that was.

The answer came to me one day while I was watching the news. There was a report from the small, enigmatic nation of Laos—a country that was closed to foreigners from 1975 until the early 1990s. Because of its seclusion, Laos still retained many of the fabled charms of old Indochina, and I wanted to see it before its inevitable modernization.

"What would you think about stopping in Laos for a few weeks on the way home?" I asked Devi.

"Sure," she replied with a shrug. "But why Laos?"

"I saw something on television, and it looked like a wonderful old-fashioned place."

"Okay," Devi said. Then she instantly added, "But if we're going to Laos, we should go to Cambodia, too."

Uh-oh. This was the type of reckless badinage that kicked off the whole round-the-world adventure in the first place. Furthermore, Devi's lightning-quick reply suggested that she'd been plotting a Cambodia expedition for some time.

"Why do you want to go to Cambodia?" I asked.

"To see Angkor Wat," she said, referring to the famed twelfth-century Khmer ruins. "It's supposed to be one of the wonders of the world."

"Isn't there some sort of factional warfare going on in Cambodia?" I asked. "Something to do with the Khmer Rouge?"

"No, it's pretty stable now, and the tourist areas are supposed to be safe."

"Are you sure, Devi?"

"Yeah. There are only a handful of Khmer Rouge guerrillas left, and they're hiding out in the jungle somewhere. It's really not a problem."

"I also read something about land mines."

"That's true," Devi replied. "There are land mines everywhere in Cambodia, but I've looked into it, and as long as we keep to well-traveled roads and paths, there's nothing to worry about."

"And there's no fighting going on there?"

"Not where we're going. I checked."

Three weeks later, we found ourselves standing on the blazing hot tarmac of Pochenteng International Airport in Phnom Penh, Cambodia. Devi's father—who zips around the world the same way other people go to the corner store—decided to join us for the Cambodian adventure. We were happy to see him, and since Betty had returned to America shortly after we arrived in Sydney, we were also glad to have some help with the kids.

As we walked through the airport, I couldn't help noticing that there were very few tourists around. In fact, there were so few visitors in Phnom Penh that we paid almost nothing to stay in a brand-new Intercontinental Hotel, and we had the place practically to ourselves.

Phnom Penh itself was a real eye-opener. The streets and markets were bustling despite the 100-degree heat, but vestiges of Cambodia's troubled past were everywhere. After all, it's been fewer than twenty years since the Khmer Rouge marched into town, annihilated any citizen who had any education whatsoever, and exiled everyone else to the countryside. That massive dislocation and the resulting famine caused at least one million deaths—roughly the entire present population of the city. Needless to say, Phnom Penh hasn't recovered from the holocaust.

Devi and I discussed whether we should take Kara and Willie to see the infamous "killing fields" of Choeung Ek or the Tuol Sleng School where tens of thousands of ordinary

Cambodians were tortured and killed. Initially, I was all for it. I thought it might be a good object lesson about "man's inhumanity to man." But Devi convinced me, rightly I think, that the children were too young to understand what happened here and that showing them a pile of eight thousand skulls wouldn't serve any purpose beyond horrifying them.

Besides, we didn't really need to seek out the horrors of war. They were all around us. When we took a taxi to Phnom Penh's huge Central Market, all of its entrances were staked out by ragtag bands of twenty or thirty maimed war veterans. Most of them still wore old army shirts, and every one of them was missing at least part of one limb. As we tried to push the children inside, they swarmed around us, begging, smiling with crooked betel-black teeth and holding their smooth stumps up for inspection. It was a ghastly, *Night of the Living Dead* experience.

It wasn't only war veterans who were maimed either. It seemed as if one out of every twenty or so men, women, and children in Phnom Penh had at least one of their hands or feet blown off by land mines. There were amputees in every shop and on every street corner. Devi wanted to do something aside from handing out a few hundred riels here and there, so we decided to buy all our homecoming gifts at a handicraft center that rehabilitated mine victims.

When we finally found the little shop and walked inside, there was only one salesgirl sitting behind the counter. She was a strikingly beautiful girl of fifteen or sixteen with refined features, a lithe, willowy body, and lustrous black hair that hung halfway down her back. When Devi asked her how much a particular purse cost, she grabbed a crutch and hobbled out from behind the counter. She wore a long Cambodian skirt in a gorgeous shade of purple. Beneath the embroidered hem she had only one foot. I don't know why, after all the dismembered people I'd seen that day, this particular girl struck me so poignantly. It was probably her tender age and delicate beauty and the fact that my own daughter was standing nearby. Maybe it was just the cumulative effect of seeing so many desperately poor, brutally maimed children all in one day. Whatever it was, I had to step outside to regain my composure.

We stayed in Phnom Penh long enough to see the city's main attractions, then we flew to Siem Riep, gateway to the vast Angkor ruins. Siem Riep is only a hundred miles from Phnom Penh, but land mines, marauding highwaymen, and roving bands of guerrillas made it far too perilous to travel by road. Our guide to Angkor, recommended by the hotel, was a polite young fellow named Kim Huch. Huch* knew the vast ruined city of Angkor like the back of his hand—particularly where the minefields were. Our first morning in Angkor, we were all walking toward the colossal Bayon Temple, when Huch approached me with a look of great discretion. He pointed toward Lucas, who was sitting in his travel stroller, and said, "What's wrong with the little boy?"

"What do you mean?" I asked.

"What's wrong with his legs?"

It took me a second to figure it out, but then I realized that Huch had never seen a stroller before, and in a desperately poor country where thousands of children are crippled by land mines every year, he naturally assumed it must be some sort of wheelchair. When I told him that Lucas could walk perfectly well and that most able-bodied American three-year-olds were pushed around in strollers, he just shook his head in amazement.

*As in many Asian countries, Cambodian family names come first, given names second.

Bayon Temple was an immense agglomeration of fifty gray stone towers set in a wide forest clearing. Its walls were adorned with nearly two hundred huge moon-faced heads of the Hindu god Avalokitesvara. Built near the end of the twelfth century, when the Khmer empire was at the zenith of its power, Bayon's narrow staircases, tumble-down passages, and countless secret rooms make it a wonderful place for children to explore. In one small chamber near the heart of the temple, the kids stumbled upon a tiny, wizened old woman with a shaved head and black betel-stained teeth. This old soul, who was only slightly taller than nine-year-old Kara, squatted in the shadows all day, tending a modest Buddha shrine and peddling incense sticks to any visitors who happened by.

Needless to say, all three kids immediately wanted to fire up some incense, so I obliged them with a small donation. The tiny guardian of the shrine helped each child light a stick and make something approximating a proper oblation before the Buddha image. Her gnarled, veiny old hands formed Lucas's chubby fingers into the traditional Buddhist prayer position. Then Lucas bowed and placed the incense stick at the base of the statue. When he toddled out of the shrine room, I asked him, "What were you doing in there?"

"I gave a stick to the Doo-dah," he said with a beatific smile.

"Why did you do that?" I asked.

"Because it makes him happy."

After Bayon, we visited Ta Prohm, the "jungle temple." To get there, we had to trek half a mile or so through dense tropical foliage. Here, we were walking in the footsteps of the nineteenth-century explorer Henri Mouhot, the first Westerner ever to set eyes on the fabulous Angkor ruins. I imagined the thrill Mouhot must have felt when he reached the end of this very path, pushed aside the extravagant jungle foliage, and saw before him a magnificent ruined temple with low square stupas, long graceful colonnades, and countless friezes depicting a pantheon of Hindu gods, demigods, and demons. Then as now, the temple structures were intertwined, heaved up, and rent asunder by roots and vines as thick as a man. Fifty-foot strangler figs grew up from the rooftops, their stout roots clutching the delicately carved temple walls like giant squids. Tropical weeds and epiphytes grew from every crack in the stonework, making Ta Prohm a particularly gorgeous symbiosis of art and nature.

For some reason—probably to prevent looting—we were escorted about the premises by a silent Cambodian soldier. He roused himself lazily from a hammock when we first arrived and followed us around halfheartedly until he satisfied himself that we were harmless. Other than him, though, we were all alone in the jungle temple, and this added to our sense of adventure. We spent several happy hours exploring the ruins while Devi's father deciphered the ancient Hindu legends set forth in the intricately carved tableaux.

In the late afternoon, we moved on to Angkor Wat itself. Constructed eight hundred years ago as a vast funerary temple, Angkor Wat is surely one of mankind's most formidable architectural accomplishments—on a par with Egypt's pyramids and the Taj Mahal.* Its sheer scale is dumbfounding. We approached the outer ramparts on a wide stone causeway spanning a two-hundred-foot moat. This is undoubtedly one of the world's most dramatic entrances, but it was only a prelude to the colossal courtyard inside. This enclosure, the size of several football fields, was spanned by an elevated stone promenade that led to the huge central temple. I don't know exactly how long the promenade was, but it took the kids more than five minutes to run full bore from one end to the other.

The central temple's most dramatic feature is a long colonnade encompassing its entire perimeter. The interior wall

---

*Also funerary structures.

of this colonnade is covered with a bas-relief depicting battle scenes, processions, gods, demons, and *nagas** from the *Ramayana* and other Hindu epics. The frieze, which covers all four walls of the central temple, is several hundred meters long, and I can only imagine how many artisans spent their lives carving it.

Angkor Wat had no barriers or signs and only a few uninterested guards, so we could pretty much wander around at will. We rambled down long porticoes once reserved for the royal priests of Shiva, and clambered up a perilously steep and crumbling staircase to the top of a decrepit pagoda. From there we could gaze out over Angkor Wat's courtyards across a perfectly flat landscape of green fields and palm trees studded with ruined towers, man-made holy mountains, and tumble-down temples. Far below, children played hide-and-seek and peddled antique bicycles amid the ruins. Peasant women scrubbed their laundry in the old imperial moat, and cattle grazed and lowed among some of the world's greatest architectural treasures.

It was hard to imagine now, but eight hundred years ago the very pagoda where we stood marked the spiritual and political epicenter of a rich and powerful empire that stretched more than a thousand miles from the South China Sea to the Bay of Bengal. Now it presided over miles of scattered ruins, some rocky cow pastures, and a few impoverished villages. I couldn't help thinking of Shelley's poem "Ozymandias," and without realizing it, I said aloud,

> "My name is Ozymandias, king of kings:
> Look on my works, ye Mighty, and despair!"

Kara looked at me like I was nuts, and said, "What are you talking about, Daddy?"

"Oh, it's just an old poem about a king who thought he

---

*Mythical snakes.

was the most powerful man in the world. In the end, though, all that was left was a broken statue with an inscription saying how great he was. Everything else was covered in sand. It's sort of like the Khmer king, Suryavarman II, who built Angkor Wat. He thought he was a god and that people would come to pay homage to him until the end of time."

"We came here all the way from California to see his temple," observed Kara, "and he probably never even heard of California."

"I suppose you're right," I said. "Maybe in the end, things worked out better for Suryavarman than they did for Ozymandias."

Kara took my hand and nodded sagely. "You need a different poem," she said, keeping me honest as usual.

Best Wishes,
David

C h a p t e r *2 3*

Subject: The Lesson of the Buddha Cave
Date: June 28
From: daylifers@aol.com (David Cohen)

Luang Prabang, Laos

Dear Friends:

After two witheringly hot days in Siem Riep, we flew back to Phnom Penh. We had a quick lunch in town, then zipped back to the airport to say good-bye to Devi's father and catch our own plane to Vientiane in Laos. The check-in line was long and excruciatingly slow, and eventually I struck up a conversation with a slight blond fellow in his thirties who was standing behind me. He was some sort of aid worker, originally from Wales, and I asked him if he lived in Phnom Penh.

"I live here," he said, "but my family is staying in Vientiane."

"Why's that?" I asked.

"Oh with things the way they are here, I thought it might be best to get them out of harm's way for a while."

That didn't sound too good, but since we were leaving anyway, and he assumed I knew what he was talking about, I didn't pursue the matter. But then I ran into another American family who'd just arrived in Phnom Penh. We'd only been comparing notes for a few minutes when their guide approached with a very somber look on her face. I excused myself quickly, but they seemed to be deciding whether they should go into town or just return to Bangkok.

Finally, by the gate, I met another American man. He looked like a cop on vacation, but he turned out to be a U.S. military officer.

"This is one crazy country," he said, making conversation. He apparently thought I lived in Phnom Penh.

"Why's that?" I asked.

"Oh, I've been flyin' around in a Cambodian army helicopter with my buddy over there, and those guys didn't have the slightest idea where they were goin'. All they had was a road map like you'd get from the AAA or something. And I'll tell you what. They got completely lost. They put us down in some little podunk village, and flew off to get directions. No kiddin'. I thought they were going to leave us there."

I thought it might be indiscreet to ask what American military officers were doing flying around in Cambodian army helicopters. Anyway, at that point, Kara and Willie ran up and asked me for some money.

The soldier looked at them somewhat confused and said, "You here with your kids?"

"Yeah," I replied. "We came up from Australia last week."

"What are you doing here?"

"We're tourists. We came to see Angkor Wat."

He stared at me as if I were insane, and said, "You plannin' on leaving now?"

"Yeah, we're going up to Vientiane for a while."

"Good thinkin'," he said. Then he walked off to tell his buddy about the lunatic he just met.

Less than twenty-four hours later, I was watching CNN in our hotel room in Vientiane, and sure enough, there was breaking news from Phnom Penh. The Khmer Rouge had deposed its leader, the infamous Pol Pot, and had defected to one of the two major government factions. That, in turn, upset the delicate balance of power between Cambodia's two co-premiers, and they settled their differences in the usual way—with rocket attacks and gun battles in the streets of the capital.

"Hey, you better come see this," I said to Devi. "It looks like all hell's broken loose in Phnom Penh."

Devi watched the screen for a while with a concerned expression and said, "Well, so much for Phnom Penh being safe. At least we got out in time, and it doesn't look like anyone blasted the Intercontinental."

Those fine distinctions were lost on my mother, who didn't know precisely when we were pulling out of Cambodia. I thought she might have seen the news reports, so I called her as soon as I could.

When I got through to Pittsburgh, I said, "Hi, Mom. I just wanted to let you know we're safe and sound in Laos."

"Oh, David, you're going to give me a heart attack," she replied. She'd obviously seen the same reports I had.

"Don't worry. It's perfectly calm here."

"Who the heck goes to Laos?" she replied. "Get out of there and come home."

"We'll be home in less than a month," I replied.

"Take care of my grandchildren," she said, sighing. "And please don't go anywhere else where there's a war. I don't think I can stand this anymore."

Fortunately, that wasn't a problem, because Vientiane seemed to be one of the most serene cities on earth. It still retained many of its old small-town charms—just as I hoped—but its backwater days were clearly numbered. We stayed nearly two weeks in all touring the city's small handful of tourist attractions, shopping for hand-woven textiles in the sprawling Morning Market and dining at sunset on the banks of the broad Mekong. Early on, we were befriended by a talented American silk weaver named Carol Cassidy, and we spent a delightful evening in her home. Over dinner, her Ethiopian husband, Dawed, told us how he fled Addis Ababa during the civil war there, and spent two years walking from Ethiopia to Rome, sneaking across borders without a passport or travel papers of any sort.

We also spent an enlightening afternoon in Vientiane's dilapidated Revolutionary Museum. There, Kara and Willie learned how the United States secretly decimated Laos during the Vietnam War, dropping more than one thousand pounds of explosives for every man, woman, and child in the country (not to mention a few hundred thousand gallons of carcinogenic Agent Orange). The kids saw faded black-and-white photographs of the carnage America wrought on this poor little land, and old wire photos of LBJ and Robert McNamara captioned, "U.S. imperialists plotting the destruction of Laos." Kara, in particular, seemed shocked that her own country could commit such despicable acts.

Despite these past aggressions, the Lao people didn't seem to bear us any animus. They were invariably kind, polite, and charming, and if anything, they were delighted to meet visitors from America. This was especially true when we flew to the remote northern town of Luang Prabang. Flying to Luang Prabang was a breathtaking experience. To get there, our Lao Aviation turboprop had to surmount a fourteen-thousand-foot mountain range, and the pilot didn't waste fuel flying any higher than he had to. After we scraped over the peaks, we dropped into a verdant jungle valley where the sparkling Khan River wound its way past golden stupas to join the broad muddy Mekong. At the confluence of these two rivers stood Luang Prabang, ancient capital of Lan Xang,* a once-glorious kingdom that antedates modern Laos.

If the goals of our journey included traveling to the far ends

---

*Literally, the Land of a Million Elephants.

of the earth, showing our children exotic cultures and exploring hidden Shangri-las, then Luang Prabang was a wonderful place to end up. A town of less than sixteen thousand people, it boasted a rather compact but very elegant royal palace, a holy mountain in the center of town, and more than twenty Buddhist wats occupied by hundreds of saffron-cloaked monks. It was a lovely peaceful place where run-down French colonial buildings lined the riverfront and colorfully clad Meo tribeswomen descended from the hills to sell their handicrafts.

As we strolled down the main street, which was practically devoid of cars, people actually came out of their homes and motioned us inside. Although the gentle residents of Luang Prabang are pretty well used to Western backpackers, foreign children—especially children as young as Lucas—were apparently a rarity. On our first evening in town, we accepted an invitation to step inside a little two-room house where a circle of ten or twelve men, women, and children sat on woven mats. The women blushed and giggled whenever I looked at them, but they enjoyed playing with Lucas. The men chain-smoked cigarettes and graciously offered us beer and water. After a while one of the men broke out his guitar, and the whole group sang lilting Lao folk songs as dusk fell. I couldn't imagine a friendlier, sweeter, more joyful group of people. Though we were as far away as possible, we all felt completely at home.

On our last day in Luang Prabang we visited Wat Xieng Thong, a peaceful sixteenth-century Buddhist compound set at the confluence of the Mekong and Khan Rivers. We ogled the wat's famous reclining Buddha and its huge funeral carriage. Then we discovered a long staircase that led down to the Mekong. Near the top of the steps we were approached by a man—remarkably forward by Luang Prabang standards—who offered to sell us a boat ride to the renowned Buddha caves of Pak Ou, about thirty kilometers upriver. It seemed like a pleasant enough day for a river trip, so we all piled into a rickety green long boat and cruised slowly up the mighty Mekong.

Since it was the dry season, the water level was particularly low, and we had to zigzag back and forth across the river to avoid sandbars and shallows. Along the way, we could see children bathing, women washing their clothes, and men bringing their muddy oxen down to the water to drink. Occasionally, we passed little villages consisting of rough wooden houses set on stilts. Everyone we passed invariably smiled and waved.

In two hours, we came to a place where the wide river ran between high forested hills. There, off the port bow, we spotted a large round cave set forty feet high on a limestone cliff. A steep whitewashed staircase ascended from the riverbank to the cave. The captain docked his creaky old boat by the foot of the steps, and we all climbed up. Inside the cave, we found what must have been a thousand bronze and wooden Buddha images set cheek-by-jowl on a series of natural and man-made stone shelves. The images ranged in size from a few inches to several meters high, and nearly all of them were the lithe, standing Buddhas typical of this region. The cave was relatively shallow, and the roof was high, so most of the statues were illuminated by daylight. From the back of the cave, we could gaze out over the river and the forested hills beyond, with countless Buddhas standing in the foreground in fluid silhouette.

After a while, we found another set of steps leading even further up the cliff. There was a second cave at the top. This one was dark and deep, and it was lit only by the occasional flickering candle. Inside, it was damp and still and the further we walked, the darker it got, until eventually we were just stumbling around in the gloom. I meant to bring a flashlight, but I forgot, so I fumbled around in my camera bag until I found a pack of matches. When I lit a match, it formed a small circle of light around us. In that circle hundreds of tall thin Buddhas stood sentry. Each time I lit another match this gentle army sprang to life, and each time it flickered out, we were plunged back into darkness.

It was a remarkable effect, very spiritual, and it made me consider how far we'd come in the last year. It was almost a year ago, exactly, that we were living a pretty ordinary life in the suburbs of San Francisco. Now we found ourselves 1,500 miles up the Mekong River, igniting matches, one after another, in a pitch-black cave surrounded by a thousand carved Buddhas. It all went by so quickly, this journey of ours—just one brief luminous scene after another.

We lit a match, and we were in the mountaintop forests of Costa Rica watching the clouds fly by. We lit another, and we were in the hills of Sardinia enjoying a sumptuous feast. A flash of light and Devi and I were standing hand in hand under a crescent moon on the banks of the Golden Horn. Flash again, and we were traveling across the sere plains of Africa. One flash of light after another and we were in the vivid Rajasthan desert, the desolate Nullarbor Plain, the crumbling ruins of Angkor Wat.

Then it struck me that life was like that, too. You light a match, and you're just a child. Light another, and you're married with children of your own. A few more brief, bright flares, and your babies have left home. A few more after that and your pack is used up. That might be why, at the end of our journey, we found ourselves standing in the Buddha caves of Pak Ou. To learn that we only have one pack of matches. To understand that we have to be in the best possible place when we light each one. To know that we must make each brief combustion a bright, shining moment that pierces the darkness and illuminates a thousand gods.

It was time to go home.

And the end of all our exploring
Will be to arrive where we started
And know the place for the first time.

— T. S. ELIOT, "LITTLE GIDDING"

On the way home from Laos, we stopped off in Hong Kong to witness the British hand over their last colony to China. It wasn't a stroke of genius to visit one of the world's most crowded, expensive cities during the one week when it would be more crowded and expensive than usual. Our tiny Kowloon hotel room had a panoramic view of a brick wall and went for at least double its usual price. To make matters worse, it rained every single one of the ninety-six hours we were there.

Still, we promised the children the greatest fireworks display of their lives, so several hours before the big handover ceremonies, we pushed and shoved our way through huge milling crowds to an esplanade overlooking Hong Kong Harbor. There we joined more than two million other people waiting patiently in the rain. When the extravaganza commenced, we all craned our necks skyward to see millions of dollars' worth of fabulous pyrotechnics explode haplessly into a low-lying cloud bank. You could make out some of the explosions muffled up inside the clouds. Some you couldn't see at all, yet we somehow felt we were present at a historic occasion.

After Hong Kong, we made brief stops in Tokyo and Hawaii. Then, one year and twenty-six days after we first left home, our plane banked sharply over San Jose and headed up the bay toward SFO. As I gazed out the window at the old familiar sights, I had distinctly mixed feelings. It was good to be home, of course, and I was anxious to see our friends and family after such a long time, but I also felt disoriented and slightly melancholy that our long family journey was finally over. I wondered whether I'd miss the traveling life—the constant sense of adventure and intense family togetherness we shared. I wondered how difficult it would be to return to conventional reality—or whether I wanted to return at all. And now that the journey was over, I wondered if it had been worth all the time, money, and effort we spent zigzagging around the globe.

During our first six months back, I would have been hard-pressed to answer any of these questions. The resettlement process didn't leave much time for reflection, and matters like these always take a while to percolate. But now that we've settled down, I think I can discuss at least some of the lessons I learned during this long journey.

The first lesson is pretty obvious in retrospect: If you want to gain fresh perspective on your life, you should make a clean break from your regular routine for a meaningful period of time. It's practically impossible to ponder—or even be fully aware of—the course of your life when you're negotiating rush-hour traffic, dealing with company politics, picking up children, making dinner, supervising homework, mowing the lawn, cleaning the house, buying groceries, and doing all the other quotidian tasks that consume your days. When Plato said the unexamined life is not worth living, he couldn't possibly have imagined the frantic pace of life in twentieth-century America where there's always pressure to see more, be more,

and do more and never enough time for contemplation and re-
newal. If a doctor told me I had a terminal illness and six
months to live, I'm sure I'd find time to sit down and sort out
what's meaningful in my life and what isn't. But other than
that, taking a good, long time away from it all may be the
most effective means to reassess your course and recalibrate
your heading.

Other cultures provide this sort of sabbatical as a matter of
course. Most Thai men join a monastery for several months
of instruction and meditation sometime in their lives. Australian Aboriginals "go walkabout" for an indeterminate
length of time in order to think things over in the bush. Even
Europeans get five or six weeks of vacation a year to recharge
their batteries. But here in North America, we expect to regain our equilibrium and sort out our lives during a six-day
family holiday.

In order to ponder the course of my own life with any sense
of perspective, I had to completely relinquish my routine—mentally as well as physically. And that took a while—at least three
months into the trip. After that I began to see aspects of my life
and career with increased clarity, and only then could I reevalu-
ate old patterns and assumptions. This was in no way a labori-
ous or even a methodical process. In fact, I didn't work at it at
all. I was just open to change at the outset of the journey, and the
rest came naturally. If I'd stayed home, my original impulse toward reevaluation and growth would have probably been
buried under the inexorable flow of everyday events.

In some ways, taking this sort of midlife break may be even
more important for men than it is for women. Men tend to be
less introspective in their twenties and thirties when they're establishing families and careers. Then they hit forty or so and often have this dramatic midlife crisis when they question all the
decisions they made during the first half of their lives. It can be
a rocky time, and in my case at least, taking a good long time
off was an immense help.

Another good reason for taking a long journey is that it just takes a while to get the knack of it. The first three weeks on the road with our children were pure, screaming hell. They fought with each other unstintingly, and complained about nearly every place we went—no matter how spectacular it was. If we had tried to predict what our year off would be like on the basis of those first few weeks, we never would have continued the journey. Only persistence and patience got us through the initial phase.

Which leads me to something else I learned on the road—how to be more patient and how to let go. Again it took several months, but I gradually learned that I couldn't micromanage everything that went on during our journey. Planes were canceled. Reservations got lost. Rooms were dirty. The laundry didn't get done for weeks at a time, and schedules mean nothing to small children. In short, life on the road was chaotic, messy, and haphazard. After a while I realized that I'd better learn to be relaxed and flexible in these matters or it was going to be a very long, very tense trip. So I started making an effort in that direction, and the more I learned to let go and utter simple phrases like "So what," "We'll do it some other time," and "It doesn't really matter" the freer I felt. It was like lifting a self-imposed and completely unnecessary burden from my shoulders. The little stuff just didn't get to me anymore—at least not to the same degree.

Unfortunately, I began to lose some of this equanimity upon my return, and the longer I'm home, the more difficult it is to draw upon. Still, I now have a touchstone I didn't have before, and whenever I'm irritated by a small problem—something that really shouldn't bother me—I think back to our time on the road, and say to myself, "I coped with these little problems then, so why should they bother me now?"

This journey also taught me that we could happily get by with less—less money, less luxury, fewer status symbols, and far fewer belongings than we previously imagined. For more than a year of our lives, our possessions consisted solely of what we could carry in a suitcase or a backpack, and the whole family had to live together in a small hotel room—often without television, stereo, air conditioning or any other modern conveniences.

That was an education in its own right, and it was buttressed by something I observed during our travels, specifically, that millions of people live joyful, productive lives with far fewer possessions than most middle-class Westerners have. If you don't believe me, drive across India. All along the roadside, in tiny villages, you'll see scores of children smiling, waving, and generally having a wonderful time without benefit of $100 Nikes, CD-ROMs, or Sony Play Stations. Do I understand these children often don't get proper medical care or a good education? Of course I do, and there is such a thing as minimum requirements. But I also realize that a big car, a big house, a big-screen TV, or the latest fashions from the Gap probably wouldn't make those kids one iota happier than they are now.

Of course, now that we're back in America, we're not going to live like Rajasthani villagers, but our many months in less developed countries like India, Laos, and Cambodia have given us a new perspective on the American consumer culture. We realize, far more than we used to, that the size of our house and the brand of car we drive just aren't that important. Upon our return, we bought a much smaller house. We got bicycles and tried to get by with one car. The one-car thing didn't work out (much to our friends' delight, since I was so preachy about all this), but for the most part, we've cut way down on expensive restaurants, trendy clothes shops, and fancy hotels. I realize this doesn't exactly qualify us for the Mahatma Gandhi asceticism award—and clearly some of our new penury has to do with the fact that we spent so much money on this trip. But compared to our pretrip days we've reduced our cost of living significantly.

The sad thing, though, is that I know this can't last. Every day in this country we're bombarded by an unrelenting torrent of advertising and promotion all designed to make us spend more, use more, waste more. It's everywhere you look and listen, and it would take a great deal of spiritual strength to swim against the cultural stream—particularly when you have children. I doubt we'll be the ones to do it.

Now for the big questions: How did this journey change our lives, and weighing everything, was it all worthwhile in the end? Remember for a moment that this whole fandango began as a somewhat spontaneous effort to reclaim the adventurous spirit of my youth. I was fed up with my work and a suburban lifestyle that felt increasingly meaningless, and I set out to search for something more.

Well, there's no doubt we found adventure on our trip around the world (sometimes too much), and on the whole, it was a rejuvenating experience. Adventure, per se, is undoubtedly a worthwhile pursuit, one that will always call me, but I found out on this trip that it isn't the be-all and end-all. In retrospect, the lessons I learned in the shadowy Buddha caves of Pak Ou and the fierce riptide off the Queensland coast seem more meaningful. Namely, that you have to live every moment—no matter where you are and what you're doing—as if it were truly important. That you must always strive to be in a good place—a place of purpose and integrity. And that you have to do these things right now because life is short under any circumstances and in some cases it can be plucked away at a moment's notice.

Could I have learned these particular lessons without zigzagging around the world for a year. Probably—but maybe not in the same salient fashion. And now that I accept these lessons, how do I apply them? Probably in ways I don't know or understand yet, but I have made some small changes in the interim. For example, I'm no longer producing coffee-table books like I did before I left.

I began to lose enthusiasm for the whole process before our departure, but when I got back I found that I couldn't really abide the endless selling and fundraising involved, and that I no longer craved the adrenaline-pumping pressure that accompanied my old Day in the Life projects. Instead, I took on two separate jobs that were far less stressful, but more rewarding. The first was writing this book. The second was mentoring and handling certain business affairs for a young artist/computer genius who invented a fantastic new graphics program at the MIT Media Lab.

These jobs together pay significantly less than my old line of work, and neither offers the same prestige I got from being the old coffee-table-book guru. On the other hand, I have far more time to spend with my family, and I wake up each morning eager to start the day. Now, when Willie goes off for his touch football class after school, I drop whatever I'm doing to go with him. I sometimes take Lucas to soccer in the middle of the day and I cook dinner most nights. The boys love it when I tag along—but not for long—so I'm going to enjoy it while it lasts. (At eleven, Kara's already too old and too social to hang out with her dad.)

And now that the trip's over, am I still searching for the lost passion and adventurous spirit of my youth? Not in the same way. I will always love traveling and searching for new places and new experiences, and I'm glad that we reinvigorated our lives with this trip, but it's no longer a compulsion. It may be that I've made the necessary transition from young adulthood to middle age, and that this journey was my rite of passage. Now that it's out of my system, I've calmed down considerably.

Strangely, the journey had the opposite effect on Devi. When we finished our globe-trotting, and she settled back into the role of full-time wife and mother, Devi began to miss all the adventure and excitement—especially now that we had to stay home and watch our pennies. In response, she took up a very adventurous avocation called mountain bike triathlons. Devi began running, swimming, and biking two or three hours a day until she got herself into amazing shape, and now she travels around the western United States engaging in grueling four-hour races that include a 1.5-kilometer swim, a 10-kilometer run, and a 35-kilometer bike ride up and down a mountain. Personally, I think she's nuts, but I admire her resolve and I'm proud of her achievements. Devi is five years younger than I am, and she may be beginning the transition process I just finished.

So in the final analysis, were the rewards worth the risks? Before we left, Devi and I both downplayed the possible hazards of this trip—to our friends, our family, and ourselves. But now that we're back safe and sound, I'd have to admit that we were both apprehensive about the many things that could go wrong on the road. We worried that one of our children would get sick or hurt someplace where we couldn't get proper medical care. We worried that we'd screw up, lose our way, and end up someplace dangerous. We worried that too much family togetherness would cause tension, and I particularly worried that I'd fall behind—monetarily and career-wise—during our long sabbatical.

I'd love to tell you that all these fears were groundless and few things went awry during our year off. But in fact, most of what we feared actually happened—at least to some degree. Willie broke his ankle in Sydney. Kara's fingers were crushed in Bangkok, and she nearly drowned in Queensland. We displayed a remarkable talent for getting lost wherever we went—Nice, Rome, Athens, Cape Town, and Tuscany to name a few. We stayed in some truly awful hotels. Our reservations got lost or confused at least a dozen times along the way. And yes, there is such a thing as too much family togetherness.

As for my career and my bank account...well, when we finally got home, we discovered our local real estate market had taken off like a rocket, and the house we sold before we left had appreciated at least 10 percent during the year we were gone. We had to buy back into a raging seller's market—

which meant less house for the money. And as for my career, there's little doubt that I missed out on some good business deals and that we lost several years on the way to a comfortable retirement.

I'm not telling you this out of disappointment or regret. It's just that many of the things Devi and I feared most about this trip actually occurred, and one way or another we dealt with them. And what we got in return seems like more than a fair trade—a new outlook on life, a spectacular opportunity to see the wonders of the world while we're still reasonably young, and the chance to shape our children's lives and expand their horizons at an age when they're receptive to these lessons. We also got to forge intense, meaningful, and positive relationships with our kids during their formative years. In short, we shared an experience that Kara, Willie, Lucas, Devi, and I will remember for the rest of our lives, an experience that will always bind us together as only shared experience can and one that will always make our lives feel special. I don't know what that's worth—but I think it's probably priceless.

Of course, saying the rewards were worth the risks doesn't mean that the risks weren't substantial, and anyone who's considering a trip of this sort should weigh these perils carefully. Keep in mind that Devi and I were both experienced international travelers before we left, and that Devi carefully researched our destinations for months in advance. Even so, our motorboat could have stalled when the hippo charged us in Botswana. A hyena could have invaded our bush camp in Zimbabwe. One of the kids could have wandered off the path and stepped on a land mine in Cambodia, and, of course, Kara could have drowned in Queensland. In fact, any number of potential disasters could have turned this journey into the greatest disaster of our lives instead of the greatest joy.

That being said, would we do it again, if we could? Would we reup for all the aggravation, risk, and expense? Would we toss sleeplessly in fleabag hotels, eat disgusting food, wear dirty clothes for a week, get sick from Indian air pollution, suffer long, crowded flights, listen to children whine and cry all day before collapsing exhausted into bed?

In a heartbeat. Because after thirteen months, sixteen countries, and more than fifty thousand miles on the road, Devi and I both know that we barely scratched the surface.

Four Frequently Asked
(and Unasked) Questions

Whenever Devi or I mention we traveled around the world with our children for a year, people generally want to ask us four questions:

"Where was the best place you went?"

"What would you do differently?"

"How much does it cost to travel around the world for a year?"

"How do you get along with your spouse twenty-four hours a day, seven days a week?"

Actually, most people are too polite to ask the third question and only women ask the fourth...but since everyone wants to know the answers, here they are, more or less.

Where was the best place you went?

It's difficult to pick just one best place. Practically everywhere we went had its particular charms, but I've managed to narrow the list to twelve contenders.

1. The wildlife safari at Chobe National Park in Botswana—thirty thousand elephants and all the romance of Africa.

2. The Pushkar Camel Fair in Rajasthan, India—spectacular color, magic, and mystery, but unless you book years in advance, you'll have to rough it.

3. Istanbul at night—simultaneously sublime and funky.

4. Diving the Great Barrier Reef in Australia—a magical world of fish and coral in every color of the rainbow. Even better than we imagined.

5. Driving across the Australian Nullarbor—stark and spiritual, but you must endure days of tedium until the desert reveals its power.

6. The Taj Mahal—once you work your way past the touts, beggars, the leper hospital, and the horrible putrid stream next door, you find yourself in the presence of one of the world's greatest architectural achievements.

7. Sipping a cappuccino in Siena's shell-shaped piazza—overrun with hordes of tourists, but it still somehow manages to conjure the romance of the Middle Ages.

8. White-water rafting on the Zambezi River in Zimbabwe—not for the faint of heart (or sane of mind...or weak of leg), but it's an adrenaline rush ne plus ultra.

9. The Burgundy canals by houseboat (France)—languorous and serene, *et le vin, c'est magnifique!*

10. Touring the Angkor ruins in Cambodia—stifling heat, bad accommodations, and the imminent threat of land mines, revolution, and bandits, but still a wonder of the world on a par with the Taj Mahal or the pyramids.

11. Luang Prabang and a boat ride up the Mekong to the Pak Ou Buddha caves in Laos—all the charm and mystery of old Indochina, but probably not for long.

12. Ancient Ephesus in Turkey—the best classical ruins in the world with the possible exception of Pompeii and Cappadocia. Nowhere else did we get such a feel for the classical age.

What would you do differently?

We enjoyed some aspect of nearly every place we went, but there are some things we'd do differently, and here are the top three:

1. We would never go back to Venice, Florence, or anywhere in Tuscany during the tourist season. It was just too abominably crowded.

2. With a few exceptions (again, see the section on Florence), we would never book another packaged tour. The markup is too high and we didn't like all the hand holding. Booking tours on the spot is a different story. What I'm talking about is the two-week package tour.

3. We wouldn't take nearly as much luggage! We didn't need half the clothes we brought, and most of the problems we encountered while we were traveling were somehow connected with our monstrous pile of suitcases. Even though we only had one large suitcase and one backpack each, that still made a dozen bags. If you don't absolutely need it, leave it at home.

How much does it cost to travel around the world for a year?

This is a very difficult question to answer. It's like asking, "How much does a house cost?" or "How much is a car?" With trips, as with cars, there are Yugos and Mercedes, and after you cross a certain minimum threshold, you can spend as much or as little as you want.* Remember, college kids back-pack around the world all the time for $5,000 or $6,000 apiece (or less), and even though they stay in $25-a-night dives, they see the same Eiffel Tower, the same Taj Mahal, and the same sparkling-white Australian beaches as the swells who sleep in thousand-dollar-a-night suites.

After we'd been on the road for several months and gained some knowledge and confidence, we began to book increas-ingly modest accommodations with relatively few adverse effects. Even though I was a confirmed Hilton/Hyatt guy before we left, I learned that downscale inns, pensiones, and smaller hotels worked just as well. Of course, not all our cheap accom-modations were charming and picturesque. But when we did end up in a bad hotel, we simply spent less time in the room and more time exploring. I can tell you from personal experience that the Acropolis is just as impressive when you're sleeping in a $45-a-night dump as when you're staying in a luxury suite. The few times we did go the deluxe route, we usually regretted the expense. We found the amenities weren't worth all the ex-tra dough, and we just insulated ourselves from the real life of the country. I can also tell you, by the way, that without a mort-gage, property tax, utility bills, and two cars to operate, it actu-ally cost us less to travel for a year than it would have cost to stay at home for the same period of time. Thirteen months on the road set us back around $125,000. About $20,000 of that was purely discretional, so I'd say that six people could com-fortably travel for one year for well under $100,000.

There is, however, one other thing to consider when you're budgeting for a trip like this. It takes far longer than you'd ever expect to disengage and reengage. This came as a real shock to us. Somehow I thought it would take two or three months at the front end to plan the trip and close down the

---

*This is especially true if you avoid travel agents, buy guidebooks, and do the research and bookings yourself. Devi cut the cost of our South African safari by more than 60 percent this way.

house and business and then another month or two when we returned to plug everything in again. In fact, we needed five months to prepare and another five or six months to reestablish ourselves. This meant that our thirteen-month trip actually took closer to two years.

Of course, this was largely due to the fact that we sold our house before we left and bought another home when we returned. There were a few advantages to this: It made us feel as if we were really making a clean break. We used some of the equity in the house to pay for our trip, and we bought a smaller house in a better location when we got back. But, frankly, it took too much time and effort to move. We had to pay large, unnecessary real estate commissions, and since the real estate market took off while we were gone, we took a hit financially. We should have just rented our house out for a year and gotten a home equity loan to help pay for the trip.

How do you get along with your spouse twenty-four hours a day, seven days a week?

Frankly, it isn't always easy and a trip like this simply won't work if you're not on very good terms with your spouse. Neither Devi nor I would have made this journey together if we weren't getting along, and even then, there were tense moments—especially at the outset. Believe me, when all of your social interaction takes place within a very small hermetic group for months on end, little peccadillos become incredibly irksome, and slights are easily magnified. If anything, we learned that a trip like this accentuates problems rather than solves them. Consequently, it wouldn't make much sense to travel with your spouse for a year if you're having difficulties to begin with, and it would be truly suicidal to think a trip like this will resolve any marital problems. Of course, if you do manage to spend twenty-four hours a day with your spouse for a year and live to tell the tale, then I think you can assume that your marriage is on very solid ground.

Bibliography

I guess there's no need to tell you that this is in no way a scholarly work. In fact, I gathered most of the factual information I needed from commercial guidebooks and a motley assortment of handouts, brochures, pamphlets, maps, and other assorted odds and ends I picked up along the way. These bits of paper eventually filled a small duffel bag that became my very own ball and chain as we traveled around the world. I also depended on sixteen hours of videotape I shot during the trip as well as *The Academic American Encyclopedia,* a CD-ROM, mostly suitable for schoolchildren. Though it lacked depth, its search engine allowed me to answer questions like "When was the Acropolis built?" instantaneously. Later Devi gave me the *Britannica* CD by Encyclopaedia Britannica. This served the same purpose, but offered more depth.

Books

Biliorsi, Massimo. *A Tour Around Siena.* Venezia: Storti Edizioni, 1996.

Bourgogne, Franche-Comté, Guide Fluvial. Graulhet: Editions CBL.

Brosnahan, David. *Turkey—A Travel Survival Kit.* 4th ed. Hawthorn, Victoria, Australia, and Oakland, California: Lonely Planet Publications, 1993.

Cimrin, Hüseyin (translated by Bilgi Altiok). *Ephesus, The Metropolis of the Antique Age.* Antalya, Turkey: Güney Kartpostal Veturistik Yayincilik, 1997.

Costello-Cortes, Ian. *The Dorling Kindersley World Reference Atlas.* New York: Dorling Kindersley Publishing, 1996.

Cummings, Joe. *Laos—A Travel Survival Kit.* Hawthorn, Victoria, Australia, and Oakland, California: Lonely Planet Publications, 1996.

Das, Dr. Asok K. *Discover Rajasthan.* Department of Tourism, Art, and Culture, Government of Rajasthan, 1996.

Dominguez, Joe, and Vicki Robin. *Your Money or Your Life: Transforming Your Relationship with Money and Achieving Financial Independence.* New York: Penguin, 1992.

Finlay, Hugh. *India—A Travel Survival Kit.* Hawthorn, Victoria, Australia, and Oakland, California: Lonely Planet Publications, 1996.

Gibbons, Gail. *Sea Turtles.* New York: Holiday House, 1995.

Hoeffer, Hans, et al. *Insight Guide: Thailand.* Singapore: APA Publications, 1989.

Jones, James W. *In the Middle of the Road We Call Our Life: The Courage to Search for Something More.* San Francisco: HarperSanFrancisco, 1995.

Maitland, Derek, and Alain Evrard *Insider's Guide to Vietnam, Laos and Cambodia.* Edison, New Jersey: Hunter Publishing (by arrangement with Nuovo Editions, S.A.), 1995.

Malan, Rian. *My Traitor's Heart.* New York: Atlantic Monthly Press, 1990.

Photinos, Spyros (translated by Tina McGeorge and Colin

MacDonald). *Olympia: A Complete Guide*. Athens: Olympic Publications, 1989.

Porter, Darwin, and Danforth Prince (eds.). *Frommer's France*. New York: Macmillan, 1996.

Porter, Darwin, and Danforth Prince (eds.). *Frommer's Italy*. New York: Macmillan, 1996. (Author's note: This book contained certain erroneous information.)

The Quotable Traveler. Philadelphia, Pennsylvania, and London: Running Press, 1994.

Rivas-Micoud, Miguel et al. (eds.). *Insight Guide: Tokyo*. Singapore: APA Publications, 1991.

Sinclair, Toby. *India, Continent of Contrasts*. Chicago: Passport Books, 1991.

Swaney, Deanna. *Zimbabwe, Botswana and Namibia—A Travel Survival Kit*. Hawthorn, Victoria, Australia, and Oakland, California: Lonely Planet Publications, 1996.

Tettoni, Luca Invernizzi. *A Guide to Chiang Mai and Northern Thailand*. Bangkok: Asia Books, 1992.

Türkoglu, Sabhattin (translated by Nükhet Eraslan). *The Topkapi Palace*. 21st ed. Istanbul: Net Turistik Yayinlar A. S., 1996.

Willet, David et al. *Greece—A Travel Survival Kit*. 3rd ed. Hawthorn, Victoria, Australia, and Oakland, California: Lonely Planet Publications, 1996.

Wolf, Stephen (ed.). *Fodor's South Africa*. New York: Fodor's Travel Publications, 1996. (Also see: http://www.fodors.com/)

Wolf, Stephen (ed.). *Fodor's Australia and New Zealand*. New York: Fodor's Travel Publications, 1995. (Also see http://www.fodors.com/)

CD-ROMS *and Internet Sites*

The Academic American Encyclopedia (1995 Grolier's Multimedia Encyclopedia Edition), Danbury, Connecticut: Grolier, 1995; CD-ROM.

The Animals, Software Toolworks, Arnowitz, Inc., and the
Zoological Society of San Diego, 1993; CD-ROM.

Britannica CD, version 97.1.1, Encyclopaedia Britannica,
1997.

Greenspun, Philip, "The Costa Rica Story," available at
http://webtravel.org/cr/arenal; Internet.

Poás, Costa Rica page on the Volcano World Web site available at http://volcano.und.nodak.edu/vwdoc.hamerica/
costarica/newpoas.html; Internet.

Acknowledgments

·

So many people helped us find our way around the world, including many kind strangers. Devi and I are grateful to all, but we'd like to offer special thanks to the following:

Dominick Anfuso and Ana DeBevoise of Simon & Schuster, for seeing the potential in this project and agreeing to publish this book in the first place.

Khun Prapansak Batayond of the Imperial Queen's Park Hotel in Bangkok for his generous hospitality.

Bret, Christina, Sophie, and Alexander Burton for their friendship in Sydney.

My mother, Hannah Cohen, for generously and diligently keeping our affairs in order while we were gone. It would have been impossible for us to take this trip without her help.

My father, Norman Cohen, for many things.

My brother, Dan Cohen, for organizing our tours of the U.S. Capitol and the White House, and his wife, Stacey Cohen, for her help.

Rick and Bettina Cullen, barristers, vintners, and bon vivants, for their wonderful hospitality in Perth and Margaret River, Western Australia.

Lois Eagleton, Devi's mother, for providing the example and inspiration for this trip. And to her husband, Mark Eagleton, for his hospitality in Arizona.

Lisa and Phil Feldman for letting us stay in their home and for coming all the way to Australia to visit us.

Kathy Fitzgerald for vetting my Italian.

Yuri and Zhenya Fridman for their help and friendship.

Hope Gladney for her hospitality in New York City.

François Hebel for a wonderful dinner in Paris.

Giancarlo and Pia, Gianni and Anna Maria, and Mino and Birghit for their world-class hospitality in Sardinia.

Rosie Harris and Mike Reese for showing us their Perth. (See Rosie, I told you I wasn't going to say anything bad about Perth.)

Catherine Hurst, Kerri Kennedy, Annik LaFarge, Ruth Lee, Peter McCulloch, Victoria Meyer, Melissa Milsten, Toni Rachiele, Jackie Seow, and all the other wonderful people at Simon & Schuster who worked so hard on this book.

Anna Kamdar and Todd Simmons for their hospitality in Oregon.

Mira Kamdar and Michael Claes for their superb hospitality in New York.

Pete Kamdar, Devi's father, for his great generosity and hospitality in both Sardinia and Bombay, and his help with the kids in Cambodia.

Pravin Kamdar and Caroline Koff for their hospitality in Colorado.

Dipu, Dipti, and Usha Kamdar for their gracious hospitality in Bombay.

Jill and Steve Kantola for putting us up (and putting up with us) for an inexcusable length of time in their Tiburon home—and for smoothing our way in Perth.

Harlan and Sandy Kleiman of Tiburon, Bill and Terri Higgins of Mill Valley, and Douglas and Françoise Kirkland of West Hollywood—all for hosting sayonara parties before we left on this journey. Each was a beautiful affair reflecting the creative and generous nature of the hosts. The Kleimans and the Kirklands were also kind enough to let all six of us stay at their homes. And the magnificent Françoise Kirkland once again for correcting my French spelling.

Hiroko Koff and her sister Taka-san for a wonderful dinner in Tokyo.

Larry and Lacy Lang for their warm (and I do mean 116 degree warm) hospitality in Phoenix.

Franz Lanting, the renowned wildlife photographer, for referring us to the Chobe Game Lodge in Botswana, one of the best stops on our trip.

Lee, Josh, Cassy, Bez, and Boris Liberman for their hospitality in Melbourne, Australia, and also for the use of their lovely place in Surfer's Paradise.

Jain Lemos for her smart, competent assistance.

Sara Loyster, DeAnn Tabuchi, Lois Giono, Diane Karabochos Burt, Renee Hayes, Keven Madvig, Shannon Sheppard, and the other librarians at the San Anselmo (California) Public Library who provided helpful reference assistance.

Diana and John Mack for putting up the whole brood in Pacific Palisades.

My agent, Carol Mann, and her assistant, Christie Fletcher, for finding a publisher for this beast—not an easy task.

Holloway McCandless, Andy Belt, and Toby McCandless for their gracious hospitality under difficult circumstances. I hope, in a similar situation, I would demonstrate the same degree of graceful equanimity.

Doug and Teresa Menuez for letting us use their Mill Valley home for three weeks when we returned to America after our trip.

Kevin Monko and Nick Kelsh of Kelsh Wilson Design for receiving, processing, and filing all the film from our trip.

The Hon. Patricia O'Neill, legendary for her kindness, class, and charisma, for an unforgettable lunch and tour of her magnificent estate, Broadlawns, near Cape Town, South Africa.

292 o DAVID ELLIOT COHEN

James O'Reilly, Lisa Bach, Susan Brady, Kathy Meengs, and the other fine people at Travelers' Tales, the publisher of this paperback edition.

Publisher John Owen for his assistance in Sydney.

Rasik Pareck for his hospitality and assistance in Mumbai.

Liz Perle, Susan Wels, and Susan Moffett—all smart, capable publishing professionals—who read and commented on the proposal for this book.

Elaine Petrocelli, for her early encouragement.

Spencer Reiss, a top editor at *Wired* magazine, who actually knows something about writing and offered much good advice. It was Spencer's idea to write this book in the form of e-mails.

Cornel Riklin and family, for their hospitality in Sardinia—and to Susie, who had to stay back in London.

Joan Ryan and Barry Tompkins, for our Welcome Home party.

Computer genius Robert Silvers, for letting me ride his tiger.

Heidi Swillinger and Kay Kirby at the *San Francisco Chronicle* for publishing the first installment of this book.

Erick Steinberg, Lisa Miller, Mark and Annie, who gave us a home away from home when we returned to Northern California.

Sara Timewell, Jim Sano, and the folks at Geographic Expeditions for helping us during the planning stages.

The legendary Australian publisher Kevin Weldon and his wonderful wife, Glenda, for helping us settle in Sydney.

Eric and Janet Weyenberg for their hospitality in Honolulu.

. . . and lastly, to our seventy or so correspondents who faithfully read installments of this book in e-mail form and offered invaluable comments, suggestions, and encouragement.

About the Author

A graduate of Yale College, David Elliot Cohen has edited or co-edited three *New York Times* best-sellers including *A Day in the Life of America*. He has appeared on numerous national programs including *The Today Show, Good Morning America, Morning Edition,* and *20/20* and has won awards from organizations as diverse as the American Society of Media Photographers, the Catholic Press Association, the government of Spain, and the National Jewish Book Awards. Cohen lives in Marin County, California, with his wife, Devyani Kamdar, and their three children, Kara, Willie, and Lucas. Since taking One Year Off, he has accomplished less and enjoyed life more. You can reach him at daylifers@aol.com.

Books edited or co-edited by David Elliot Cohen